Exulting in Jesus on every page, J[...] authority of Christ not only bolsters [...] one's spirit to worship Jesus, even when me is nard [...] seems improbable. Dripping with Scripture, the case Shaw lays out will serve as bedrock for believers under persecution and will enable not just surviving, but actual thriving in severe circumstances. May the view of Christ presented in this book spread and ignite white-hot worship among all peoples!

Bob McNabb, Executive Director, Launch Global and author of *Spiritual Multiplication in the Real World*

Wow. Read at your own risk. If you pick up and read *All Authority,* you will learn about the authority and power of Christ, who rules over all. Your heart will be filled with deep emotion—joy, sorrow, and hope. Most of all, you will be challenged with fresh motivation to make disciples of all nations both personally and corporately. I believe generations for years to come will be reading this book, as they consider the enormous privilege, responsibility, and call to go to the nations with the good news of a crucified Lamb, an empty tomb, an occupied throne, and a soon-coming King. I plan on using it at our local church, and pray that we may also see a movement like Joey has described.

Tony Merida, Pastor for Preaching and Vision, Imago Dei Church, Raleigh, North Carolina

In recent years The Austin Stone Community Church has sent more than one hundred of her members to live and serve Christ among the nations. Believing that "biblical mission is biblical doctrine applied," Joey Shaw offers us an important look at the theology and thinking that drives the mission efforts of a church that is literally impacting the world.

Eric Geiger, Vice President, LifeWay Christian Resources

All Authority rings with truth and conviction. Joey writes with a double-pronged purpose. First, he masterfully develops from Scripture the doctrine of our Lord Jesus Christ's authority. Second, his first-person narratives about how this authority intersects with mission serve as an impassioned plea for Jesus' followers to trust him and follow him, wherever he leads, whatever the personal cost. Reading this book may be risky.

Kendell Easley, Professor of Biblical Studies
Director of Graduate Programs, School of Theology and Missions, Union University

Don't try to devour this feast of applied biblical truths at one sitting. Nearly every page is a meal for serious reflection. Our Sovereign King Jesus, with all his authority, commands that we persevere in making disciples of all peoples . . . including among those who hate his messengers and his authority, and will kill us if they cannot drive us away otherwise. Whatever it takes . . .

Greg Livingstone, Founder, Frontiers

There could not be a more relevant, timely, or thrilling concept for us to consider than that of the authority of Christ. Especially in my role as a wife and mom, I cannot think of a more important theme for my marriage or parenting. If the Lord wills, this book will inspire such confidence in his Son that unprecedented waves of gospel proclamation will begin to break on the darkest of shores.

Gloria Furman, Cross-cultural worker (UAE) and author of *Treasuring Christ When Your Hands Are Full*

Many believers today lack confidence in the gospel, first for themselves and especially in sharing it with people in their family, communities, and the nations of the world. In *All Authority* Joey takes the reader into the beauty and freedom of Jesus' lordship with a depth and insight that I think will help a lot of people experience the power of their own salvation. This book will lead them to actually discover joy and confidence in sharing the life-giving hope of Christ with the people around them. This book is a great invitation to have confidence in the one who is lovingly Lord of all.

Rick McKinley, Lead Pastor, Imago Dei Community and author of *The Answer to Our Cry* and *This Beautiful Mess*

No other book unpacks the last words of Christ as skillfully and powerfully as *All Authority*. It will change you!

Todd Ahrend, Founder, The Traveling Team and author of *The Abrahamic Revolution* and *In This Generation*

A lot has been written on the Great Commission, but much of it has focused on pragmatic ways in which to accomplish God's mission. Joey Shaw's book goes beyond the pragmatic to what empowers, ignites, and excites the mission of God, which is the authority of Jesus Christ. Christ's authority is often assumed and overlooked, but as Joey makes clear, it is the very basis by which Christians spread the gospel of Jesus Christ. Joey writes not merely from research, but from personal experience in facing the trials and persecution that come with participating in God's mission. He speaks on the authority of Christ because he rests in that authority as the source and strength of his ability to cross cultures and spread the gospel. This is an essential book for the church that longs to see the mission of God unleashed in every neighborhood, network, and nation.

Logan Gentry, Lead Pastor, Apostles Church, Union Square, New York Center

The only way to be involved with persistence and joy in the Great Commission is to be resolutely fixated on Jesus, the Great Apostle. This book contains stories and insights that can help Christ-followers focus their attention afresh on Jesus, the magnificent world evangelizer.

Steve Hawthorne, Director, WayMakers

ALL

AUTHORITY

ALL

AUTHORITY

JOEY SHAW

B&H
PUBLISHING GROUP
NASHVILLE, TENNESSEE

To my parents:

Sam and Ruth Shaw

If faith is the fruit of the Vine,
Then you have been my vineyard.

Acknowledgments

My Lord, this book is for you. Thank you for loving me. Please use this book to lead many to "gaze and proclaim."

For the time to write this book and for her endless encouragement, I am indebted beyond words to my beautiful wife, K.S.

Every single day I enjoy the friendship of hundreds of coworkers in the kingdom of God who serve among the nations. Because most of them serve in very sensitive contexts, I am unable to thank them by name here. But their camaraderie is one of the most precious gifts from God to me.

I am thankful to so many for their love, support, patience, and kindness to me. Many have encouraged me along the way in this project: the pastors of The Austin Stone (Austin, TX), the pastors and staff of The Orchard Fellowship (Memphis, TN), Dan E., our Advocacy Team, S. B., our financial supporters, and many others. Travis Wussow was a huge support and advocate for me throughout this project. Thank you to Kevin Peck and the elders of The Austin Stone for trusting my leadership. Thank you to Matt Carter for graciously writing the forward to this book and supporting me. Thank you to Ken Easley, Lindsay Funkhouser, N.B., John Hervey, N.C., Todd Ahrend, and my faithful brother and rock star Charlie Shaw for reviewing the manuscript and providing very helpful comments. I'm very grateful to Devin Maddox, Toby Jennings, and the folks at B&H Publishing Group for their hard work putting this manuscript to print, as well as their encouragement and belief in me.

I am who I am because of the incalculable investment and influence of my parents, Sam and Ruth Shaw. They model joyful submission to the authority of the Lord Jesus to me, as well as many thousands of other people. I dedicate this book to them.

Contents

Foreword

SEVERAL YEARS AGO OUR INTERNATIONAL MINISTRY PASTOR AT THE Austin Stone Community Church shared with me his idea on how our local church might play a part in God's global work. His idea, really more like a dream, was to call, equip, and send 100 people from our church to the nations for the name and purpose of Christ. The more he talked, the more outlandish the idea sounded. Not only was he asking me if I thought it would be feasible to send 100 people from our church to nations, but that specifically these 100 people would go to an unreached people group. These are people groups with little to no presence of indigenous believers in Christ.

I initially thought he was crazy. At our church, we have a hard enough time getting 100 people to sign up to work in our kids ministry, much less leave the comfort and safety of their home to go to a place where very few have ever even heard the name of Christ. But the more I talked to him, the more he made me believe that it was possible. The last thing I said to him before the meeting was over was that if he would lay the groundwork and prepare the training, funding, sending, and caring networks for these 100 people, then I would preach a sermon on it to see if there was any interest.

Five years and a lot of blood (literally), sweat, tears, and work later, The Austin Stone sent their 100th person to the nations in the name of Jesus. This process has stretched and grown our church in ways none of us could have ever imagined. For instance, one of my closest friends was murdered. He was among these first 100 people to go to the nations for our beloved Savior.

The pastor who met with me that day in my office is the author of this book, Joey Shaw. His passion and vision to see Jesus exalted among the nations is contagious and has sparked a movement in our church that is literally changing the world.

In the pages of this book, Joey skillfully explains why the supreme authority of Jesus is not only the foundation for ministry, it is also the very message that we proclaim in ministry. "Jesus is Lord" is good news!

"Jesus is better" is the anthem that we sing at our church; and it is the anthem of the heavens. This is the anthem that Joey declares with this book.

I encourage you to read this book. I challenge you to carefully consider how the doctrine of the authority of Christ upholds the mandate that Jesus still gives to all of us: "Go, therefore, and make disciples of all nations" (Matt. 28:19). And as you read, I challenge you to ask yourself what role God would have you fulfill in this great task of magnifying his name among all peoples, even in the ends of the earth.

Dr. Matt Carter
Pastor of Preaching
The Austin Stone Community Church
Austin, Texas

Then Jesus came near and said to them, "All authority has been given to Me in heaven and on earth. Go, therefore, and make disciples of all nations, baptizing them in the name of the Father and of the Son and of the Holy Spirit, teaching them to observe everything I have commanded you. And remember, I am with you always, to the end of the age." (Matt. 28:18–20)

All of life for nothing less
Than Christ, his worth my years profess.
My fortune sealed, the interest yields
Eternal gifts, his oath my shield.

No hope in life, no assets mine
Except my scars, and joy sublime.
What's rest in life I humbly give
To him whom sinners' souls forgive.

No waste but that which given here
To build a chest of greed and fear.
What good is there in earthly best
If without him and all the rest?

My home with him, my mansion there.
Here nothing but a song and prayer.
He builds a city rich with gold.
It in our faith we now behold.

Gaze and Proclaim

JESUS CHRIST HAS BEEN GIVEN ALL AUTHORITY IN HEAVEN AND ON earth. His authority is supreme and it is glorious. On the basis of his authority, he commissioned his people to go and make disciples among every people group on earth. This is an impossible commission if it were not for the promise that he is with them forever.

A Blessed Scar

Suffering makes us ask the question, "Who's in charge?" For weeks after September 11, 2001, churches were packed with people longing to hear a preacher say, "He's got the whole world in his hands."

On November 8, 2009, in New Delhi, India, two others and I were attacked and robbed by a small gang of Indian men. Unexpectedly, one of these men knifed my left cheek with a straight razor. The wound was four inches long and an inch deep, spanning from about my left sideburn to the left corner of my mouth. I bled profusely all over the place and looked horrific. We ran for safety in the middle of the city, pleaded with locals for help, and finally ended up in the emergency room at a local hospital where a doctor stitched up my face with approximately eighty stitches in three layers. Fortunately, the two other men with me were physically unharmed.

This attack happened just weeks after we at The Austin Stone Community Church decided to launch the campaign to send 100 people to the nations. Weeks before the attack, we prayed for the nations with the thought in mind that one day someone from these 100 people would shed blood for Jesus. I never thought that the first person would be me. And I never thought that a few years after that my own close friend and fellow pastor would die for Jesus in Libya.

When the plastic surgeon inspected my scar post-surgery, he asked me if I wanted to try blurring the scar using some high-end plastic surgery technique. I immediately knew my answer was no. Let the scar remain as is.

I wanted the scar to remain because three months before being knifed, my wife gave birth to our first son. I had been nervously thinking about how to model for my son what it means to follow Jesus. Now I knew the answer. I want my scar to remind my son (now three sons!) every time that he looks at me that we follow Jesus on the road to glory, called the Calvary Road. The Calvary Road is not a path merely to endure, but is to be *embraced* with joy and hope, because Jesus himself walks with us there! On Thursdays we pray over our sons that they would "embrace the way" of this Calvary Road.

That straight razor may be the greatest blessing of that year for my family and me as it reminds us that Jesus is in control. He is not only in charge—reigning with supreme authority—he is also good to keep his promises. As we ran from the gang of thugs that dark night, my face bleeding freely, I remembered his promise, "I will be with you." Jesus was there with us that night!

So, I am thankful for my scar. It leads me one step further on the Calvary Road and reminds me every single day of the truth that Jesus declared in Matthew 28:18, "All authority has been given to Me in heaven and on earth." I do not command my destiny. I am not the captain of my ship. "Jesus commands my destiny," as we sing in the song "In Christ Alone."[1] The scar also reminds me that he is keeping all of his promises to me.

What's the "Therefore" There For?

The supreme authority of Jesus is the biblical foundation for local and global mission. Consider "The Great Commission" in Matthew 28:18–20. First, in verse 18, Jesus declares his supreme authority over all, "All authority has been given to Me in heaven and on earth." *Then,* Jesus gives the famous mandate (vv. 19–20): "Go, therefore, and make disciples of all nations, baptizing them in the name of the Father and of the Son and of the Holy Spirit, teaching them to observe everything I have commanded you." It is no coincidence that the doctrinal declaration of Matthew 28:18 precedes the mandate of Matthew 28:19; for the authority of verse 18 is linked with the power needed to fulfill the mandate in verse 19. Truth is the bedrock of mission.

Notice that most English translations of Matthew 28:19 start with "Therefore" or "Go, therefore." So what is the "therefore" there for? This "therefore" helps the reader make the connection between the authority of Jesus and the mission of the church. Without the truth that Jesus has "all authority," our mission to "make disciples" of all peoples is not only impossible, it is fatally foolish. The entire gospel hinges on the authority of Jesus. If his authority is not supreme, the gospel crumbles and the church—as well as the world—loses all hope.

Fulfilling the mission of Matthew 28:19–20 will be difficult! Living to fulfill this mission will inevitably come with trials, discouragements, complexities, confusions, setbacks, and suffering. Jesus knew that this would be the case, so he reminded his disciples of his absolute authority that was delegated by his Father in full and that is executed on earth today by the Holy Spirit. The "therefore" in Matthew 29:19 connects doctrine with living on mission with God.[2]

It is also no coincidence that Matthew 28:20 comes after Matthew 28:19. Even if Jesus is supremely authoritative, if he is not present with the church, the church loses hope of accomplishing the Great Commission.

Without the truth of verse 18 and the promise of verse 20, we lose all hope of completing the mandate of Matthew 28:19–20. This book explores the connections between the truth of Matthew 28:18, the commission of Matthew 28:19–20, and the promise of Matthew 28:20.

Mission Is Doctrine Applied

In 2009, we pastors at The Austin Stone Community Church felt God leading us to take a huge risk as a church. So in the late fall of 2009, we decided to officially ask for 100 people from our church to move to an unreached people group to declare and demonstrate the gospel for at least two years or more. We asked for 100 people to make this commitment sometime in 2010. We then asked for every other person in our church to serve the nations as a "Sender" or "Mobilizer." By the end of 2010, we had just over 100 committed, and over a dozen launched already to the nations. Four years later, by God's grace, our 100th "Goer" got on a plane destined for disciple-making ministry among one of the world's most unreached peoples. During those four years, momentum built as more and more people decided to obey the Great Commission. As of the writing of this book, we have launched 142 Goers and we have about 100 in the pipeline very seriously preparing to launch in the next twelve to eighteen months.[3] While we aim to continue mobilizing and sending out hundreds to the nations, our goal now is to launch 100 multiplying churches among unreached people groups. We pray that God would allow us to realize this vision.

We often get questions like, "What motivates your church to send your best and brightest to the ends of the earth?" It surprises many to hear that the root of our confidence among the nations is not pragmatism, or strategy, or an easy opportunity to bear lots of disciple-making fruit. Rather, our confidence is rooted in truth. This truth is the supreme authority of Jesus Christ.

We believe that biblical mission is simply biblical doctrine faithfully applied. What we *know* about Jesus shapes what we *do* for Jesus. The reverse is also true. When we live for Jesus, it shapes our understanding of what we know about Jesus. Martin Luther said, "Not understanding, reading, or speculation, but living . . . make a theologian."[4] This is why theology is not primarily for academicians; rather, "theology is a matter for the church."[5]

The problem for most of us is that doctrine is tough to chew on. This is the case for at least three reasons. First, doctrine implies truth. And in our present age there is no lack of postmodern prophets who scoff at the notion of "absolute truth." Second, knowing doctrine means that we have to think, and thinking is hard. It makes for slow reading. But doctrine should be unpacked carefully and precisely, for it is the truth on which we base our eternity. Third, doctrine always demands change in us. Doctrine demands that we adapt the way that we think about God, the world, the devil, eternity, and mankind to truth.

In this book, I have tried to make the doctrine of the supreme authority of Jesus Christ clear and beautiful. To do this, I explain the biblical meaning of the word "authority" as it applies to Jesus in the New Testament. Jesus' use of the word "authority" in Matthew 28:18 is intentional, so in this book I outline the connections between his authority and the rest of the "Great Commission."

The practical thread that runs through this book is the importance of abiding in Christ. He is the Vine. We are the branches. If we abide in Christ, and Christ in us, we will bear much fruit, for apart from him we can do nothing (John 15:5). The power to magnify Christ while demonstrating and declaring the gospel to all nations comes from an abiding relationship with living and ruling Jesus Christ.

I have introduced each chapter with one of my poems. Poetry is, for me, a way to express the inexpressible and lead others to do the same. It gives me a taste of the food that only the saints at the feast of heaven eat. Poetry should be read out loud, and slowly. Therefore, I encourage you not to read these poems too quickly. Perhaps read them out loud to your spouse or friend. Take a moment, quiet down, breathe deeply, and smell the feast of the saints with me.

Gaze and Proclaim

My invitation to you in this book is to behold the glory of Jesus Christ. Here we will study one of his diverse glories: namely, his authority. My prayer is that the Holy Spirit will use this book to help you gaze upon the beauty of the Lord (Ps. 27:4), and as a result, you would "proclaim the praises of the One who called you out of darkness into His marvelous light" (1 Pet. 2:9). Pray that your eyes would be opened to "see" his glory and be "amazed" (John 17:24; 5:20).

Do not be put off by the density of some of the chapters. We want to carefully observe the glory of Christ so that we may cherish him more. You will not be incidentally struck by the beauty of the morning dew and moss in a dense forest while waiting in your car on the side of the highway. You must get out of your car and go walking. You must enter the thick forest. You must apply yourself diligently to careful observation.

With this book, I invite you to get out of your car and go walking with me. Walk slowly and carefully. Let us gaze together on the glory of the supreme authority of Jesus Christ, and then let us proclaim this glory, as well as his other manifold glories, to the ends of the earth.

Gadaffi

Crowned with treasures, green glories
Hardly moved by Sirocco's
Thick blow. Like Franklin trophies
Each leaf sounding greed's echoes.

None venture bark this tree's frame—
Brown, dirty, bane, a man's cut.
But envy not this hound's name,
His vain life's worth hardly Phut.

Roots sound Brother Leader's mort,
Ravaging the desert's drought.
Each day piercing his old fort,
Like rebels' bids for spoil's clout.

Stiff and dead this fair tree's source.
Cold, packed in to the freezer.
He that ruled lies with, perforce,
Alexander and Caesar.[1]

——— Chapter 1 ———

The Supremacy of the Son's Authority

EVERYBODY WHO FOLLOWS JESUS WILL ENCOUNTER A MYRIAD OF "authorities" that directly challenge the authority of Christ. These other "authorities" may be parents, teachers, bosses, presidents, institutions, religions, or ideologies. In order to stay firm in devotion to Jesus, we must believe that he has supreme authority over all. The doctrine of the authority of Jesus upholds the work of his church. So we begin this book considering why we believe Jesus Christ is the supreme authority in the universe.

A growing number of our Austin Stone disciple-makers among the nations are experiencing regular suffering. Some have been evacuated under threat of being killed by terrorists. Some have had car engine shrapnel go through their kitchen window from a nearby explosion aimed at killing Christians. They have been held at gunpoint, harassed, robbed, interrogated, put in jail, and accused of false crimes. In addition, some live under the daily threat of kidnapping, extortion, murder, sexual harassment, sickness, and eviction. They constantly have to move their young families from home to home, dealing with many difficulties in obtaining visas and incarnating among unreached peoples. They face endless unknowns about their work and future, and on top of that, they must raise their own support to do this work. One of these "Goers" wrote of his experience in North Africa:

> After settling with my family in North Africa, we realized that the neighborhood we moved into was a drug trade neighborhood. So we had to walk in front of our children to make sure they didn't step on needles. That wears on you. We had active gangs among us. One night, they took over our street. I was threatened to my face with a machete. I saw fistfights or knife fights about three to five times a week. Often these fights happened under our apartment window. We watch the Arab Spring protests and riots from our kitchen window as they happen in our neighborhood. We fall asleep to gunfire most nights, often machine gun fire. My wife has been grabbed on her behind. My sons have been harassed. On my team we've had one guy held at gunpoint. Another guy had about ten armed militia men harass him and search his house. Our women have been verbally and physically harassed by men. On top of that we live under threat every day of kidnapping, assassination, robbery, and harassment. Every single day.

I do not write all of this to elevate our global workers, or to boast in their resilience, but rather to pose the question, "What motivates a person to risk for the cause of making disciples of Jesus Christ?" Or, "What motivates people to shift their resources, make practical sacrifices, and refocus their energy on making disciples of all nations?" We might ask the same type of question about a church: "What motivates a church to send out their best people to the ends of the earth where they will face a myriad of sufferings and even death?" The doctrine of the authority of Christ is at the heart of the answers to these three questions. We have found that the more people cherish the doctrine of Christ's authority, the more they are willing to risk and endure along the way.

The *Exousia* of Jesus

In Matthew 28:18 Jesus uses the Greek word *exousia*, which most English translations translate as "authority." *Exousia* is a common New Testament word; it occurs 102 times in the New Testament. The ESV translates *exousia* with the words "authority, power, right, jurisdiction, charge, disposal, control, claim" and "domain." Together these English translations give us a deeper sense of what *exousia* means in the context of the New Testament. The Gospel writers use the word *exousia* forty-four times in thirty-four verses. Twenty-eight of those are in reference to Jesus. When not applied to God the Father or Jesus, *exousia* in the Gospels always refers to governing rulers and, once, to supernatural darkness that was given "power" during the crucifixion.

The word *exousia* has a long history of usage in ancient Greek. In religious texts, the word "shows a strong preference for supernatural authority, whether divine or demonic, or for the investiture of royal authority."[2] *Exousia* normally refers to the royal, free, and magisterial authority of God or for kings, priests, Israel, the covenant, Jerusalem, or other supernatural powers such as Satan, all of which derive their authority directly from God.[3] Important for our understanding of *exousia* in the Gospels, the pre-Christ religious and nonreligious texts use *exousia* or its Hebrew equivalents to emphasize that the "authority" is either supernatural or directly God-given.[4] Thus, the Gospel writers clearly intended to represent the authority of Jesus as stunning and unique because they use *exousia* so frequently in reference to the *man* Jesus Christ.

It is hard to overstate the importance of the Gospel writers' use of *exousia* to distinguish Jesus Christ as the Son of God. The concept of the *exousia* of Jesus is central to understanding the very nature of Jesus. I agree with professor James Edwards who states, "I should like to suggest that the essential and distinctive characteristic of Jesus is to be found in his *exousia* and that his authority is perhaps the most significant example of implicit Christology in the gospel tradition."[5]

Honest readings of the Gospels will not allow any denigration of the supremacy of Jesus Christ. As will be discussed in more depth in chapter 9, the *exousia* of Jesus could not be more relevant to a postmodern age that has tried numerous iterations of sidewinding scholarship to diminish the glory of Jesus. Modern and postmodern raves to "re-discover" Jesus as impotent and non-supernatural are futile. Again, James R. Edwards states, "Evidence of Jesus' consciousness of divine sonship and *exousia* appears in all layers of the gospel traditions . . . as well as in Paul. Its recognition not only makes the Gospels intelligible but also is the primary reason why the quest for the non-messianic Jesus remains unsatisfied."[6] At the center of the Gospel writers' argument for Jesus' supreme glory is their promotion of the supreme *exousia* of Jesus Christ.

How Is the Son's Authority Supreme?

The authority of Jesus Christ is supreme because it is innate, foretold, real, founding, unimpeded, empowered, exclusive, and legitimate. Let's look at each of these descriptions of his authority.

Innate. Jesus is supreme over all other authorities because his authority is not only given to him by his Father. It is also innate to himself as the second person of the Trinity. It is intuitive for a monotheist to associate supreme authority with God. He is the one sovereign ruler of all existence. He says, "I am the LORD, and there is no other, besides me there is no God" (Isa. 45:5 ESV). But what about the Son of God? He too is fully God. He is the "son . . . given to us" in Isaiah 9:6 who is the "Mighty God." On his shoulders the "government," or authority, rests. And his throne will last forever (Isa. 9:7).

Foretold. When we wait for something, we communicate that the worth of that thing is greater than the expense of the wait. This is why we commonly say, "It was *worth* the wait!" Waiting does not make something special; it demonstrates that something already is special. It would be strange for a mother to say of her newborn, "Oh, the baby is nice, but not worth the nine months of waiting!" No, a child is worth every day of that nine-month wait. This is because the baby has an intrinsic worth greater than those nine months of waiting.

The Messiah has been foretold and awaited from the beginning of human existence. And Jesus the Messiah was worth every minute of waiting! God organized the very genealogy of mankind in preparation for the coming of Jesus (Matt. 1:1–17). The Old Testament awaits an authoritative Messiah who will forever sit as the divine Son on the throne of David at the Father's right hand and have all enemies under his feet (Ps. 45:6–9; Dan. 7:13–14). This Messiah will be sent from God to speak God's words to the world (Deut. 18:18; Isa. 7:14). He will have the strength of God to bring justice, righteousness, and salvation to the nations (Isa. 9:7; Jer. 23:5–6). He will triumph over all of his enemies, including death (Pss. 16:10; 49:15). His kingdom will be forever (Dan. 2:44–45; 7:13–14, 27). He will be worshiped and obeyed as Lord by all the kings and nations on earth (Gen. 49:10; Ps. 22:27–28; Isa. 49:7).

Awaiting something magnifies the worth of that thing. The degree to which something is waited for is the degree to which that thing is magnified. Jesus is magnified as the most supremely worthy Person because his first coming was the most awaited event in the history of the world. What joy and relief there must have been among the angels when the Savior was born in Bethlehem. It is fitting that at the birth of the most awaited person in the history

of the world the angels would burst out of heaven singing, "Glory
to God in the highest heaven!" (Luke 2:14). We can almost imagine the angels saying to themselves, "Jesus was *worth* the wait!"

Real. Most of us have likely encountered a person who is a real
know-it-all with colleagues, and especially subordinates, but completely useless when the boss shows up. This can be aggravating,
especially if he or she has no real authority over you. The authority
is not real, but only a figment of the person's imagination.

Jesus was not a magician, a con man, or a wannabe leader. His
authority was not imagined by him, the apostles, or the church.
His authority is supreme over all others because it is real, and he
spoke of it and demonstrated it in a real way. This is clear in the
first direct reference to Christ's authority in the New Testament:[7]

> Then they went into Capernaum, and right away He
> entered the synagogue on the Sabbath and began to teach.
> They were astonished at His teaching because, unlike the
> scribes, He was teaching them as one having authority. Just
> then a man with an unclean spirit was in their synagogue.
> He cried out, "What do You have to do with us, Jesus—
> Nazarene? Have You come to destroy us? I know who You
> are—the Holy One of God!" But Jesus rebuked him and
> said, "Be quiet, and come out of him!" And the unclean
> spirit convulsed him, shouted with a loud voice, and came
> out of him. Then they were all amazed, so they began
> to argue with one another, saying, "What is this? A new
> teaching with authority! He commands even the unclean
> spirits, and they obey Him." News about Him then spread
> throughout the entire vicinity of Galilee. (Mark 1:21–28)

Jesus was teaching in the synagogue near the beginning of his
ministry.[8] The religious teachers and leaders as well as the people
were still getting introduced to this unusual rabbi. This was the
carpenter, Jesus son of Mary, after all. They noticed immediately

that Jesus was not a typical religious leader, "because, unlike the scribes, He was teaching them as one having authority" (Mark 1:22).

Scribes were expert interpreters and teachers of the Scripture, but their authority rested on the Scripture, not in themselves. Scribes were only interpreters of God's authority through the law. Being only human, they could not claim universal knowledge of God and his law. Their commands to others were more like pleading, because they had no authority or power to make others obey them.[9]

Jesus spoke so differently from the scribes, with an unprecedented completeness of knowledge and with authority and power over creation. He spoke with the authority of a divine command. Whereas scribes obtain their authority through reference to the tradition of the fathers (Mark 7:8–13), Jesus receives his authority directly from the Father (Mark 1:11).[10] He was not just an impressive teacher who mastered the law, he spoke as the one through whom the law was created. He knew it intimately, like a painter knows his own painting.

When Jesus speaks and rules today, he does so as the one who created all things, "in heaven and on earth, the visible and the invisible, whether thrones or dominions or rulers or authorities—all things have been created through Him and for Him" (Col. 1:16). When the Father through Jesus said, "Let there be light," there was light. Likewise when Jesus commands his people, "Don't be an unbeliever, but a believer," as he did to the apostle Thomas, his people respond with belief saying, "My Lord and my God!" (John 20:27–28).

Jesus is the only one who could ever say, "You have heard that it was said . . . But I say to you" (e.g., Matt. 5:17–48). No scribe or leader could ever say that with even the slightest legitimacy! This would be blasphemy for any religious leader of the time to say. The Old Testament prophets prefaced their inspired words with, "Thus says the LORD." But Jesus begins his statements with, "Truly I say to you," or in Greek transliteration, *"amēn amēn legō hymin."*[11] In Jewish custom, saying "amen" at the end of a prayer, statement, or blessing signified personal agreement with the will of God. But as the very "Amen" of God (Rev. 3:14), the "yes" of God to all of his promises (2 Cor. 1:20), Jesus could legitimately preach with the authority of God himself.[12] Jesus is the only person in history who has the legitimate right to say "Amen" at the beginning of his sentence, rather than at the end.[13]

Is it possible the people were just fooled by a charismatic man with an impressive grasp of the Scriptures and reason? Perhaps the Gospel writers and the apostles were fooled as well. That may be a reasonable charge, except that Jesus didn't merely speak with authority. He did not merely teach. He also healed, and he did so with the authority of God alone. His power proves the authority of his words.

Immediately after Jesus astonishes the people with his teaching, a man with a demonic spirit appears in the synagogue. And whether as a defensive strategy or instant submission, the demon cries out that which is actually true of Jesus: that he is of Nazareth and that he is the Holy One of God. After Jesus casts out the demon, the people are amazed again, saying, "What is this? A new teaching with authority! He commands even the unclean spirits, and they obey Him" (Mark 1:27). They had seen with their own eyes that Jesus had *real* authority. He was a "Prophet powerful in action and speech before God and all the people" (Luke 24:19).

The people had encountered new teachings before. Exorcists had appealed to the God of Abraham, Isaac, and Jacob perhaps, or to a host of other deities through Hebrew history. But the people had no category for a man like Jesus. Jesus did not appeal to a deity; he did not employ a spell or technique. He spoke. And with that word, the demon obeyed. As Martin Luther wrote in one of the greatest hymns ever written, "A Mighty Fortress Is Our God":

> *And though this world, with devils filled,*
> *should threaten to undo us,*
> *We will not fear, for God hath willed His truth*
> *to triumph through us:*
> *The Prince of Darkness grim, we tremble not for him;*
> *His rage we can endure, for lo, his doom is sure,*
> *One little word shall fell him.*

Founding. One of my favorite titles used for Jesus in the New Testament is the Greek word *archegos*. It is used four times, always referring directly to Jesus, and there are three senses in which it is used.

First, the word means a person who rules and commands a people with authority. The *archegos* is the leader, prince, or chief. In ancient Greek, Zeus was called *archegos* because he was the chief of all the gods. This is the sense in Acts 5:31, "God exalted this man [Jesus] to His right hand as ruler [*archegos*] and Savior, to grant repentance to Israel, and forgiveness of sins." Jesus is the prince of God who rules from the Father's right hand.

Second, *archegos* means pioneer, captain, champion, or trailblazer. This is a person who goes ahead and opens the door for others to follow, like a captain of an army who boldly goes forth, defeats the enemy, and leads his army into victory.[14] The army follows in the triumph of their captain and shares in his spoil. An Old Testament picture of this is when David defeated Goliath. Though David was not officially a captain in the Israeli army, he went before the army and defeated their foe. Or in ancient times, the best swimmer on a boat might also be called an *archegos*. If a ship got caught among rocks, or in waves so fierce that it could not land, this able swimmer would tie a rope to the ship and to himself, jump into the water and guide the boat to shore.[15]

Jesus is the truest and highest *archegos* in this sense. He is our great Captain who entered the darkness of death, broke its reign over us (Heb. 2:14–15), and invites us to follow in his triumph. "For in bringing many sons to glory, it was entirely appropriate that God—all things exist for Him and through Him—should make the source [*archegos*] of their salvation perfect through sufferings" (Heb. 2:10).

The third sense of *archegos* describes a founder or originator. In ancient times, the founder of a city or of a school of philosophy was called its *archegos*. To use a modern illustration, we might say Steve Jobs is the *archegos* of Apple. Adam might be called the *archegos* of humanity, and Abraham might be called the *archegos* of the Hebrews. Likewise, Jesus Christ is the *archegos* of the family of God. He is "source [*archegos*] and perfecter of our faith" (Heb. 12:2). He did not merely open the door for salvation to us who believe, he is even more the "source [*archegos*] of [our] salvation" (Heb. 2:10). He is the very "source [*archegos*] of life" (Acts 3:15). Jesus is supreme in his authority because he is our supreme *archegos*.

Unimpeded. Jesus has no natural or supernatural rivals. He has final, unimpeded, and supreme authority over every square inch of existence. Nothing can stop him when he acts.

Mark 1—8 focuses on showing the unimpeded authority of Jesus Christ over all things.[16] Consider the following chart from Mark 1—8:

Jesus has supreme authority over . . .

Satan	1:12–13; 3:22–27
Demons	1:23–28; 3:11; 5:1–13; 7:25–30
Religion	(Scribes, Pharisees) 1:21–22, 32–35; 2:16–17; 7:1–12; 8:11–12
	(Tradition) 2:18–22; 7:1–12
	(The Sabbath) 2:23–27; 3:1–6

His Disciples	3:13 (he "called to him those whom he desired" ESV)
Social Order	3:21–35
Nature	4:39; 6:51
Natural Elements	6:35–44, 47–52; 8:1–9
Sickness	1:29–34; 6:55–56
Disease	1:40–45; 3:10; 5:25–34
Physical Disability	2:11–12; 3:1–6; 7:32–35; 8:22–26
Sin	2:1–12
Death	5:21–24, 35–43

All human authority is limited by geography, the ability to exercise power, and time. No one has ever been able to claim universal authority over all things.

Consider the case of Alexander the Great. He is renowned as perhaps the greatest military commander in history. He amassed the greatest geographical expanse of authority of any single leader in history; the sheer extent of territory is almost unfathomable considering the difference in technology, communications, and travel between the fourth century BC and today. Using today's maps, he ruled over some or all of Afghanistan, Pakistan, Tajikistan, Kyrgyzstan, Uzbekistan, Turkmenistan, Iran, Iraq, Azerbaijan, Armenia, Turkey, Bulgaria, Macedonia, Albania, Greece, Serbia, Romania, Cyprus, Syria, Lebanon, Israel, Palestine, Jordan, and Egypt! Though he had an impressive expanse of power, nobody ever bowed their knee to him in the Americas, China, Australia, Western Europe, or most of modern Russia. How many people never even heard of him! The authority of every commander is limited by at least geography.

The authority of every leader is limited in the execution of their authority with power. Julius Caesar, perhaps one of the most influential leaders in human history, was declared "dictator in perpetuity" and ruled most of Western Europe and the northern coast of Africa. Yet even someone as powerful as Julius Caesar could not maintain control even over his own Senate. In the end, a large group of senators stabbed and killed him, and his death precipitated the fall of the Roman Empire. Even though he had expansive authority, he lost the ability to exercise it with power.

Lastly, the authority of leaders is limited by the extent of their rule through time. Every leader in history has eventually died, except one. Consider a modern example. Mu'ammar Gaddafi ruled Libya from 1969–2011. His forty-two years of power made him the longest living ruling leader in Africa and the Arab world by 2011. But revolution erupted on February 15, 2011, in Benghazi in the context of the broader Arab Spring. The authority of Gaddafi disintegrated quickly. By October 2011 he was dead at the hands of his enemies. Even with nearly unrivaled personal control over the vast oil reserves of Libya, Gaddafi could not overcome his enemies. Death finally took him.

The world's most powerful kings and leaders have always been limited in their authority. They are limited by geography, power, and time. After the death of Gaddafi, I read Psalm 37:35–36, "I have seen a wicked, violent man well-rooted like a flourishing native tree. Then I passed by and noticed he was gone; I searched for him, but he could not be found." Reflecting on that passage, I wrote the following poem:

> *Crowned with treasures, green glories*
> *Hardly moved by Sirocco's*
> *Thick blow. Like Franklin trophies*
> *Each leaf sounding greed's echoes.*

> *None venture bark this tree's frame—*
> *Brown, dirty, bane, a man's cut.*
> *But envy not this hound's name,*
> *His vain life's worth hardly Phut.*

Roots sound Brother Leader's mort,
Ravaging the desert's drought.
Each day piercing his old fort,
Like rebels' bids for spoil's clout.

Stiff and dead this fair tree's source.
Cold, packed in to the freezer.
He that ruled lies with, perforce,
Alexander and Caesar.

Alexander the Great, Julius Caesar, and Gaddafi are all dead and their kingdoms are long gone. But King Jesus defeated death, and his kingdom continues to overcome all limits of geography, power, and time.

Empowered. One with authority but not power is like an exiled king who has legitimate authority over his people, but no power to exercise it. But Jesus has both infinite power and perfect authority. He is "far above every ruler and authority, power and dominion, and every title given, not only in this age but also in the one to come" (Eph. 1:21). He will fully display his authority and power on Judgment Day when he "abolishes all rule and all authority and power" (1 Cor. 15:24). Forever he reigns at the Father's right hand "with angels, authorities, and powers subject to Him" (1 Pet. 3:22).

Exclusive. There can be only one *supreme authority.* As Jesus has supreme authority, nothing in all existence rivals, or will ever rival, his authority. Jesus does not lack any amount of supreme authority, and no other being has any amount of supreme authority. The demons once grasped for authority beyond their assigned place in the heavens, and for that God cast them away (Jude 6).

The exclusivity of salvation in Jesus is a function of the exclusivity of the authority of Jesus. If there were, for example, another being that had authority over sin, death, and eternal condemnation, then that authority would be another path for human salvation. Using the same logic, if Jesus alone has authority over sin, death, and condemnation, then he alone can save people from eternal death. This means that someone who struggles accepting that Jesus is the "only way" to God really struggles with the claims of Jesus to supreme authority. Faith in the exclusivity of Jesus demands faith in the exclusivity of salvation in Jesus.

Faith in the exclusivity of the authority of Jesus also brings a person into conflict with the people, institutions, ideologies, and spiritual forces of darkness contending for the seat of authority. This is so because a person's thoughts, actions, and affections all depend on the allegiance of his or her heart. One may permit several authorities, or "idols," to compete for supremacy in his or her heart, but when Jesus enters the scene he rejects all other authorities and demands total surrender. The throne of the heart was crafted for only Jesus to sit and rule on it.

Authority demands a response; either submission or rejection. Followers of Christ not only war in their hearts for daily allegiance to Christ, but they also contend in their lives and societies for the purity of their public devotion to Christ.

The story of the seventeenth-century Covenanters in Scotland highlights the inevitable conflict of earthly authorities with the authority of Christ. In 1625 Charles I took the throne of England, Scotland, and Ireland. He believed in the divine right of kings, the idea that God rules directly through the king, and therefore, the king rules above the people and the law. Charles I began to demand that the Church of Scotland adhere to a monarchy-controlled Anglican church. The Scottish Christians were appalled, believing that the supreme leader of the church, and the world, was not the king of England but King Jesus himself. Tension between the king and his clergy with the Church of Scotland erupted into violence in 1637. Backed by the Archbishop of Canterbury, the king declared that opposition to the use of the Anglican Book of Common Prayer in the liturgy would be considered treason. On

July 23, 1637, when the Dean of Edinburgh began the Anglican liturgy in St. Giles church, a local street market vendor, Jenny Geddes, threw her stool at the head of the king's man and cried out, "Devil cause you colic in your stomach, false thief! Dare you say the Mass in my ear?!" Riots broke out at the church and continued. This eventually led to a group of resisters to the Crown, called the Covenanters, signing a covenant in 1638 declaring allegiance to Jesus Christ and his church above the king. A Covenanter recognized only one supreme ruler—Jesus Christ—and refused to the death to recognize a king who claimed to be "supreme over all persons, and causes, ecclesiastic as well as civil." Their covenant led to a season of merciless violence and killings. An estimated 18,000 Covenanters died, were imprisoned, or were forced from their homes for their allegiance to King Jesus.[17]

In our pluralistic society, this story may seem like a petty disagreement about church government. But at the time, it was no such disagreement. By adopting the Anglican episcopacy in their time, the Scottish Covenanters would have been understood as endorsing the king of England with the license to act outside of the law and as a sort of mediator between God and man. But they believed—even unto death—that though Jesus has authority over the law, he submitted to it, fulfilling it completely, and thus proved himself the only mediator between God and man.[18] The story of these brave Scottish Covenanters reminds us that when we say that Jesus Christ has all authority in heaven and on earth, we not only recognize him as supreme, but we declare that all other authorities should, and will, bow their knee to him.

Legitimate. Legitimacy is a concept at the very heart of authority. Legitimacy is so central to the establishment of authority that this whole book could be framed as a defense of the legitimacy of the authority of Christ.

The exchange between the scribes and elders with Jesus in Mark 11:27–33 is a potent story about the legitimacy of the authority of Christ.

> They came again to Jerusalem. As He was walking in the temple complex, the chief priests, the scribes, and the elders came and asked Him, "By what authority are You doing these things? Who gave You this authority to do these things?" Jesus said to them, "I will ask you one question; then answer Me, and I will tell you by what authority I am doing these things. Was John's baptism from heaven or from men? Answer Me." They began to argue among themselves: "If we say, 'From heaven,' He will say, 'Then why didn't you believe him?' But if we say, 'From men'"— they were afraid of the crowd, because everyone thought that John was a genuine prophet. So they answered Jesus, "We don't know." And Jesus said to them, "Neither will I tell you by what authority I do these things."

The chief priests, scribes, and elders saw Jesus demonstrate his power indisputably, and they hated him for it.[19] They heard him teach with unique authority and wisdom. They met the men and women that he healed and saw the power of Jesus manifested, but they resisted acknowledging that Jesus was from God. Their hardness of heart produced envy, jealousy, slander, hatred, fear, and unbelief against Jesus. In Mark 11:28 they directly ask Jesus about his authority, "By what authority are You doing these things? Who gave You this authority to do these things?" They ask two questions that are really one. First, they ask who gave him the *right* to do "these things," which is almost certainly a reference to at least his act of cleansing the temple (Mark 11:15–18). They wanted to know his credentials. Yes, he had indisputably demonstrated his supernatural power, but did he have a right to walk into the very temple of God and denounce its leaders? The Jews had asked him a very similar question attacking his credentials the first time that he cleansed the temple early in his ministry: "What sign of authority will You show us for doing these things?" (John 2:18). The second question from the Jewish leaders was about the source of his authority: "Who gave You this authority to do these things?" (Mark 11:28). They thought that the power of Jesus came from Satan (Mark 3:22–30).

Jesus seemed to enjoy silencing his opponents with a counter question:[20] "I will ask you one question; then answer Me, and I will tell you by what authority I am doing these things. Was John's baptism from heaven or from men? Answer Me" (Mark 11:29–30). Jesus reframes the question about his authority into a question about John the Baptist's authority. Why? If John the Baptist was from God, then Jesus was from God, because John's ministry prepared the way for Jesus, and John the Baptist testified that Jesus was the Son of God (John 1:19–34). Not only is the preaching of John the Baptist inseparable from the divine authority of Jesus, but John the Baptist represents the prophesied one who prepares the way for the Messiah sent by God. He was born to "make ready for the Lord a prepared people" (Luke 1:17). Finally, referencing the baptism of John no doubt reminded his audience of the pinnacle of John's ministry: the baptism of Jesus Christ himself! In that baptism, all three persons of the Trinity are gloriously manifested in public display of the divine approval of Jesus Christ as the beloved Son of God. So, by referring to John's baptism, Jesus authoritatively shuts down his opponents and points to God Most High as well as his own innate position as the Son of God as his credentials. The gospel that we declare and demonstrate to the nations rests on the doctrinal foundation of the legitimacy of Christ's authority.

The legitimacy of Jesus' authority reflects the righteousness of God. The upholding of God's righteousness is central to his holy administration of history. This is part of what Romans 9:21 means, "Or has the potter no *right* [exousia] over the clay, to make from the same lump one piece of pottery for honor and another for dishonor?" (italics added). Romans 9:21 means that God has the legitimate authority to do what he wills with every person and every people—if he damns some or saves some, that is his legitimate decision. The righteousness of God is central as well to the gospel itself. The righteousness of God is the foundation of our hope for salvation (Rom. 3:21–26). Our legitimacy as children of God depends on whether Jesus is legitimately God's Son. This is why John 1:12–13 uses *exousia* as well: "But to all who did receive Him, He gave them the right [*exousia*] to be children of God, to those who believe in His name, who were born, not of blood, or of the will of the flesh, or of the will of man, but of God." In other words, as the legitimate Son of God, Jesus gives legitimacy to God's children. This is why Revelation 22:14 also uses *exousia*: "Blessed are those who wash their robes, so that they may have the right [*exousia*] to the tree of life and may enter the city by the gates." The right of believers to inherit eternal life depends on whether their robes are washed in the blood of the Lamb, a blood that is trustworthy and sufficient because it comes from the legitimate Son of God.

Is His Authority Dependent on the Acceptance of the People?

A common definition of legitimacy within the social sciences is the *acceptance* of authority as right. One might argue that fundamentally the queen of England is only the supreme "royal" in as much as the people accept her as royal.

But what if people do not accept Jesus as the Son of God? Does this discredit his authority? A friend said to me, "If Jesus is Lord, then why do so many people not follow him? Isn't the fact that people do not universally recognize Jesus as Lord mean that he is, in fact, not the Lord? Doesn't his right as king depend on having followers who accept his rule?"

No. This is where modern discussions within the social sciences on authority and the biblical portrayal of the authority of Jesus part ways. The authority of Jesus does not depend on our acceptance of him or his rule. His authority, power, and legitimacy are independent of anything anyone ever says or thinks about him. He can never be deposed. There never has been and never will be a successful *coup d'état* against him. No matter the extent of our sin, the force and power of God's enemies, and no matter if the will of all humanity is joined together against God himself, Jesus is still supremely Lord.

The Son of God, Jesus Christ, is the supreme authority over all existence. Jesus needs no vindication from reason, facts, history, or consensus. He never doubts himself. There has never been nor will there ever be any shadow of doubt in the Father as to the truthfulness, perfection, glory, completeness, and authority of Jesus. The Spirit always testifies to the authority of Jesus. There is no unknown fact, no revolutionary argument, no surprising revelation, no unseen reality, no innovative discovery, and no new thought for the Lord Jesus Christ, eternal *logos* of God.

My sons, look! There comes from the mountain way,
Beyond the shadows, past our dreary land.
Put down those toys, my Lord this is the day!
Arise and out the door, just as we've planned!

Ev'ry pain will cease—so fast!—the tears will dry!
My body feels to run a thousand miles!
I wish to fly to him—Lord, now I fly!
There fly with me my sons—I look—they smile!

Since Adam's fall the world has groaned for now.
He's heard the rocks, the clouds, the beasts, and trees.
The earth has set its course by heaven's vow
That one day old will burn and new will be.

Heaven's Farmer once took his plough and sowed.
He scattered seeds across his harvest fields.
So grew the wheat, but with it weeds soon showed;
The Farmer's foe had come to damn his yield.

So sons you see the Farmer had to wait
For harvest season. He waits because he cares.
He'll send his workers to the fields of fate
To sift and gather wheat, but burn the tares.

No one knows when the harvest season starts.
But now, today, the reapers rend the skies.
He knows the deeds of man, he knows their hearts.
He knows who's his, the rest will surely die.

The Son of Man beside his Father sits.
His garment white as snow, his throne like fire.
All knees are down, the peoples all submit.
The books are opened, his judgment transpires.

In the crowning of the age, the King is crowned.
The Father beams in the praise of his Son.
The Spirit fills the saints, so that they sound:
"All glory to the Godhead, three in one!"

---- Chapter 2 ----

"Has Been Given to Me"

PLEASE JOIN ME ON A STROLL DOWN A TYPICAL STREET IN THE ARAB world. As we exit our home, we immediately smell the fresh bread from the bakery next door owned by the friendly Abd al-Rahman. Having just returned from prayers, a customer greets Abd al-Rahman with, "May God accept you." Moving along, we pass the primary school wall on our left. Spray-painted on the wall is the familiar slogan, "There is no might or power except in Allah." Across the street there is a house of a Christian family. On the outer wall there is a spray-painted verse from the Qur'an, "Say, 'Allah, He is One. Allah, the Eternal Refuge. He neither begets nor is born. Nor is there to Him any equivalent.'"[1] Moving along, we look up at a makeshift sign for the neighborhood cafe called, "Tawheed." The word *tawheed* refers to the doctrine of God's infinite oneness and, by implication, a rejection of the Trinity. Finally, having reached the corner of our street, we approach a beggar who raises his hand to us and repeats in desperate repetition, "There is no god but Allah. May Allah reward you for your good works, if Allah wills. There is no god but Allah."

One can hardly walk a city block on the average Arab street without being barraged by religious and cultural affirmations of

the oneness of God and, either implicitly or explicitly, denounce-
ments of the doctrine of the Trinity. There is nothing more
strange, and frankly, more offensive to Islam than Jesus' claim
to have "all authority in heaven and on earth." For if he has all
authority, then he must be divine himself, for only God has all
authority. Millions within the Muslim world sincerely wonder,
"How can these Christians claim that 'the Father' gave Jesus all
authority and at the same time Jesus is equal with the Father?
Furthermore, as a prophet, what right does Jesus have to claim
divine authority for himself? Prophets are given authority, but that
does not make them divine."

Christian workers in the Muslim world often face direct questions about the Trinity, and Jesus' place within the Trinity, because
authority is at the heart of the Trinity. In the Bible, authority is
one of the few topics from which we learn about the nature of the
Trinity.[2]

In both the Muslim and non-Muslim world, the issue most
often of concern is not that "God" might claim supreme authority
over creation, for if he exists, it is reasonable to assume that he has
at least some measure of divine authority. The concern is, rather,
that the historical man Jesus Christ claimed to have the divine
authority of God in full. Referencing a generalized "God" is a
fairly benign cultural artifact even in "secular" society. In Muslim
contexts, references to God are nearly ubiquitous in daily life. But
Muslim communities and secular communities unite in their shock
at any direct reference to the supreme authority of Jesus Christ.

What does Jesus mean that all authority "has been given" to
him? Who gave it to him? For what purpose was it given? If Jesus
is God, how can someone else give him authority? And if the
authority was given to Jesus, does that not imply that the giver
of authority is superior to Jesus? These are the questions that this
chapter will answer.

Through a study of John 5:19–30, we will see that authority was given in full to Jesus the Son by God the Father in the context of divine love and for the accomplishment of the triune God's redemptive purposes.

> Then Jesus replied, "I assure you: The Son is not able to do anything on His own, but only what He sees the Father doing. For whatever the Father does, the Son also does these things in the same way. For the Father loves the Son and shows Him everything He is doing, and He will show Him greater works than these so that you will be amazed. And just as the Father raises the dead and gives them life, so the Son also gives life to anyone He wants to. The Father, in fact, judges no one but has given all judgment to the Son, so that all people will honor the Son just as they honor the Father. Anyone who does not honor the Son does not honor the Father who sent Him. I assure you: Anyone who hears My word and believes Him who sent Me has eternal life and will not come under judgment but has passed from death to life. I assure you: An hour is coming, and is now here, when the dead will hear the voice of the Son of God, and those who hear will live. For just as the Father has life in Himself, so also He has granted to the Son to have life in Himself. And He has granted Him the right to pass judgment, because He is the Son of Man. Do not be amazed at this, because a time is coming when all who are in the graves will hear His voice and come out—those who have done good things, to the resurrection of life, but those who have done wicked things, to the resurrection of judgment. I can do nothing on My own. I judge only as I hear, and My judgment is righteous, because I do not seek My own will, but the will of Him who sent Me." (John 5:19–30)

Does Jesus Have the Right to Have All Authority?

At the heart of the attack on the authority of Jesus in John 5:19–30 is the question of the legitimacy of his claim to authority. What right does he have to say that he has "all authority"? Without legitimate authority, according to his own Jewish law, Jesus was nothing but a devil-filled hoax. But if his authority is legitimate, Jesus is the very Messiah, the Son of God and Son of Man.

The question is whether Jesus *has the right* to minister on the Sabbath day and whether he *has the right* to "[make] Himself equal with God" (John 5:18). The Jews were infuriated at Jesus because he was speaking and ministering with the authority only attributed to God himself. They were angry with Jesus because they did not believe he had the right to work on the Sabbath. Only God has that right. And because Jesus claims to be one with God, he has that right as well. To establish the legitimacy of his authority, Jesus appeals to his identity as the Son of God and Son of Man.

As the Son of God

How does the giving of authority from the Father to the Son build the legitimacy of the Son's authority to work on the Sabbath and his claim to be divine? Very simply, as the "One and Only Son" (1 John 4:9), Jesus rightly *inherits* all authority from his Father. If God the Father has the right to minister on the Sabbath, so does the Son of God.

The moment my first child, Nehemiah, was born, he became my legal, legitimate heir. If my wife and I had died even a minute after he was born, he would have received legal ownership of all our assets, to be granted at the appropriate age, simply because he is our child. As the eternal Son of God, Jesus possesses all things from the Father. Authority is part of his eternal (past and future) inheritance from the Father. And as such, he has the full legal right to possess this authority.[3] The legitimacy of Jesus' authority is based on his being the Son of God.

The Father gave "all authority" to the Son because the Father loves the Son with an infinite and eternal love. "The Father loves the Son and has given all things into His hands" (John 3:35). The Father did not give the authority to the Son for a specific work, but because of a specific relationship that they share. In this way, the eternal giving of authority by the Father to the Son highlights the glory of the Son as one with God.

The Father's happiness in the glorification of the Son highlights the Father's love for the Son. "Father, I desire those You have given Me to be with Me where I am. Then they will see My glory, which You have given Me because You loved Me before the world's foundation" (John 17:24). Nothing is more pleasing to the Father than when his Son is exalted above all things.

Just as the Father loves the Son, the Son loves the Father. The Son's love for the Father is illustrated in the delightful submission of the Son to the Father. "For whatever the Father does, the Son also does these things in the same way" (John 5:19). The Son lives for the glorification of the Father, because the Son loves the Father (John 17:4).

Because the Son loves the Father, the Son walks in step with the Father and derives all authority from the Father. The Son is not a rogue agent working independently from God. The heavens had already seen that kind of rebellion before, and it led to the fall of many angels (Jude 6). Jesus was not ministering on the Sabbath in rebellion to the Father. On the contrary, he was sent by the Father and has been given all things by the Father. As such, an attack on the authority of Jesus is an attack on the authority of the Father since Jesus was sent from the Father and works in perfect unity with the Father. "Anyone who does not honor the Son does not honor the Father who sent Him" (John 5:23).

Do not speed past the significance of this connection between the authority and sonship of Jesus. The world's nearly two billion Muslims believe it to be the most God-belittling and damaging lie in the history of the world. The greatest sin that a Muslim can commit is to elevate Jesus, or any other person, to the position of God. Islam fundamentally denies that Jesus is the Son of God, and so by virtue of that, all sects of Islam deny that Jesus inherits the full authority of God.

This connection between the sonship of Jesus and his authority is critical to disciple makers. When we explain the authority of Jesus to others, we must explain it—as Jesus does in John 5—in context of Jesus' relationship with the Father. Without the doctrine of the Trinity, there is no doctrine of the authority of Jesus.[4] The interpretive framework of a Father-Son relationship is indispensable for understanding texts like John 5:19–29. Without it, the text simply would not make sense. The Muslim world rejects the sonship of Jesus ultimately because it splits the precious oneness of God. Hence, one of the most quoted Qur'anic verses in the Muslim world is an implicit rebuke of the idea that Jesus is God's "son": "Say, 'Allah, He is One. Allah, the Eternal Refuge. He neither begets nor is born. Nor is there to Him any equivalent.'"[5] While Islam rebukes sonship of Christ in order to magnify the glory of God, we embrace the sonship of Christ in order to magnify the glory of God. For if we lighten the meaning of Jesus' divine "sonship" in order to make the identity of Christ clearer, we may inadvertently work against ourselves since the sonship of Christ is the fundamental concept from which we learn about the unity of God. In sum, without divine sonship, there is no divine unity.

As the Son of Man

Replying to the questioning of his authority, Jesus argues that he has the authority to issue divine judgment over all mankind, because he is the Son of Man. "And He has granted Him the right to pass judgment, because He is the Son of Man" (John 5:27). This is a surprising remark from Jesus, for we might naturally assume that eternal judgment should be issued by the "Son of God." But in referring to himself in this context as the Son of Man, he is clarifying that he has the Father's authorization to issue the final word of judgment on every person, either to eternal life or eternal death.

Jesus' authority to issue eternal judgment is central to the meaning of the term Son of Man. It will be the Son of Man who will come, "with His angels in the glory of His Father, and then He will reward each according to what he has done" (Matt. 16:27). The Son of Man will "appear in the sky, and then all the peoples of the earth will mourn; and they will see the Son of Man coming on the clouds of heaven with power and great glory" (Matt. 24:30). On the Day of Judgment, the Son of Man will sit "on his glorious throne" (Matt. 19:28) and either acknowledge a person before God or be ashamed of a person before God (Mark 8:38; Luke 12:8).

When Jesus refers to himself as the "Son of Man," he references not only his divine role in judgment, but also in the history of redemption. He makes clear that he is not merely a rabbi ministering on the Sabbath and stirring up trouble. He is the Messiah, the very one awaited since Adam and Eve. Using the term "Son of Man," Jesus echoes back to the prophet Ezekiel who spoke of the destruction of Jerusalem and restoration of the kingdom of God (Ezek. 4, 7, 10, 22, 40—48).[6] He also reminds the Jewish listeners of the prophet Daniel's vision of the coming of the Son of Man:

> I continued watching in the night visions, and I saw One like a son of man coming with the clouds of heaven. He approached the Ancient of Days and was escorted before Him. He was given authority to rule, and glory, and a kingdom; so that those of every people, nation, and language should serve Him. His dominion is an everlasting dominion that will not pass away, and His kingdom is one that will not be destroyed. (Dan. 7:13–14)

No matter how we might place this passage in the context of the end times, one fact is sure: the Ancient of Days gives authority to the Son of Man to rule over all and "every people, nation, and language should serve Him" (v. 14).

What Does the Son of God/Son of Man Do with This Authority?

With this authority what does the Son of God/Son of Man actually do? Jesus' response to the Jewish leaders in John 5 focuses on two great works: the granting of life and the execution of eternal judgment. These are the two primary works that Jesus says will make us all "marvel" (John 5:20 ESV).

First, *Jesus has the authority to give life.* Jesus "gives life to anyone He wants to" (John 5:21). On the basis of hearing his word and believing in the Father, one will obtain eternal life (John 5:24). "I assure you: An hour is coming, and is now here, when the dead will hear the voice of the Son of God, and those who hear will live. For just as the Father has life in Himself, so also He has granted to the Son to have life in Himself" (vv. 25–26).

Someone might object that man should not put their hope in another man for eternal life; only God holds the keys to eternal life. Someone might say that putting our faith in another man lessens our assurance that we will be given eternal life. But what does the Bible say? The Bible actually says just the opposite. Because we share in humanity with our brother, our friend, our Lord and Savior, we are *all the more* assured that he will save his people on Judgment Day because as a human, he conquered death (Acts 17:31). He destroyed death, and now the Father has put "everything under His feet" (1 Cor. 15:27). It is both right and loving of God the Father to judge humanity through the Son of Man.

Second, *Jesus has unique authority to "execute judgment"* (John 5:27 ESV) *on all mankind.* This judgment will be the final word for every man, determining whether they enter hell or heaven. "The Father, in fact, judges no one but has given all judgment to the

Son" (John 5:22). When Jesus speaks, the dead will rise. Then Jesus will judge: "I judge only as I hear, and My judgment is righteous, because I do not seek My own will, but the will of Him who sent Me" (John 5:30). In the Day of Judgment, the whole world will know that Jesus is the Son of Man and Son of God and that the Father has given all authority in heaven and on earth to him. But how precious this proof will be for the children of God, who have waited for this day for so long! For in that day, we will all live in the presence of God and see with our own eyes—as Jesus said—that, "I am in My Father, you are in Me, and I am in you" (John 14:20).

Let us never forget to be grateful that we are the people of God, who one day will be forever united with God in Christ in paradise! Let us also not forget that the time is short to call people to follow Christ with us. A number of years ago, I was having coffee with a few believers in Christ in a beach café in Tunisia. We sat in the midst of hundreds of Muslim Arab men who were enjoying the pleasant evening in the community of their good friends. It occurred to me at that moment, as we were chatting about the glory of God and the preciousness of his Word, that our table was almost certainly the only table with followers of Christ on that entire beach. I was forcefully struck with the vision of us all dying in that very moment, approaching the judgment seat of Christ, and every one of those men being condemned to an eternity of hell! Only our table would be saved! Indeed, most of us live every day in the company of hundreds, if not thousands, of people who will spend eternity in hell. Will we not do everything we can to tell them the good news of this Son of God and Son of Man?

Subordination of the Son to the Father

Some might be concerned that such extreme exaltation of Jesus may, in turn, elevate Jesus over the first person of the Trinity, the Father. But this is a misplaced concern about the trinity; for each person of the Trinity lives to exalt the other Persons. The Father exalts the Son above all, and the Son exalts the Father above all. The Son exalts the Father through his eternal subjection to the Father.

One of the main points in John 5:17–30 is that while the Father and Son are equal in being, the Son is subordinate in his role to the Father. And this will be the case for all of eternity (1 Cor. 15:24–28). The exact meaning of the subordination of the Son to the Father has been the point of much controversy in the history of the church. But for now, we must simply restate the orthodox teaching of the church: Jesus is the *Son* of God, and is naturally subordinate to his Father in that role. Though the illustration is admittedly insufficient, my own son is no less equal with me in worth, but he is subordinate to me in authority because I am his father and he is my son. Likewise, Jesus is subordinate in authority to his Father. "The Son is not able to do anything on His own, but only what He sees the Father doing. . . . I can do nothing on My own" (John 5:19, 30). In this sense, the Son does not independently call the shots. The Son's authority is forever linked to the Father's authority.[7]

Does Subordination Mean Inferiority?

Now, does the subordination of the Son in authority to the Father mean in any sense that his authority is any less than the Father's? No. For the Father has granted "all authority . . . in heaven and on earth" to the Son. Does the subordination of the Son to the Father mean that the Son is inferior in glory to the Father? This is, in fact, one of the main counterattacks of Islam against the doctrine of the sonship of Jesus. For one of God's incommunicable attributes is his absolute independence from all other beings. So how can Jesus be equal with God and simultaneously "do nothing" on his own (John 5:30)? To this question, I give four responses. In response, I give four reasons.

First, *it fits with the role of a father to give authority to his son* without delineation of worth or honor between the two. God the Father delegates to God the Son because delegation fits with his role as Father. The Son naturally represents the Father and exhibits his nature to mankind. Just like in an earthly family, the Father is responsible to delegate authority and the Son is responsible to execute that authority. So everything is from the Father, through the Son (1 Cor. 8:6). Wayne Grudem helpfully articulates this dynamic:

> The role of commanding, directing, and sending is appropriate to the position of the Father, after whom all human fatherhood is patterned. (Eph. 3:14–15). And the role of obeying, going as the Father sends, and revealing God to us is appropriate to the role of the Son, who is also called the Word of God (cf. John 1:1–5, 14, 18; 17:4; Phil. 2:5–11). These roles could not have been reversed or the Father would have ceased to be the Father and the Son would have ceased to be the Son. And by analogy from that relationship, we may conclude that the role of the Holy Spirit is similarly one that was appropriate to the relationship he had with the Father and the Son before the world was created.[8]

Second, *the Jews did not hear Jesus claiming to be inferior to God, but, in fact, equal to God!* Jesus' Jewish audience thought that Jesus was claiming to be equal with God by calling God his Father (John 5:18). Orthodox Muslims would never refer to God as their "Father." In their minds, if we call God our Father, then we are saying that we share with God in his glory as his children. But that would be heresy, because God shares his glory with no one. Similarly, the Jews needed no explanation that when Jesus said, "My Father is still working, and I am working also" (v. 17); he was clearly "calling God his own Father, making Himself equal with God" (v. 18).

Third, *the Father works in perfect accord with the Son*. The Son is not independent of the Father, nor is the Father independent of the Son. The mystery of the Trinity is that there are three distinct persons in the Godhead, each fulfilling unique roles, each in perfect unity with each other as one God. So Jesus is in step with the Father in the giving of life and the execution of judgment, and the Father is in step with the Son in the giving of life and in judgment. The "Father, in fact, judges no one but has given all judgment to the Son" (John 5:22). At the same time, the "wrath of God remains" on him who "refuses to believe in the Son" (John 3:36).[9] In this sense, the Son's authority is entirely legitimate because he works in perfect unity with the Father and the Spirit.

Fourth, *there is no tension in the Bible between the glory of Jesus and the glory of the Father*. Though, God says numerous times through his prophets, "I am Yahweh, and there is no other, there is no God but Me," the Father pours out his divine praise onto his Son. During the first days of the Son's earthly life, the Father even brought the "wise men" from the ends of the earth to worship before the Son. Moreover, the Father has commanded his angels to worship the Son (Heb. 1:6).

So we agree with the Jews that Jesus was "making Himself equal with God" (John 5:18), for indeed he was! He is equal with God in being and glory, but distinct from the Father in the role that he plays within the Trinity.

The Role of the Subordinate Son in Redemptive History

Here it would be helpful to clearly trace the authority of the Son through redemptive history. First, from eternity past, Jesus was the pre-incarnate Word of God who dwelt in eternal and infinite happiness in the community of the Trinity. In the act of the creation, Jesus wielded divine authority, since "all things have been created through Him and for Him" (Col. 1:16). In the incarnation, the Son humbled himself, descending to take to his own divine nature also a human nature. During his earthly ministry, the Son of God/Son of Man executed authority in accord with the redemptive purposes of his Father. Jesus delegated authority to his disciples to use in their ministry. In his crucifixion, at the very moment it appeared Satan had defeated him, Jesus was actually authoritatively crushing Satan underneath his feet. When he rose from the dead, he demonstrated his limitless authority by disarming "the rulers and authorities and disgraced them publicly; He triumphed over them by Him" (Col. 2:15). When he ascended, he declared for all to hear that he has universal authority from the Father.

At Pentecost, Peter exclaimed to the crowd, "God has made this Jesus, whom you crucified, both Lord and Messiah!" (Acts 2:36). Presently, he rules in authority over his church as it completes the Great Commission. The gospel goes forth to all people groups through the manifold display of the authority of Christ over unbelief, sickness, evil spirits, Satan, temptation, and even death. In the consummation of history, we will see the Son of Man at the right hand of the Father. He will be there, as it was when Stephen the martyr saw him, ready to descend and complete the task of destroying the devil. At that time, God will finish putting all of his enemies under his feet (1 Cor. 15:25). Then finally, at the end of the old earth and the beginning of the new earth, the "Son himself will also be subjected to him who put all things in subjection under him, that God may be all in all" (1 Cor. 15:28 ESV).

The Father delegated all authority to the Son for the accomplishment of redemption for his people. That is one of the reasons that Jesus upholds the Great Commission, "Go and make disciples" with, "All authority has been given to Me in heaven and on earth." The triune God has a grand agenda, called redemption, and each person in the Trinity plays a critical role in that agenda. The Father delegates his authority to the Son. The Spirit executes the authority of the Son in perfect accord with the will of the Father on earth. Together, the Godhead authoritatively rules all creation in joyful unity for his redemptive purposes.

Ezekiel 1:4

You have sent the wind with the sand,
   A herald from the north.
Its train the cloud that you command,
   With judgment you bring forth.

Like red chariots with their captain,
   Onward on triumph's trail.
The swift warrior made to glisten,
   Like clouds in a bright veil.

The rain an oracle of love,
   Drops from the prophet's brow.
"Oh Israel, my first son, my dove,
   You're lost, but now be found!"

Fire flashes like the prophet's tongue,
   The bush ablaze now speaks.
Gleaming amber at center strong,
   The sharpened sword unleashed.

A tempest in the wake of wind,
   A blessing from the north.
If we but sought some sunshine, then,
   Lord, make the wind your course.

Chapter 3

The Son's Authority as Prophet, Priest, and King

JESUS IS THE FINAL AND EXALTED PROPHET, PRIEST, AND KING. EACH of these three offices highlights his supreme authority in a new way. Christ properly fulfilled each of these offices throughout his earthly ministry; now he continues to minister in them from his heavenly throne.

It might seem that authority is most directly linked to Christ's kingship. But we will see authority is the central connection point between all three offices of prophet, priest, and king. As a study of the three offices of Christ sheds light on his supreme authority, so also a study on his authority sheds light on his supreme fulfillment of the work of each office.

Anointing

The thematic link between the three offices is the very title that we ascribe to Jesus: the *Christ*. Christ, or *Christos* in Greek, is the translation of the Hebrew word *Messiah* (John 1:41). As a title, Christ means "The Anointed One." The Hebrew root of

Messiah is used throughout the Old Testament to describe the sacred anointing of prophets (1 Kings 19:16), priests (Lev. 4:5, 16), and kings (1 Sam. 24:6, 10). To assume the office of prophet, priest, or king in Israel meant that God had set one apart from the community for a special role under God's leadership. This role required unique designation, authority, and power for its proper fulfillment. So when we say that Jesus is the "Christ," we are saying that Jesus is the awaited and anointed prophet, priest, and king—the Savior!—of God's people.

In the Old Testament, the prophet, priest, and king were all ceremonially anointed with oil. This anointing symbolized their investment by God with authority. Jesus was anointed as the prophet, priest, and king of his people, but not with oil. He was anointed with the Holy Spirit. This anointing took place at his baptism. "After Jesus was baptized, He went up immediately from the water. The heavens suddenly opened for Him, and He saw the Spirit of God descending like a dove and coming down on Him. And there came a voice from heaven: 'This is My beloved Son. I take delight in Him!'" (Matt. 3:16–17). The anointing of Jesus was greater than the prophets, priests, and kings of old because God the Father himself anointed him (Acts 10:37–38). The baptism of Jesus was God's public endorsement of Jesus for the work of ministry.

Because authority and power are symbolized by the anointing, it is not surprising that immediately after his baptism his authority and power over sin was on trial front and center in his desert temptation. The devil knew the significance of his baptism, so he sought to strip Jesus of the very meaning of his anointing. If Jesus gave in to that temptation, he would have lost his authority as prophet, priest, and king over his people.

But that would not be so. For Jesus was the "shoot . . . from the stump of Jesse" of whom the prophet Isaiah said, "The Spirit of the LORD will rest on Him—a Spirit of wisdom and understanding, a Spirit of counsel and strength, a Spirit of knowledge and of the fear of the LORD" (Isa. 11:1–2). He would triumph over temptation, trial, suffering, and even death.

The three offices of Jesus are all necessary for the completion of God's redemption mission. Thus, the mission of God is the mission of Jesus as prophet, priest, and king. As Jesus fulfills the work of each office, he accomplishes our eternal salvation. Thus, fulfilling all prophecy, Jesus could legitimately say, "The Spirit of the Lord is on Me, because He has anointed Me to preach good news to the poor. He has sent Me to proclaim freedom to the captives and recovery of sight to the blind, to set free the oppressed, to proclaim the year of the Lord's favor" (Luke 4:18–19).

Christ the Prophet

The work of Christ as prophet is to serve man on behalf of God. Thus, his teaching was not his but was God's (John 7:16). His authority as prophet was the authority of God himself. "Don't you believe that I am in the Father and the Father is in Me? The words I speak to you I do not speak on My own. The Father who lives in Me does His works" (John 14:10). The prophet of God speaks and expects the people of God to listen and obey. But as we know, the people of God throughout the Old Testament were bent toward disobeying God's words. Something greater was required than a mere prophet to communicate the word of God. So God provided not merely a person to speak the word of God; he provided as a person the very Word of God. Jesus not only brings revelation from God; he *is* the revelation of God. The authority of his words not only derives from the endorsement of God but from the fact that he is God himself, and all that God says is forever true. This is why Jesus never adopts the familiar preamble of the Old Testament prophets, "Thus says the LORD." Instead, he affirms the very deity of his being with the words, "I say to you," for his prophetic ministry is that of God himself.

As the Word (*Logos*) of God, Jesus speaks and effectively calls his people to himself. Those whom God elects, Jesus calls, and those whom he calls, the Spirit empowers to obey. The prophet Jesus speaks with authority so great that it pierces to the very soul of man and commands the life, power, and transformation to produce obedience. This is the good news of the New Covenant, and it is our only hope in calling the nations to repentance and faith in Christ.

The accuracy of a prophet's words is the test of whether he is truly of God (Deut. 18:22). According to the Law of Moses, if a supposed prophet speaks in the name of other gods, he shall die (Deut. 18:20). Knowing this, Jesus spoke in the name of the one true God and accurately prophesied.[1] Everything that Jesus said is true and will be one day proven as such.

The works of Jesus also prove his authentic prophethood in public view. "These very works I am doing testify about Me that the Father has sent Me" (John 5:36). It may seem strange to hear Jesus referred to as a "prophet," as that title can feel implicitly downgrading of the glory of the one we also know as Immanuel—"God with us." This is true especially when we interact with Muslims who consider Jesus to be no more than one in a succession of prophets, finalized in Muhammad. But in terms of the Bible, the title of prophet is not only fitting for Jesus, it in fact glorifies him as the long-awaited one of God. Moses foretold of the final Prophet of God who would come and speak the words of God (Deut. 18:15–19).[2] This is why Jesus says, "For if you believed Moses, you would believe Me, because he wrote about Me" (John 5:46).[3]

This is where we begin to seriously confuse our Muslim friends. What right does Jesus have to claim that his words alone are divine revelation? Muslims are taught that only God has the right to endorse a prophet with authority. But the Bible teaches that Jesus is not only the authority *from* God, he is the authority *of* God. In Islamic thought, the highest blasphemy is for a prophet to claim that he is himself divinely authoritative. Instead, a prophet should insist that he has no authority in and of himself; he is, rather, merely a messenger from God. But Jesus claims to be more than the mere messenger. He is the message itself. He is the long-awaited prophet (Deut. 18:15); he is the very *Logos* of God. Thus, the foundational discord between the biblical gospel and Islam is rooted in the authority of Jesus.

Christ the Priest

While a prophet serves man on behalf of God, a priest serves God on behalf of man. Priests must be holy, as they present sacrifices to God for the sin of the people. Priests intercede for the people to God and they steward the tabernacle of God. So when we say that Christ holds the office of our High Priest, we mean that he is holy, that he presented the sacrifice for our sin, he intercedes for us, and that he rules over the church, which is the true tabernacle of God. Likewise, as the church is "a chosen race, a royal priesthood, a holy nation, a people for His possession" (1 Pet. 2:9), the church should present sacrifices of worship to God, intercede for the nations, and steward the gospel of God.

The issue of the authority of Christ as priest and the authority of Christians as priests goes straight to the heart of present-day theological divisions between Christians. I believe in the supreme authority of Christ as priest and his delegation of that authority as priests to all of his people. For we all now have access with "boldness to enter the sanctuary through the blood of Jesus" (Heb. 10:19)! He is our High Priest who grants us all full access and favor! Praise God for this free access to the throne and delegated authority to minister as priests to the nations. What a privilege!

The priesthood of Christ is precious for saints who are persevering through affliction. Because Jesus is a greater priest than those of the Old Covenant, we have greater confidence, assurance, endurance, and faith as we suffer in this world. His unique, greater authority as High Priest produces confidence in us by faith that no matter what happens, "Jesus is better." This confidence has a "great reward" in the world to come (Heb. 10:35).

We must dwell on the connections between his authority and his priesthood to build our confidence to follow Jesus in the midst of opposition. In the words of the writer of Hebrews to a people enduring great affliction, "Therefore, since we have a great high priest who has passed through the heavens—Jesus the Son of God—let us hold fast to the confession" (Heb. 4:14).

We will see that Christ has supreme authority as priest. His authority as our priest derives from his greater *qualification* as a priest, his greater *presentation* of a greater sacrifice, his greater *propitiation* of the wrath of God, and his greater *intercession*. As a result, Jesus is indeed the *highest* Priest who mediates between God and man according to a greater covenant.

His Greater Qualification

Just like the high priests of the Old Testament, Jesus was "appointed in service to God for the people" (Heb. 5:1). Unlike these high priests, though, he was appointed as High Priest "according to the order of Melchizedek" by God himself since he was the very Son of God. Melchizedek was the mysterious king-priest of God Most High over Salem whom both King David and the writer of Hebrews depict as a type of Christ (Ps. 110:4; Heb. 7). Abraham offered his tithe to Melchizedek and received his blessing. Because Melchizedek seems to appear from nowhere to meet Abraham and then disappear again afterwards, the writer of Hebrews uses him to argue that Jesus has no beginning or end. He is qualified as the High Priest of God not "based on a legal command concerning physical descent but based on the power of an indestructible life" (Heb. 7:16). Due to the eternality of his life, Jesus has supreme authority to offer a single sacrifice for all time.[4]

. The priest and the sacrifice should be holy in order to successfully appease the wrath of God. In Jesus, the priest and the sacrifice come together in one body. Jesus offered up the sacrifice of himself. And his body was uniquely qualified to fully save God's people.

His Greater Presentation

The sufficiency of a priestly sacrifice relies on the quality of the sacrifice itself, as well as the quality of the one presenting it. If the sacrifice is in any way blemished, it is ineffective and might bring greater wrath from God (Deut. 17:1). It is therefore critical for the writer of Hebrews to establish Jesus' sacrifice as qualitatively superior if it is to be effective for all time and for all peoples. So he writes: "For this is the kind of high priest we need: holy, innocent, undefiled, separated from sinners, and exalted above the heavens. He doesn't need to offer sacrifices every day, as high priests do— first for their own sins, then for those of the people. He did this once for all when He offered Himself" (Heb. 7:26–27). Therefore, Jesus' sacrifice presented to the Father was infinitely superior in its atonement for sin.

His Greater Propitiation

John Stott eloquently asks, "How could a righteous God forgive sinners without compromising his holiness"? He calls this question "the problem of sin."[5] The answer is found in Jesus' propitiation of the Father's wrath for sinners. "Propitiation" simply means the appeasement of wrath by the offering of a sacrifice. Jesus propitiated the wrath of God for his chosen people. As a result, there is no wrath left for us his children but only favor. The propitiation of God in the Old Covenant was temporary, in that the sacrifices were merely a foreshadowing to the final propitiation of God in the event of the cross. Jesus did not merely enter a material tabernacle in Jerusalem, but into the very spiritual presence of the Father. Jesus' sacrifice sufficiently propitiated the wrath of God because of the superior quality of his sacrifice—his own self! In that one sacrifice, Jesus successfully secured the eternal redemption of whoever believes in Christ (Heb. 9:12). His propitiation of the wrath of God was, indeed, "finished" (John 19:30)!

His Greater Intercession

Unlike his propitiation that was once and for all completed, his intercession is perpetual for his people. "Therefore, He is always able to save those who come to God through Him, since He always lives to intercede for them" (Heb. 7:25). If Christ died for a people, will he not also live to intercede for them throughout this life?

How can we be assured that the intercession of Christ for us is heard and always answered perfectly by the Father? Our assurance is that Christ has "all authority" before the Father due to his being the Son of the Father and his being the proven Savior of all his people. In other words, we trust his perpetual intercession because we trust his singular propitiation.[6] How precious is the doctrine of Christ's intercession for us! When we are at the end of our wits with suffering, or when we feel entirely useless in shame, depression, and insecurity, or when we fight the hordes of Satan's army in temptation, let us be comforted that the Spirit intercedes for us in the theater of our hearts and Christ intercedes for us in the theater of heaven (Rom. 8:26–27, 34)!

His Greater Compassion

The role of a priest is not only to offer sacrifices but also to help the people. The problem with the priests of the Old Covenant was that they were enslaved to sin as much as the people. They were fatally weak in their compassion and in their counsel for a struggling Jewish people. But Christ is greater. As the High Priest of God over his bride, the church, he pastors her with the authority of one who has faced the same struggles that she has faced, but overcome them all. Because he was "tested in every way as we are, yet without sin," he is able to "sympathize with our weaknesses." Therefore, we can "approach the throne of grace with boldness, so that we may receive mercy and find grace to help us at the proper time" (Heb. 4:15–16).

When we are tempted we need a king to make us submit, a prophet to declare God's word to us, and a priest to come beside us and help us. We know that authority resides not only in a position but also in experience. As John Bunyan's protagonist "Christian" says in *The Pilgrim's Progress*, "No man can tell what in that combat attends us, but he that hath been in the battle himself."[7] A priest's practical authority with his people relies on his shared experiences with them.

The pastoral work of Christ the priest in helping his people overcome sin and temptation relies on his propitiatory work already accomplished at the cross. In other words, he helps today the one whom he won yesterday. "Therefore, He had to be like His brothers in every way, so that He could become a merciful and faithful high priest in service to God, to make propitiation for the sins of the people. For since He Himself was tested and has suffered, He is able to help those who are tested" (Heb. 2:17–18). We see, again, that the redeeming work of Christ consists of his once-and-for-all offering of himself as well as his perpetual intercession.

His Priestly Rule over the Church

As our High Priest, Jesus rules over his church with the authority of the throne of God. So the "royal priesthood," the church, is ruled by a royal High Priest. The writer of Hebrews could not be more explicit on this point, "Now the main point of what is being said is this: We have this kind of High Priest, who sat down at the right hand of the throne of the Majesty in the heavens" (8:1). Jesus sits on his throne at the right hand of the Father because his priestly work of offering the atoning sacrifice is complete. He offered one sacrifice—himself—and he offered it only once. After that, "he sat down at the right hand of God, waiting from that time until his enemies should be made a footstool for his feet" (Heb. 10:12–13 ESV).

His Greater Assurance

The people of the Old Covenant had to trust their priests to know and follow the law properly for the atonement of their sins. The community's favor with God depended on their sinful priests doing the right things! What a dangerous predicament they were in, for the priest could be secretly sinning, or there might be sins within the community, or perhaps the priest did not know the right rituals to perform. How then does Jesus as High Priest improve this situation?

Jesus guarantees our eternal salvation by means of the very integrity of his priesthood. And the integrity of his priesthood rests on his anointing from God in the declaration of his sonship at his baptism: "None of this happened without an oath. For others became priests without an oath, but He became a priest with an oath made by the One who said to Him: The Lord has sworn, and He will not change His mind, You are a priest forever. So Jesus has also become the guarantee of a better covenant" (Heb. 7:20–22). So we have assurance in Jesus as our High Priest and we have assurance from God the Father that Jesus is a perfect High Priest.

Every time that we are tempted to trust in our works for our salvation, we should remember that Jesus operates as Priest within the New Covenant. To the rebellious, we plead, "Trust in Christ's offering and lose not hope because of your sin." To the rule follower we plead, "Trust in Christ's offering and lose not hope because of your pride." For there is no hope of salvation, of knowing God, of getting through this life replete with trials, of fulfilling the Great Commission, of parenting well, or of doing anything else for the glory of God and our joy if we are not trusting in our New Covenant High Priest.

Christ the King

In the Old Testament, the Israelite king rules over the people on behalf of God. As God's appointed leader of a people, he should minister to the people on behalf of God and minister to God on behalf of the people. The king has authority over the prophets and the priests. Thus, in biblical terms, the most righteous king also fulfills the role of priest and prophet.

Jesus was prefigured by Melchizedek, who was the priest-king of Salem (Gen. 14:17–20). David, who was a prophet-priest-king in the order or Melchizedek (Ps. 110:4), also prefigures Jesus. David was a messenger of God's Word (thus, many of the Psalms). He not only ruled over the priests as their king, but he also occasionally performed the tasks of the priesthood, and that without condemnation (1 Sam. 21:1–6; 2 Sam. 6:12–15). As a descendent of the line of David, Jesus is the King of the throne of David (Matt. 22:41–46; 2 Sam. 7:12–16).

It is not by chance that the Gospel of Matthew emphasizes Jesus' words, "All authority has been given to Me in heaven and on earth" (28:18). One of the unifying themes of the Gospel of Matthew is that Jesus Christ is King. Matthew opens and closes his Gospel utilizing this image of Christ. The opening verse connects Jesus with Abraham and David the king. The book closes with Jesus declaring his sovereign authority. For his audience of Jews, Matthew wanted to ensure they understood that although the kingdom of God arrived in Jesus very differently than they expected, Jesus is still legitimately and entirely, "The King of the Jews."

Matthew was not out of place to focus on Jesus as the King. The title of *Christ* is inseparable from the imagery of a king. The Jews knew that the Messiah would usher in a new and long-awaited kingdom from God—a kingdom that he would rule forevermore (Pss. 2; 110; Isa. 11). They would finally be vindicated as God's people, and the enemies of God would be judged. Jesus came as King but in a very different way. He inaugurated his kingdom, and opened the door for people to enter into his kingdom and enjoy its benefits, but it remains until Judgment Day yet to be consummated.

The meaning of "the kingdom of God" has been widely debated among evangelicals. Because the meaning of this theological phrase has such wide-ranging implications for Christian engagement in the public sphere, discussions about its meaning have ranged from cordial to vicious. Thankfully, as Russell Moore argues, there seems to be a growing consensus among contemporary evangelicals over a central base of meaning for the kingdom of God, largely contingent on the idea that the kingdom is "already but not yet."[8] This "already but not yet" perspective means that the kingdom of God in Christ has been inaugurated, but is yet to be consummated. That consummation will happen in the end times. The "already but not yet" paradigm provides a way for Christians to recognize that Jesus is Lord and has been crowned King of kings, but is still actively at war against his enemies till one day "at the name of Jesus ever knee will bow—of those who are in heaven and on earth and under the earth—and every tongue should confess that Jesus Christ is Lord, to the glory of God the Father" (Phil. 2:10–11). He has been crowned "already" in heaven as Lord and Christ and his rule as king will one day be universally recognized.[9]

The Coronation of the Ages

When Jesus ascended back to heaven, he was received at the right hand of the Father in the coronation of the ages (Eph. 1:20). Jesus reported to the Father the perfect fulfillment of his work, in which opened the way to salvation for God's people and secured their faith necessary to receive that salvation. There in heaven, having died "once for all," and never to offer himself again, he intercedes for the saints at the right hand of the Father, always to have his prayers fully answered.

What great pleasure there is in considering heaven's welcome-back party for the resurrected Jesus after ascended. We can only imagine the pomp and majesty of Christ's crowning by the Father. As the second person of the Trinity, Jesus was already sovereign over all. The whole world was created "through him" (Heb. 1:2). But now he was recognized as the obedient God-man who triumphed over Satan and all his forces, and finished the atoning work of salvation for all of God's people! I imagine the angels crying out, "He did it! It is finished! All hail King Jesus!"

The coronation of Jesus is for the benefit of the nations. A friend in Manchester, England, recently showed me a picture of his father walking behind Queen Elizabeth II during her royal coronation. He was the page of a high-ranking admiral so he enjoyed the right to trail in the new Queen's path. My friend beamed with pride that his father participated in this monumental event! And so he should be proud, for a coronation is not merely a ceremony of investiture, it is a ceremony that should bless a nation! Likewise, the coronation of Jesus was for the display of the splendor of his kingdom, with a view toward the blessing of not one nation, but all nations!

His Reign

The connection between Christ's authority and his kingship is intuitive, but it is not without nuance. Though Christ is supreme

King, not everything has been subjected to him. He rules, but he is still at war. One day he will gain victory over all, but that day is not yet.

Scholars have helpfully distinguished between the different ways that Christ is King. First, as the eternal Son of God, he reigns in power over all things in all times in all places. Second, he reigns in grace over his church. He leads his church to triumph over all enemies and to accomplish the very agenda of Christ the King. Third, he will one day hand over "the kingdom" to the Father after destroying all of his enemies, including death (1 Cor. 15:24). From Judgment Day forward, he will reign over a triumphant church forevermore from the new earth. So we might think of his *reign of power* over all things, his *reign of grace* over his church, and his *reign of glory* beginning on Judgment Day.[10]

Jesus reigns in power. Jesus has always ruled over all peoples and places in power, therefore we will never go anywhere or speak to anyone outside of the rule of the living Christ Jesus. This offers us great hope and peace that when we launch out in mission to the roughest places on earth—where there are absolutely no Christ followers, and darkness seems to cover every home and heart— Jesus still reigns there in power.

I remember as a young boy dreaming about the honor of being imprisoned for Christ, or the honor of going somewhere where there are no other Christians for hundreds of miles and making disciples. I remember the peace and joy of thinking that when I face that lack of community in Christ, all I have to do is find something living—a mere plant, or an insect, or a beetle—and there, with that living thing, I would find community as one who submits to Christ. Even the rocks submit to him! Then, one day I found myself running lost in New Delhi from a gang of young men, who had just robbed my friends and knifed me in the face. As I ran, lost, not able to speak three words in Hindi, bleeding profusely, and not having any idea what to do next, I remember the peace and joy of knowing that Jesus rules on every street in New Delhi. With that faith, I was comforted and freed to pray in love for my attackers. What comfort there is in knowing that Jesus is King over all in power!

Jesus reigns in grace over his church. He reigns in light of his mediatorial work on the cross for his people. While living in Beirut in 2006, my wife and I attended a very small Lebanese church in a very poor area of the city. On average there were ten to fifteen people sitting in the pews. Sometimes this discouraged me and left me thinking, *How in the world are these few people going to make any difference in this complex and intense city?* But when those ten people opened their mouths to pray and sing, I was reminded that Jesus is King over this church. He is the head of that small, aging church in Beirut as well as the impressive megachurches of America.

As King over his people, Jesus leads his church on mission to the ends of the earth. When he said, "All authority has been given to Me in heaven and on earth" in Matthew 28:18, he not only looked forward to his re-entrance into the throne room of God in heaven, he also knew that his authority over the church was the indispensable hope of the apostles to do the task that he was going to give them in verse 19: "Go, therefore, and make disciples of all nations." In other words, the exaltation of Christ over the church is the hope of the church for its expansion among the nations.

This is why when we suffer or face opposition in making disciples, the kingship of Christ becomes so precious to us. Suffering and opposition make us bow to our knees and remember that Jesus rules at God's "right hand in the heavens—far above every ruler and authority, power and dominion, and every title given, not only in this age by also in the one to come" (Eph. 1:20–21).

The extreme Islamic group ISIS is renowned for its extreme brutality and its militant enforcement of its strange vision of Islamic law. Recently, I was talking with a Christian friend who is serving the Kurdish people of northern Iraq with his wife and young child. He told me that while life continues as normal in his small city, he is taking precautions with his young family in case the civil war against ISIS bleeds into his city. He recently wired extra cash to himself, packed a food bag, bought some extra water, and packed an emergency supply bag. Pondering the instability in this country, he remarked, "Sometimes I don't even know what to pray but I'm glad Jesus is King of the world and of all the armies." YES! That is right. His faith in Jesus the King and the already-but-not-yet coming of his kingdom has given my friend hope, peace, and joy to continue serving the people with love and sacrifice.

The church on mission for an exalted Christ spreads the sweet music of worship among the nations. I love the story of how God saved the life of E. P. Scott. Scott was an American Baptist missionary to India in the mid-nineteenth century. He felt God leading him to reach the Naga tribes of east India. The problem was that the Naga tribes were renowned for their savagery as head-hunters. Tradition holds that before a Naga man could marry, he had to kill thirty of his enemies, shrink their heads, and wear them on his neck to prove his bravery. The British officers in the region heard of Scott's plans and urged him not to go to Naga territory, since he would most assuredly lose his life. Nevertheless, he felt God's call and set out with a few supplies as well as his treasured violin. Several days into his journey, he came upon twelve men of the head-hunting tribe and they immediately surrounded him with their spears aimed at him. He had no weapon with him. So, assured of his impending death, he pulled out his violin, closed his eyes, and began to play and sing the hymn "Am I a Solider of the Cross?"

Am I a soldier of the cross,
A follower of the Lamb,
And shall I fear to own His cause,
Or blush to speak His Name?

Amazingly, as he played and sang he realized that he was still alive! He opened his eyes and noticed the twelve tribesmen dropped their spears and eagerly asked that the music go on. They afterward welcomed Scott to stay in their land as long as he had his violin.[11] As in the amazing story of E. P. Scott, when we go to the nations we spread the pleasing music of worship of our King.

So Jesus reigns over all in power, he reigns over his church now in grace, and one day, *Jesus will reign over his church in the new earth in glory.* When the gospel of the kingdom has been preached as a testimony to all nations, Jesus will return to earth in judgment. He will judge and destroy his enemies. He will rule in submission to his Father over all of his redeemed people from all nations of mankind forever and ever.

What hope there is for us who try to make disciples among the most distant and difficult peoples on earth? No matter how unresponsive they may be, we are assured that there will be a remnant of Christ followers among them, or else Christ himself will be made a liar! Our hope in the triumph of the church among all peoples is the Father's upholding of the honor of King Jesus over all peoples.

The King's Agenda

Kings have the right to have an agenda for their kingdoms. So what is the agenda of Christ the King? First, he will destroy his enemies, including death itself, from all the nations. "For He must reign until He puts all His enemies under His feet. The last enemy to be abolished is death" (1 Cor. 15:25–26). Second, he will receive worship from all the nations and all the angels (Heb. 1:6). Third, he will "reign wisely as king and administer justice and righteousness in the land" (Jer. 23:5). Fourth, he will graciously rule over his church as he builds it from all nations (Rev. 5:9–10). Lastly, he will ready his kingdom of grace to hand over to the Father, so that "God may be all in all" (1 Cor. 15:28).

A Spiritual King

The nations rage and mock King Jesus because they do not see him as he is. The nations respect strength, but Jesus came in weakness. The nations want exuberant confidence. Jesus came in humility. The nations want epic displays of power, but Jesus came to die. Jesus speaks now to the nations with the same words he said to Pilate: "My kingdom is not of this world. . . . If My kingdom were of this world, My servants would fight . . . As it is, My kingdom does not have its origin here" (John 18:36). In other words, since I am the King of heaven, my servants do not fight to establish my earthly kingdom. Because I am King of heaven, I can establish my kingdom on this earth at my appointed time.

As we make disciples among the nations, we need to remember that our King and his kingdom is not of this world, and neither are the weapons that we use. Living in the Muslim world makes the contrast between the acts of faith in a spiritual rather than earthly kingdom all the more apparent. Included in historically orthodox Islamic doctrine is the command that Muslims should defend their faith with war if necessary. This is codified in the doctrine of *jihad*. So-called Christians have adopted the same attitude for generations in the past. For instance, Roman and Byzantine emperors sought to defend Christendom by the sword. Not to mention the implicit influences of Christianity in motivating leaders toward modern conflict, such as in twenty-first-century Iraq. But we are not of the sword; we are of faith. Instead of killing others to take the nations for our religion, we choose to die to take the nations for our King. We give ourselves as holy sacrifices to God on the altar of the nations. We sacrifice for the nations boldly, knowing that our Lord has "raised us up and seated us in the heavens" together with him (Eph. 2:6).

The Endurance of the Church

The endurance of the church depends on the endurance of Christ's reign as King. As long as Christ is on his throne, we have hope that the church will never cease to exist and the expanse of his rule will grow. Hope for the church is never lost. Every door to every "closed" country will one day be open. Doors and gates are made to keep things in and out. The gates of hell are made for darkness to stay in and the hope of the gospel to stay out. But these gates will not prevail against the advance of Christ's kingdom into darkness (Matt. 16:18).[12]

For All Peoples, for All Time

The glory of kings and queens is measured by the extent of their authority over time and space. The greater the extent of their authority, the greater their glory. The Scripture takes advantage of the inherent territorial connotations of the image of a king and his kingdom to magnify the universality of the kingship of Christ.[13] King Jesus shines like an infinitely bright sun over a dark land of rivaling kings and queens because his throne is everlasting!

Consider Psalm 2, one of the most referenced Old Testament passages in the New Testament. This psalm is about the royal coronation of the Christ as King. The nations "rebel and the peoples plot in vain" (Ps. 2:1). They fight endlessly for greater control and power. They conspire together on how to defeat God and his Anointed. But God Almighty just laughs at their foolish audacity, for he has invested his King to rule over all. At Christ's coronation, the Father will issues a regal decree over Jesus: "You are My Son; today I have become Your Father" (Heb. 5:5). Unlike the kings of the earth, Christ can never be stripped of his royal authority, because his kingship rests on the pronouncement of God himself. His authority is forever and over all the nations. "Ask of Me, and I will make the nations Your inheritance and the ends of the earth Your possession" (Ps. 2:8).

It is quite humorous to hear kings and leaders boast of the expanse of their authority in light of the infinite authority of Christ. There is only one thing that they all have in common: death. Death plagues all men, including the highest ranking of us all. Death is the reason that having children is so important not just for monarchs but also for their nation, for someone has to rule when the ruler dies! But unlike every other king and queen, Jesus rules forever.

All peoples understand the connection between supreme authority and worship. This is why the list of earthly rulers throughout history who have demanded the worship of the people is nearly endless. My favorite illustration of this is the "wise men" story in Matthew. These men came from Persia to pay homage to the child king Jesus. They saw his star in the east and they came to find him so that they might worship him (Matt. 2:2). Isn't it remarkable that some of the first worshipers of this King of the Jews were from a far-off nation? They were, in our nomenclature, from an "unreached people group"! And that is entirely fitting, since as the long-awaited Davidic King of the Jews, this Jesus is the King over all peoples!

The Prophet, Priest, and King Blesses Us

As we grow in our understanding of the threefold office of Christ, we grow in our experience of the freedom we have in Christ. Consider the shame that we so often carry for past sins. Christ the prophet rebukes our shame, Christ the priest represents us to the Father, and Christ the king rescues us from shame. We need to hear this, because shame paralyzes us, keeps us in fear, and as a result shuts down our ministry. The tragedy of sin is not just in its consequence of displeasing God, but also in the shameful paralysis it brings in mission. Every disciple maker, except for Christ himself, is a sinner. And the intent of Satan is to gnaw at our confidence one temptation and one failure at a time. The more failure is left unresolved by the precious blood of Christ, the more shame untouched by the remembrance of our complete and final justification, the more paralysis to our ministries.[14]

Instead of boldly calling other sinners from all the nations to the cross where they might find their sins washed away and their lives reborn, we often hide from them thinking to ourselves, *What right do I have as a sinner to call others to holiness in Christ? What standing do I have to proclaim the worth of following Jesus when I so often do not myself? There is no way God will use me now since he knows the depth of my sin against him.* So we shrink away, and we stifle the gospel-exalting power of the Holy Spirit.

As commissioned ambassadors of King Jesus who call other sinners to be reconciled to God, we need to daily rely on the gospel, namely, that Christ justifies the ungodly. We cry out with Micah: "Do not rejoice over me, my enemy! Though I have fallen, I will stand up; though I sit in darkness, the LORD will be my light. Because I have sinned against Him, I must endure the LORD's rage until He argues my case and establishes justice for me. He will bring me into the light; I will see His salvation" (Micah 7:8–9). Yes, because of our prophet, priest, and king, Jesus the Christ, we trust that God himself will plead our cause and anoint us to make disciples in his name. Our vigor in making disciples is not found in ourselves, but in the anointing that we have of God. It is in this anointing of the Holy Spirit that we find power in and with Christ to proclaim good news to the poor, to proclaim liberty to the captives, to bring sight to the blind, to set at liberty those who are oppressed, and to proclaim the year of the Lord's favor to all nations (Luke 4:18–19).

We Are Coworkers with Christ

We are not only anointed with the Spirit but we are coworkers with Christ as prophets, priests, and kings. And it takes all three offices working together in harmony to make disciples of the nations. Often we fill our teams with people just like us. So if we are prophetic in our ministry, we join teams with others who are too. But the beauty of the church is that Christ is among us as prophet, priest, and king. Therefore, we need each other working together in mission as his body. The prophet speaks, the priest intercedes, the king manages. I have seen this work so beautifully on disciple-making teams. Some groups might even ensure that every team in their church or ministry is filled with at least one of each office. We need each other. The nations need us to work together. In this way, we as the church may fulfill all three roles of prophet, priest, and king.

Christ Is All We Need

As our great prophet, priest, and king, Jesus Christ is all sufficient for leading us in disciple-making ministry. Do we need anything else but Christ to thrive and to be fruitful in our task of disciple making? Do we rely on the amenities of ministry—technology, resources, and status—to make disciples? Or do we rely on the all-sufficient Christ? Who or what is our hope for both staying on task and thriving in mission? Have we not been blessed in Christ by the Father "with every spiritual blessing in the heavens" (Eph. 1:3)?

I lead and coach many disciple makers living in the most difficult environments on earth among the most difficult peoples. I have found just one secret for contentment and fruitfulness in life and ministry in these places: abiding in Christ! Be not tempted to think that Christ is a cliché for life. No! Christ is all that we have and all that we hope in. How futile is every moment spent calling people and cultures to repentance from centuries of darkness and satanic enslavement if we are not filled with Christ and clinging to him! The weapons of the world just do not work to make disciples! We place our lives at risk in the hope that Christ would be made all in all. If we die while making him all in all, let us die with the radiant joy of Stephen, looking above to heaven where our kingly, prophetic, priestly Christ stands ready to return. Death is not, as Hamlet bemoaned, the "undiscovered country from whose bourn no traveler returns."[15] Death is, rather, our precious bridge to meet our Redeemer face-to-face in the celestial kingdom that he has been preparing for us. Because of our confidence even in the face of death, we can thrive and stay on task as we "go, therefore."

Though few around observe your labor,
Christ sees all—the best and least.
One day those few you sought with vigor,
Will sing with you at the Feast.

—— Chapter 4 ——

"Go Therefore"

WHILE FOLLOWING THE LORD ON MISSION, WE MUST TAKE CARE TO thrive as human beings. We must also stay focused on the task of making disciples. Both thriving and staying on task are immense challenges for us in a world that is dark, oppressive, and full of distractions. Jesus knew this would be the case. So he gives us the dual promises of Matthew 28:18 and 28:20 to keep us thriving and staying on task while living on mission with him.

It is in light of the enormity of the task of Matthew 28:19–20 that Jesus comforts the disciples with doctrine in verse 18 and a promise in verse 20. Without the promises of Matthew 28:18 ("All authority") and 28:20 ("I am with you always"), Matthew 28:19–20 ("Go therefore") is a task so impossible that it is absurd.

Imagine the objections from the disciples:

Jesus: "Go."
Disciples: "But we have no resources to just pick up and go."

Jesus: "Make disciples"
Disciples: "You yourself taught us that only God can save men, how then are we supposed to make disciples?"

Jesus: "of all nations"

Disciples: "But we are Jews! First of all, how are we, being clean, to go among the Gentiles, being unclean? Second of all, there are only a few of us, how are we to go to 'all nations'?"

Jesus: "Baptizing them in the name of the Father and of the Son and of the Holy Spirit."

Disciples: "If we do this, we will be killed just like the prophet John who came before you."

Jesus: "Teaching them to observe everything I have commanded you."

Disciples: "How are we, being uneducated, to remember all that you have commanded us. One of us has already betrayed you!"

Jesus: "And remember, I am with you always, to the end of the age."

Disciples: "Okay, but wait a minute, you are ascending!"

Risk for Gain

In light of the promises in Matthew 28:18 and 28:20, we must adjust our perspective on risk from what may be lost to what may be gained. Justin and Sarah, and their young children, are serving in a highly restricted Muslim country. Recently, gunmen set off a deadly car bomb, attacking a community center close by Justin and Sarah's home. That day we quickly got ahold of Justin and Sarah to make sure they were okay. They were safe, but shaken. They were at the community center literally minutes before the explosion and fighting. Part of the engine of the car that blew up went through their kitchen window just moments after Sarah moved away from it. They were distraught and sorrowful for the locals who died in this attack.

After returning from a period away, they returned only to face another violent incident head-on. Just a month after the car bomb, a gunman killed multiple foreigners in their country as they went to work. They were there to serve the poor, sick, and needy of the country, and in the end, they gave their lives for the people. So again, Justin and Sarah were evacuated.

Their teammates, Will and Rachel, are also close friends of mine. Will and Rachel evacuated this time in shock and mourning, as they were very close friends with those who died. For months after, Will and Rachel and their young children struggled with depression, grief, and nightmares.

The morning of the first attack, Will was leading worship for his small group that met near the community center. During that worship time, before the attack, the Lord brought Matthew 28:18 to his mind and he shared with the group that they should take comfort because, no matter what happens, the authority of Jesus still stands. After the attack, not knowing yet that I was working on this book, Will e-mailed me, "A verse the Father has continually brought to mind is 'all authority on heaven and earth has been given to me.' That includes what's happening now."

Justin and Sarah, and Will and Rachel are risking their lives and the lives of their children. They are thriving and staying on task with making disciples because they set their minds on the promises of Christ's authority and his presence. They count all else as loss for the "surpassing value of knowing Christ Jesus my Lord" (Phil. 3:8).

Face Jesus, Not Fear

It is common to believe that the way to conquer fear is to face it head-on. For instance, if you are afraid of falling, you should bungee jump off a bridge. If you are afraid of the dark, you should close yourself in a dark room until you realize that you will be just fine. There is even a television show that puts people into the contexts of their worst nightmare. But in reality, fear is more often like the face of Medusa. If you look it in the face, it will turn you to stone, paralyzing you. To conquer fear, we have a better tactic. Instead of staring fear in the face, we must look to the face of Jesus and trust him.

When I was a little boy struggling with fear of the dark, my parents taught me to pray to Jesus and remember that he is Lord. This was excellent parental counsel! And so, when we are afraid, we must look not into our fear but into the face of our King Jesus. It was precisely when Peter turned from looking at Jesus to looking at the wind that he began to sink. Jesus reprimanded him, "You of little faith, why did you doubt?" (Matt. 14:31).

When we are tempted to fear, we might utilize the weapons of reason, encouragement of friends, or of technology. But the greatest weapon against fear is faith in Jesus. Perhaps a personal, and quite awkward, story will illustrate this.

Like all high school boys, I was insecure and desperate for the approval of my peers. The thought of rejection was terrifying to me. But one night I came head-to-head with my insecurity and had to make a choice to submit to the authority of my Lord or to the approval of my peers. It was the winter dance at my public high school. In the middle of the dance, during another rock song from the band, I felt the Spirit of God speaking to me: "Get on stage and acknowledge me."

I knew clearly what this meant. "What, God!? No way. I'm not in the student government, or on the dance organizing committee. I have no reason to get on stage, and no reasonable excuse to talk about 'God' at this public school dance!" But the Spirit continued to whisper into my ear, "Get on stage and acknowledge me."

At this point, I began to tremble in anxiety. I broke off from dancing with my date and away from my friends. I walked in circles around the dance hall trying to reason my way out of obedience. I was sweating, trembling, wandering around like a scrawny confused puppy, and terrified at rejection. Then, I looked in my heart up to the throne of Jesus and decided that Jesus was my Lord and nothing else mattered. I would obey. Shaking, I walked up and interrupted the front man of the band to tell him that I'd like to say something after his next song. He surprisingly agreed. After the song, I got on stage, looked at the sexually inflamed crowd of high school seniors, and said, "We are having a good time tonight. But there is a God in heaven who rules from his throne and he is here with us. We must not forget that he lives and rules over us. We must acknowledge him tonight as Lord." The crowd awkwardly stood there stunned. I remember seeing my principal standing in the back of the crowd shaking his head in unbelief. I walked off stage very nervous, but on fire for Jesus. Jesus was my Lord and there was nothing anyone could do about it. I loved him and he loved me and I will live with him forever. I was no longer afraid. I had conquered the fear of rejection by looking not at the fear but at the throne of my Savior.

He's Got the Whole World in His Hands

If you decide to live on mission with Jesus, at some point you will find yourself in a frightening situation, or in a dark place, explicitly because of your obedience to Jesus. Where do you turn for peace and comfort in that moment? And what about your children? What will you say when your parents scoff at your apparent lack of responsibility in taking your young children to some far-off dangerous place to take on the "impossible" task of calling others to repentance? You may find yourself moving with your kids to a drug-infested neighborhood, where they witness fights, where they see weapons on the street, and where they go to sleep to the sound of gunfire.

My wife and I have spent considerable time thinking through these things. So we decided to write a song that we memorized and sing regularly as a family. We recorded it so that our kids can listen to it on car rides and at home. It goes like this:

He's got the whole world in his hands
When the world gets kinda scary
When things get kinda hairy
Just look above
And trust in his plans

Yes there may be monsters in your room
They're demons of the dark, they lurk and loom
But on your side, for you, is the High King
With him twenty million angels who sing . . .

He's got the whole world in his hands
When the world gets kinda scary
When things get kinda hairy
Just look above
And trust in his plans

Outside there may be lions, but we still
Exit our house in his good will
We don't fear those cats when they come
For at the Name of Jesus they must run!

Oh my sons you will walk this dark field
The valley of the shadow of death
Remember that your safety was sealed
In our Savior's first resurrected breath

Listen to the valleys sing
Listen to the thunder roar
Watch the clouds form
They declare . . .

He's got the whole world in his hands
When the world gets kinda scary
When things get kinda hairy
Just look above
And trust in his plans

I love listening to my young boys sing this song by memory. When they sing, I am encouraged because the truths that they are singing have the power to uphold them in the tough times ahead.

We Are Not in Control

There is nothing more comforting in danger or tragedy than knowing that King Jesus rules over all existence. At some point, it just becomes unloving to tell a hurting person, "It'll be okay." For the reality is that the suffering may continue on for some time yet. The most comforting thing to tell a follower of Christ in his or her suffering is not, "It'll be okay," but rather, "No matter how all this turns out, Jesus has all authority in heaven and on earth and he is with you."

The evil lure of comfort is that it tempts us to think that we are in control. We must remind ourselves that it does not take much to undo us completely. It takes only a small bullet, or a small mass of cancer, or a tired heart, or little blood clot in the brain, or a car accident to end our lives. Our personal kingdoms are so fragile. It is simply asinine to trust in our personal control over our lives or that of any other. It is beyond absurd to take comfort in the size of our personal kingdoms. In a single day, the prophet Job's fortune and much of his family were lost. We must face the fact every day that we are not in control.

Consider the illustration of Eike Batista. In March 2012, Batista was Brazil's richest man and the world's eighth richest man with an estimated $34.5 billion. Batista had "supreme self-confidence." Up to the spring of 2012, his confidence was matched by proven success. He boasted to *Forbes* in 2010 that he would become the world's richest man. But the bubble of his "world class, idiot-proof assets," as he was known to boast, would embarrassingly pop in view of the whole world. In a single year, due to overconfident business decisions, he lost $25 billion! Within two years, Bloomberg reported that he had a "negative net worth." *Bloomberg Businessweek* described his quick loss of fortune as "one of the largest personal and financial collapses in history—if not the largest."[1]

The story of Batista will be the story of us all. We boast in our empires, whether small or large, but one day our empires will collapse and we will be shamed at our previous confidence. But the universal empire of Jesus Christ will never decay. Once inaugurated in the ministry of the person Jesus Christ, this kingdom has no end. "His kingdom is an eternal kingdom, and His dominion is from generation to generation" (Dan. 4:3).

Liberated to Love

As we release control of our lives, we are liberated to love. Matthew 28:18 is, thus, a good-news message of liberation from internal and external oppression. The story of Jesus and the paralytic illustrates how this liberation works. Before healing the man, Jesus declares that his sins are forgiven. The scribes scoffed, "He's blaspheming!" (Matt. 9:3). The story continues:

> But perceiving their thoughts, Jesus said, "Why are you thinking evil things in your hearts? For which is easier: to say, 'Your sins are forgiven,' or to say, 'Get up and walk'?

But so you may know that the Son of Man has authority [*exousia*] on earth to forgive sins"—then He told the paralytic, "Get up, pick up your mat, and go home." And he got up and went home. When the crowds saw this, they were awestruck and gave glory to God who had given such authority to men. (Matt. 9:4–8)

In other words, Jesus has the full authority to heal a man and forgive his sins. There is no room to fear any accuser. When you remember that the final word of forgiveness has been declared to the ends of the universe with the authoritative voice of Christ, then you will be freed from your guilt and shame to love the ends of the earth.

If one were to interview our Austin Stone missionaries, one would find all sorts of sordid pasts. However, they are now declaring and demonstrating the gospel among unreached people groups. How could that be? The moment they trusted in Christ, the final word of their justification went out from the throne of heaven and freed them from all condemnation. They are not only free to serve Christ now among the nations, they have the very *right* to serve Christ among the nations.

Look to the Blood, Not the Barriers

Jesus knew that fulfilling the mandate of Matthew 28:19 would come with mammoth challenges and complexities. One of the main barriers that people face today in accessing unreached peoples is simply obtaining visas. Most of the world's most-unreached peoples live in very difficult places to get access to. I have many friends who have gone to extraordinary lengths to obtain visas and find work in these places.

I was encouraged years ago by an elderly Egyptian woman who had followed Christ for many decades. As I complained to her about the difficulties in reaching certain places, she shook her finger in the sky and cried out (in Arabic), "*Aala hasab a-dam!*

Aala hasab a-dam!" This means, "On account of the blood! On account of the blood!" As we were focusing on the barriers to following the Great Commission, she was focusing on the blood of the authoritative Christ! Nothing will stop the blood of the One with all authority from bursting open the doors to the hardest to reach places on earth!

Focus on Worship, Not on Waste

When you follow Jesus, and especially when you suffer, you will find yourself tempted to throw in the towel believing that you are wasting your life. Certainly the world will tell you that you are wasting your life pursuing some vision of declaring and demonstrating the gospel.

There was a time when even the disciples pondered whether sacrifice for Jesus was a waste. The week before the crucifixion, Jesus was having dinner with his friends Mary, Martha, and Lazarus. In an act of overwhelming and pure love for Jesus, Mary "took a pound of fragrant oil—pure and expensive nard— anointed Jesus' feet, and wiped His feet with her hair. So the house was filled with the fragrance of the oil" (John 12:3). This alabaster jar of oil that the woman poured on Jesus' feet was worth about 300 days' wages. This was likely her dowry money saved up for her wedding. This money might have been passed down to her from generations above. Poverty was rampant in Israel at this time. This was her life's worth, her treasure. In many respects, it was her very identity.

Yet Mary breaks the jar and pours it all over Jesus. She was unreserved in her devotion to Jesus. She could have given half of her treasure (150 days' worth of wages) and we would still stand in awe of her devotion. But she held nothing back.

The disciples were angry at Mary. They asked Jesus, "Why this waste?" (Matt. 26:8). The disciples did not understand that no amount of money or sacrifice was wasteful when it was poured out in worship of Jesus. So Jesus responds, "She has done a beautiful thing to me" (Matt. 26:10 ESV). With her act of sacrificial worship, Mary was symbolically anointing Jesus for his burial.

Jesus reveals a glimpse of his authority and declares, "I assure you: Wherever this gospel is proclaimed in the whole world, what this woman has done will also be told in memory of her" (Matt. 26:13). In that moment Jesus effectively canonizes Mary's worship into the Scripture. Wherever the Scripture will be translated, taught, and read, the story of Mary's devotion will go forth.

What so profoundly affected Jesus that he would mandate that this story be told to every tribe, tongue, nation, and people? While the Scripture does not explicitly say, I believe the reason is that Mary's unreserved sacrifice sets a pattern of many stories that would mark Jesus' disciples, even to the present day. Jesus' followers should be known for the incredible sacrifice of their most precious possessions for the sake of worship of Jesus and the advance of his kingdom.

In other words, the story of Mary will be told to the ends of the earth because it will take radical devotion and sacrifice like Mary's to take the gospel to the ends of the earth. Mary's story is a small picture of what it takes to complete the Great Commission.

No Reserves, No Retreats, No Regrets

Mary's story has been repeated countless times over as disciples of Christ focus on worship, rather than on potential "waste." Consider the story of William Borden. In 1904 William Borden graduated from a Chicago high school. As heir to the Borden Condensed Milk Company (now Borden, Inc.), he inherited a fortune. For his high school graduation present, his parents gave sixteen-year-old Borden a trip around the world! As the young man traveled through Asia, the Middle East, and Europe, he felt a growing burden for the world's hurting people.

In college, Borden was a man of incredible influence. Borden's small morning prayer group gave birth to a movement that spread across the campus. By the end of his first year, 150 freshmen were meeting for weekly Bible study and prayer. By the time William Borden was a senior, one thousand of Yale's thirteen hundred students were meeting in such groups. He was the president of the honor society Phi Beta Kappa at Yale, and founded Yale Hope Mission.

Upon graduation from Yale, Borden turned down some high-paying job offers. He had decided that he wanted to be a missionary to the nations. A friend remarked that he was "throwing himself away as a missionary."

William Borden went on to graduate study at Princeton Seminary. When he finished his studies at Princeton, he sailed for China. Because he was hoping to work with Muslims, he stopped first in Egypt to study Arabic. While there, he contracted spinal meningitis.

Within a month, twenty-five-year-old William Borden was dead.

When news of William Whiting Borden's death was cabled back to the U.S., nearly every American newspaper carried the story. One wrote, "A wave of sorrow went 'round the world . . . Borden not only gave (away) his wealth, but himself, in a way so joyous and natural that it (seems) a privilege rather than a sacrifice."

Some may rant that William Borden's life was a waste. He could have done so much good, they might say, but instead he threw it away for Jesus. But on the contrary, his life and death have inspired likely thousands of Christians to give up more for Christ.

His gravestone in Cairo, Egypt, reads, in part: "Apart from faith in Christ, there is no explanation for such a life." If you were to look today at the back of William Borden's Bible, on the last page, you would see the words:

No reserve!
No retreat!
No regrets!²

A life lived and died for Jesus will be vindicated as right and good forever and ever in eternity in the presence of the church, the angels, and the triune God. When you choose to live and die for Jesus and for the cause of declaring his glory among the nations, people will smirk at you and say with their mouth and with their hearts, "What a waste of a life." They will render you irrational for taking your family and your future to die for Jesus in the desert fields of Algeria or the harvest fields of Indonesia or the "dangerous neighborhoods" on the "other side of town." Cleaving to Jesus always means leaving your earthly possessions and relationships behind in pursuit of maximizing your joy in God and your impact in his kingdom on this earth. This is what we mean when we say, "Jesus is better."

Do Not Endure the Way, Embrace the Way

Obeying Jesus will lead to suffering. When we suffer, we are forced to ask two critical questions: "Who's in control?" and "Where is Jesus in this suffering?" Jesus knew these two questions would arise in some of our toughest and darkest moments. And suffering would be the inevitable result of following him.

Does Jesus know what he is doing leading us on the Calvary Road? Is suffering really, then, good for us? Here are ten reasons why suffering on the Calvary Road with Jesus is good for us:

1. Suffering is good for our joy as we are forced to embrace God over and above the hollow and evanescent thrills that come from earthly activity.

2. Suffering is good for our prayer life because we remember that prayer is the most strategic and transformative activity in the world.

3. Suffering is good for our humility because we are desperately and dependently thrust into the mercies of God for all our needs.

4. Suffering is good for sharpening our focus on the few things in this world that really matter for eternity.

5. Suffering is good for our love of the Bible, because we learn that nothing encourages us so deeply and so lastingly as the written Word of God.

6. Suffering is good for our relationships with others, because the scars that we gain in suffering become our source of compassion for others.

7. Suffering is good for our hearts, because suffering is a sharp mirror into the heart.

8. Suffering is good for our families, because the stories of God's faithfulness in our suffering will build a lineage of faith in our children upon which they may build their own faith.

9. Suffering is good for evangelism, because our response to suffering testifies to the world about the one who is on the throne of our hearts.

10. Lastly, suffering is good for worship, because we learn to leap into the authoritative and comforting arms of our Shepherd and Savior.

Viewing suffering from this perspective changes the way we see the Calvary Road. The Calvary Road is not the lone, necessary, and unfortunate route on which we must walk to "get to Jesus." Rather, the Calvary Road is the most blessed road on earth, since it is there that we find Jesus, leading us all the way.

Because Christ walks with us on the Calvary Road, we do not merely *endure* it, but we *embrace* it. In every minute of every trial and through every impossible task that we face, Jesus is with us. He never fails in his promise. What courage, confidence, hope, joy, and glorious peace we have even in the slightest remembrance that Jesus—the one with all authority in heaven and earth—is with us forever. Jesus is *Immanuel*—God with us.

I thought it was a dream until I woke . . .
Breathing now, breathing, after passing the breathless precipice
With not a croak, but a leap.
My eyes, like kites piercing the clouds, began to weep
Their gaze upon the diamonds, which we used to call stars,
Decorating his throne.
Yes, he sits, his work complete,
His scars sealed, as a captain's jewelry that, so effulgent,
Blazes trails into the dark souls of his captives
And demands surrender.

But oh! Like the reapers scythe which once cut my throat
As I spoke my Savior's Name in the heart of darkness called Ethne—
That heart which pulsed only by the electricity of love—
As if this scythe again upon my throat I shrieked.
Might tomorrow borrow a sum and retreat my soul
Back to that lucid nightmare from which I awoke?!
Then, each gradient of glory now drunk would become further sorrow!
And my name not preserved, but reserved for the memory
of a dead man,
Would dissolve like blood in the earth!

"Fear not," said the bright unnamed creature, I think a doorman,
Unto my reborn ears.
"Look, with the fiercest faith of a new butterfly in her first flutter,
Upon the crimson mark that flies above the gate
on a wooden banner."
There, with the brilliance of a righteous king's ring
And the indelibility of his pen, was written thus:
"All arrivals."
"No departures."

—— Chapter 5 ——

"Make Disciples"

JESUS COMMANDS HIS DISCIPLES TO GO AND MAKE DISCIPLES OF ALL nations (Matt. 28:19). In this chapter we will see that submission to the authority of Christ is at the core of what it means to be a disciple of Jesus Christ. In this respect, to "make disciples" means influencing others to pledge their allegiance to Jesus as the Lord of their life.

"Disciple" Means "Follower of Jesus"

The word *disciple* means "pupil" or "follower" of a teacher. A disciple accepts the authority of a teacher and decides to follow his or her teaching. In the New Testament, we encounter disciples of the Pharisees (Mark 2:18), of Moses (John 9:28), and of John the Baptist (John 1:35).[1]

While the term *disciple* does not necessarily imply exclusivity in a person's allegiance, Jesus calls his disciples to follow him alone. Discipleship to Jesus supersedes loyalties to family, work, possessions, culture, religion, tradition, ethnicity, and everything else. Jesus was clear, "If anyone wants to be My follower, he must deny himself, take up his cross, and follow Me" (Mark 8:34). Taking up our cross means rejecting all other allegiances, including to life itself, and following Jesus on the Calvary Road.

In the Scriptures Jesus did not wait around for the disciples to start following him. Rather, he authoritatively called them to himself. When Jesus said, "Follow Me," he was not offering an invitation. He was giving a command that always rendered its intended result. "Immediately they left their nets and followed Him" (Mark 1:17–18). Contrary to the popular use of the verse, Jesus does not powerlessly "stand at the door and knock" (Rev. 3:20) while waiting around for an unbelieving person to come to the door and accept him in.[2] Rather, for those elected by God, Jesus seizes the house, defeats any powers in the house, rescues his elect, and returns them to their true home with him forever. While the invitation to Christ is universal, only those effectively called by Christ to himself will respond. Because he has all authority, he never fails to save his people.

By definition, following someone means accepting his leadership. Becoming a follower of Christ means accepting his leadership in every area of our lives. As a follower of Christ, there is absolutely no room for competing allegiances. He demands our total surrender. Therefore, making disciples means calling others to submit to the lordship of Jesus.

Disciple is not the only term for a follower of Jesus in the New Testament. Followers of Jesus also called themselves slaves, elect, righteous, saints, believers, friends, brothers, and children of God.[3] Each of those terms points to the authority of the Lord Jesus over all.

As slaves, or servants, of Christ we are bound as if by chains under his authority (Rom. 1:1; Rev. 1:1). Though bound to him, we are actually freed by him to live for him (1 Cor. 7:22). As such, we take our cues on how to live our life from the Lord (2 Tim. 2:24), and we live to please him alone (Gal. 1:10). But being the

Lord's slave is a position of honor, for we get to serve him in his household.

Disciples of Jesus are referred to as "the elect" or "the called" (2 Tim. 2:10), as we belong to God "by calling" (Rom. 1:6). We are God's "chosen ones" (Col. 3:12). We are "called, loved by God the Father and kept by Jesus Christ" (Jude 1).

We are called "the righteous" ones (Gal. 3:11) not because of the extent of our own righteousness, but because of the authoritative triumph of Christ which enables the transfer of his righteousness to us (Rom. 5:19). As the righteous of God, we live now by faith (Rom. 1:17).

Saint is a very prominent term for a follower of Jesus in the New Testament. A *saint* is a holy person set apart for God. We do not have the authority to decide the standard by which to live our lives. As the "Holy One of God" (Mark 1:24), Christ himself is our standard and so we follow him.

A *believer* (Acts 19:18) is one who trusts in the good news about Jesus Christ and follows him as a result. To be a *believer* means to trust in Christ as the supreme Lord. The term *believer* can also be translated "faithful." Believer and faithful communicate a total commitment to living under Christ's authority in all realms of life.

Jesus calls his disciples *friends* (Luke 12:4). With this term, Jesus emphasizes the intimate access that we have to God (John 15:15). Departing a bit from our standard usage of *friend*, Jesus clarifies that his *friends* are those that submit to his authority and follow his commandments, "You are My friends if you do what I command you" (John 15:14).

Brother or *brethren* is also a popular name for disciples of Christ in the New Testament. This term stresses the intimacy of fellowship that we have with each other under a unified head, that is, Christ. Our spiritual brotherhood is closer than a blood brotherhood (Mark 10:23–31).

Finally, disciples of Christ are called "children of God." God in Christ has adopted us as children on the basis of faith (John 1:12; Gal. 3:26; 1 John 5:1). Having been adopted, God is our Father and Christ is our older brother who leads us together in the household of God (Heb. 2:11). In summary, each of the biblical terms for disciples of Christ explains a different facet of what it means to follow Jesus Christ as the authoritative Lord.

Salvation and Sanctification in Submission

Being born again necessarily entails submission to Christ as Savior *and* Lord. "If you confess with your mouth, 'Jesus is Lord,' and believe in your heart that God raised Him from the dead, you will be saved. One believes with the heart, resulting in righteousness, and one confesses with the mouth, resulting in salvation" (Rom. 10:9–10). Certainly, we are all fighting daily for total surrender to Christ. Each day, by God's grace, we are able to surrender more and more of our lives. But daily surrender to Christ does not negate a once-and-for-all salvation by Christ in the confession that he is Lord.

Cherishing the lordship of Christ is the root of our strength against a myriad of daily temptations. For when we face temptations, we face a crisis of authority. Nobody can serve two masters. So when Christ is exalted to the throne room of the heart, he expunges all other deviant influences in the heart. Consider the example of my good friend Nathan. A few years ago he felt the Lord leading him to fast as a petition to God to abolish sex slavery. He decided to give up something that he enjoyed on a regular basis: coffee. Since that time a number of years ago, Nathan has fasted from coffee. Every time he says no to coffee, he points to Christ as his greater authority.

The declaration of faith in Christ is simply "he knows best." We are able to believe that declaration when we focus our minds and hearts on the gospel that Jesus is Lord. The gospel that Jesus is Lord enables us daily to say no to sin and yes to Jesus.

Our daily fight for sanctification ultimately comes down to the question, "Who is my master?" We are often like an excited puppy ready to go outside and play in the snow. We bark and scrape at the front door. But if our master says, "no," we must trust him that he knows best. He knows, after all, that we will sink in the deep snow, get lost, and suffocate.

Submission to Christ is an act of worship. Bowing down is the most graphic physical portrayal of submission. Though we do not believe that worship necessitates certain bodily movements (as in Islam), we should consider the helpful links between worship and bowing down. It is not surprising, therefore, that bowing down in submission is linked to the biblical concept of worship. Bowing to idols represents worship of idols (e.g., Exod. 32:8; Isa. 2:8). Bowing in the temple was an act of affectionate worship of God (Ps. 5:7). Upon seeing the boy Jesus, the wise men fell to their knees and worshiped him (Matt. 2:11). One day, all existence will recognize the authority of Christ and submit to him in a universal act of bowing to him and confessing his lordship (Phil. 2:10–11).

The implications for connecting disciple making with submission to Jesus are broad for disciple makers. As an example, we must be careful to evaluate a person's spiritual growth primarily in terms of his or her relationship to Jesus Christ, not in terms of their acceptance of "kingdom values" or "kingdom ethics." Faith in Christ leads to obedience in Christ. Since Christ leads us most directly through the proper application of Scriptures, obedient submission to the authority of the Bible is the clearest mark of submission to the lordship of Jesus.

We must be ready to submit ourselves to the Lord if we are to call others to submit to the Lord as his disciples. That means that we must be willing to do or say anything at the command of the

Lord. When he says, "Go to the nations," we must go. When he says, "Share the gospel with your boss," then we must share. When he says to us, "Give your money to the poor," we listen and obey knowing that Jesus has our good in mind. If we do not follow him as Lord, how will we influence others to do so?

The King and His Kingdom

By elevating the importance of submission to Jesus in the life of a disciple, I do not mean to downplay emphasis on participation in the kingdom of Christ. In my view, submission to the lordship of Christ is not in tension with participation in his kingdom. I rather mean to clarify that participation in his kingdom is contingent on submission to his lordship.

Entrance into the kingdom of God depends on being born again as a child of God (John 3:3). And being born again requires believing in Christ as Lord of all. So the apostle John writes that though Jesus came to the world from heaven, the world did not recognize him as from God. We have the "right," or legitimacy, to become the children of God and citizens of God's kingdom in Christ because of belief in Christ Jesus as Lord (John 1:12–13).

We need careful articulation of the doctrine of the kingdom of God and what it means to live in it. In my view, all of our discussions about the kingdom of God must relate back to the King himself. We are disciples of the King, and therefore, citizens of his kingdom, not the reverse. There is no kingdom without the king, for the kingdom is a derivative of the king who embodies it. When Jesus says, "The kingdom of God has come near" (Mark 1:15), he means, "I am near!" The good news of great joy that we declare and demonstrate to all peoples is not a new set of social ethics or a new spiritual community. But, principally, the good news is that the King has come and he offers to us citizenship in his kingdom.

Certainly those who are not disciples of Jesus may experience the fruits of Christ's kingdom. They may draw the fruit from its outer orchards, but they may not bathe in the life-giving river that runs eternally from the King's throne. That river is reserved only for those who have been washed clean once and for all by the perfect blood of the Lamb.

Submission in Relationship

Working in the Muslim world, I am constantly confronted with comparisons between a life devoted to the Islamic Allah and a life devoted to Christ. The concept of submission to God is central to both a Muslim and a disciple of Jesus. What, then, is the difference between how a Muslim relates to God and how a follower of Jesus relates to God? This difference is the nature of the relationship between a person and God, and it is the most consequential theological contrast between these two historic faiths.

The very term *Islam* means "submission." Submission to God and his prophets in a life of religious devotion is the very essence of the Muslim life. But Muslims do not call God their "Father." To the Muslim ear, calling God "Father" smacks of heresy. For God is infinitely transcendent and has never had relations with a woman. He has no biological children and is the child of no one else. He is entirely self-existent and self-sufficient.

In contrast, as the adopted children of God, we call God our "Father." The God of the Bible descended to us as a man so that we might know him in a real, dynamic, personal, and intimate relationship. He is intimate not merely because he is near, but because we have full access to him in his very throne room. We can approach him, as we are and as he is, with confidence and boldness and strength. He cares for every detail of our lives and we can be totally honest with him.

I recently met with a new follower of Christ from Saudi Arabia. He grew up in a Muslim family, fully believing in Islam. In his teenage years he began to learn about Jesus. He was drawn to watch a video about Jesus Christ. He was so attracted to Jesus because he felt that Jesus was present with him. When he prayed in Jesus' name, he felt that God heard him. Soon, he gave his life to Jesus and began a personal relationship with him.

This is not an uncommon story in the Muslim world. We submit to God in Christ because we believe that God loves us individually. There is no personal relationship with the god of Islam. But we know that God in Christ calls us to submit to him in a personal relationship.

The Return of the King

There is an important connection between the commission to "make disciples" of all peoples and the promise that Jesus is with us to the "end of the age." The connection is that the fruit of discipleship is cherishing the display of the authority of Christ. And since his authority will be displayed in its fullness to all creation when he returns, as disciples grow they will more "eagerly wait" the return of Christ at the end of the age (Phil. 3:20–21), when he will display his supreme authority in his judgment over all peoples.

Our hearts leap at the thought of God magnifying Jesus over every human and spiritual authority and power. When Jesus returns, every inch of existence will be filled with the radiance of his robe. His horse's nay will echo off the Himalayas into the homes of the Inuits in Alaska and then through the secret rooms of the Kremlin and into thousands of tiny kitchens in the slums of Brazil. His sword will smash the fiercest idols of humanity in a single sweep. He will shine like ten million suns in the splendor of his holiness. On that day, everyone will submit to him who has all authority (Phil. 2:10–11).

This eagerness motivates us to press on in fulfilling the commission to make disciples among all peoples, since the end will come when the "good news of the kingdom [is] proclaimed in all the world as a testimony to all nations" (Matt. 24:14). On the day that Jesus returns he will be "glorified by His saints" and "admired by all those who have believed" (2 Thess. 1:10). So, making disciples means influencing people to look back to the person and work of Christ and to look forward to the return of Christ one day. The more they look back and forward at Jesus, the more they will cherish his leadership and authority in the present.

Looking Forward to "The End of the Age"

Obviously, there are countless glories about the day of the return of Christ. Personally, I look forward to five glories specifically. Each of these glories relies on the Lord Jesus exercising his supreme authority and power on that day.

First, we will finally see Jesus face-to-face. I grew up as a boy in the southeastern tip of New Mexico, about one hour from Ciudad Juarez, Mexico. The religion of the land is folk Catholicism. I remember hearing reports of locals spotting the face of Jesus and the Virgin Mary on all kinds of things: the clouds, in the sand, and most memorably for me, on a tortilla. To the relief—or likely the terror—of the owner of the holy tortilla in southern New Mexico, one day there will be no more speculation as to contours of the face of Jesus. We will have to wonder no more, for "we will see Him as He is" (1 John 3:2). "They will see His face, and His name will be on their foreheads" (Rev. 22:4). May we never dull to that stunning promise. We will meet the Lord, we will see him face-to-face, and we will be with him forever.

Suffering encourages us to think about the face of Jesus. With the prophet Job we cry out, "But I know my living Redeemer, and He will stand on the dust at last. Even after my skin has been destroyed, yet I will see God in my flesh. I will see Him myself; my eyes will look at Him, and not as a stranger. My heart longs within me" (Job 19:25–27). We will behold Jesus, the Lord of infinite beauty and glory, and we will be with him.

Second, our faith, hope, and patience will be realized. Faith, hope, and patience are temporary. Singer/songwriter Andrew Peterson sings about the day when there is "no more faith":

> *I say faith is a burden*
> *It's a weight to bear*
> *It's brave and bittersweet*
> *And hope is hard to hold to*
> *Lord, I believe*
> *Only help my unbelief*
>
> *Till there's no more faith*
> *No more hope*
> *I'll see your face and Lord, I'll know*
> *That only love remains*[4]

It is easy to grow weary of living by faith in the supreme authority of Christ when the world goes awry and suffering comes like a tsunami over the little space that we call "home." This is why we are admonished to not give up (Gal. 6:9). We now seek a homeland (Heb. 11:14). We will be *entering it* on that Day. Our faith, hope, and longings will be realized. We will receive all that has been promised (Heb. 11:39–40). And we will enjoy the most satisfying rest from our faith for all eternity.

Third, when Christ returns, the suffering of the saints will be completely avenged. Have you ever felt a holy desire for avenging the persecution of the saints or the mistreatment of the poor and weak by the strong? Have you ever felt a holy hatred of Satan and the way that he so craftily destroys people's lives? Have you ever struggled to obey Romans 12:19, "Friends, do not avenge yourselves; instead, leave room for His wrath. For it is written: Vengeance belongs to Me; I will repay, says the Lord"? Have you ever felt the cry of the holy martyrs of Revelation 6:9–11? "They cried out with a loud voice, 'O Sovereign Lord, holy and true, how long before you will judge and avenge our blood on those who dwell on the earth?" (ESV). When Jesus returns, all this longing will be fulfilled. Every evil act of men will be exposed and punished. Vengeance will come on all those who do not "obey the gospel of our Lord Jesus" (2 Thess. 1:8).

For us who have been washed in the authoritative blood of the Lamb, this will be the day of fulfillment: "But based on His promise, we wait for the new heavens and a new earth, where righteousness will dwell" (2 Pet. 3:13). As immediate, final, complete, and relentless as the judgment will come on the enemies of the Lamb, it will come in glory upon us who have been masterfully cared for by our Vinedresser in the garden of God.

Fourth, we look forward to the return of our King because on that day our physical bodies will be glorified. When Jesus returns, his followers will either be resurrected (if they are already dead) or clothed with a new, perfect and eternal physical body (if they are still alive, 2 Cor. 5:4). There will be no possibility of sickness or imperfection with this body—no Ebola, no malaria, no broken bones, no colds, no allergies, no stubbed toes, no aching, no infections, no cancer, no brain tumors, no need for glasses or hearing aids, and no tooth aches. "But our citizenship is in heaven, from which we also eagerly wait for a Savior, the Lord Jesus Christ. He will transform the body of our humble condition into the likeness of His glorious body, by the power that enables Him to subject everything to Himself" (Phil. 3:20–21).

When we suffer, we should think upon the future redemption of our bodies. We should dream about the day when our bodies will be "raised in incorruption" (1 Cor. 15:42). We should

encourage our suffering brothers and sisters in the Lord with
these truths. This is how the New Testament writers encourage
those who are suffering (James 5:7–11; Rom. 8:18–25; 1 Pet.
4:13; 1 Thess. 4:18; 1 Cor. 15:58; 1 Thess. 5:11).

This reason affects me quite profoundly as I think about my
mother. In 1984 my family was in an eighty-mile-per-hour head-
on automobile collision in the Dominican Republic on Christmas
Eve. My father fractured his neck in the wreck. My sister and I
broke our legs. My baby brother broke his nose. My other sister
fractured a facial bone. But my mother experienced the most physical damage: about half of her body was shattered from head to toe.
By God's grace and healing power, she is alive and able to do many
things a healthy person is able to do. But it has been a long, hard,
painful road for her and the rest of my family. Three decades later,
she still bears the physical consequences of the car wreck of 1984.
I asked her to describe the suffering that she regularly endures.
Below is what she wrote:

> I don't ever mind talking about the goodness of God. He
> has blessed me in many ways. The wreck is an event that
> has drawn me close to God. All of us had major injuries,
> so to say mine were the worst is only because I had more.
> The car was hit head-on with a little tilt to the right. I
> took most of the impact. The van was flat-nosed which
> was a God thing because I had no time to be thrown
> from the car. My right side was crushed. There were very
> few bones that were not broken from my head to toe. My
> left hand had some broken fingers. I had numerous cuts
> on me apparently from broken glass. My internal organs
> were moved around. I had to have five major surgeries
> immediately in order for me to be in a critical state to live.
> During this time doctors would say, "She will not live."
> Flying home on the plane I "code blue" two times. After
> a few days, the doctors would say, "Well, if she lives, she

will never be able to walk and she will have limited use of her body." Eventually, they would say, "Well, she will have to use orthopedic equipment the rest of her life to walk." Then, "Well, she will limp." Then, in 1995 I began to walk without assistance.

Degenerative bone disease began to develop very early after the accident because my body was using what calcium I had to reproduce marrow. But, I didn't have much calcium, so the disease invaded my body. How has that affected me? I fracture easy. The inside structure of my bones are very thin and, with the disease, thinning can take place at any location of my bones. And so they break easily. Aging of my bone marrow is well beyond my age. The last test I had showed the bone structure to be already aged by twenty years. What do I do with this? I have to be careful not to fall, to avoid any quick movements and high-impact exercise. I take lots of medicine.

The arthritis is the same. I lay motionless for a period of time, and then not able to move or strengthen parts of my body, arthritis settled in. Medicine helps.

The seizures continue to this day because of the impact to my head. The skull was fractured and there was swelling. I have to stay on medicine. The seizures still come but, praise the Lord, memory is not affected too much. To be able to write why and how all this relates is really something I haven't given much thought to because I have always tried to thank God for all that He has given me, and not curse Him for all that I've lost.

I long for the return of Christ in part because on that day my mother's body will be renewed. The triumphal King will rejoice as he shows off to the host of heaven when my mom runs through the gates of heaven without the slightest limp. Every time she hits a tennis ball in the new earth she will magnify the authority of Christ. May we hasten the return of Jesus for the sake of the renewal of my mother's body!

Fifth, and finally, because Jesus has all authority over all evil, everything will be set straight on that day. This comes last because it sums up the other reasons. I once visited an area of Cairo, Egypt, called "Trash City." There are multiple "trash cities" in Cairo alone. These communities gather and sort trash from greater Cairo by hand. They filter the trash for recyclable goods. The scene is unimaginable as the people literally live in a city of trash. They sleep on beds of trash. Trash lines the streets. Maggots abound. The stench is surreal. Trash-eating pigs mate with trash-eating dogs. After visiting "Trash City," I longed more for the return of Christ, because when he comes, he will set everything straight again.

He will authoritatively end injustice, avenge evil, redeem his peoples' bodies, bring an end to our faith and sanctification, welcome us into our eternal home, reveal his very face to us, put an end to death, and set everything once and for all time straight, "For God has put everything under His feet" (1 Cor. 15:27).

Our Own Shahada

The universal creed of Islam is called the *shahada*: "There is no god but God and Muhammad is the prophet of God." The *shahada* is the confession of every Muslim.[5] It is a summary of central truth of Islam, and as such it is impossible to be a Muslim without confessing the *shahada*. The *shahada* is so important, one may convert to Islam by simply stating the *shahada* in faith. Living in the Muslim world, it is possible to hear the *shahada* dozens of times in one day. It rings out in the calls to prayer, it is written on the walls of the neighborhoods, it is said before significant undertakings, it is referred to in simple conversation, it is cried out when someone is afraid or astonished or passionate or content. There is simply no context in the life of a Muslim or in the community of Muslims that the *shahada* is irrelevant. The entire corpus of Islamic theology boils down to this single confession, the *shahada*.

I make this point about the Islamic *shahada* to highlight the importance of our own *shahada*. We have a confession that unifies us as a family of believers around the world throughout all time. This confession is the foundation of our faith and it is universally relevant to all of life. All of our faith and hope and joy depend on this confession. We should hear it declared, explained, and exulted every single day in every context of our lives. It is the banner that flies over our lives. This confession is simply three words: "Jesus is Lord."

When unceasing storms arise
And the bruised mast tilts
The battered ship nears capsize
The sails ripped to their hilt.

Think not like common men
On such thund'rous nights
Who look into the wind
And think they've lost the fight.

Look rather to the ballast
This time in human flesh
His pow'r more than amplest
Though he looks as if he rests.

This Ballast keeps you steady
Firm and focused through the storm
With him you will be ready
For every tempest that may form.

Chapter 6

The Cross and Courageous Obedience

WHERE DO WE FIND THE FAITH, COURAGE, AND CONFIDENCE TO SUB-mit in joy to the supremely authoritative Jesus Christ? If we follow Jesus' command to "Go, therefore, and make disciples of all nations" (Matt. 28:19), we will inevitably encounter a multitude of complex decisions, intense obstacles, and perhaps even severe oppression. How then do we stay the course and daily submit to his leadership, even when the stakes are high? How we answer that question, and the power upon which we draw, indicates the authority in our lives. In this chapter, we dwell on the completed and perfect work of Christ on the cross to find the courage and confidence to walk faithfully with Christ.

For example, suppose that a husband has grown calloused over the years toward his wife. His relationship with her is business-like. He can deal with coming home every day and staying in the same house, but he does not come home to serve her, love her, and romantically pursue her. She is "over spiritual," he is "under spiritual," and every morning he feels a little relieved when he leaves for work. Then he is confronted with the biblical command, "Husbands, love your wives, just as Christ loved the church and gave Himself for her" (Eph. 5:25). How does he find the confidence and courage to obey God's Word and do what it takes to break up this calloused heart of his and lead his wife toward a restart of the marriage where he loves and pursues her, as Christ to his church?

Or, suppose that a wife has had growing romantic thoughts about her trainer at the gym. She has kept these thoughts secret from her husband, fearing his response. The trainer is charismatic, confident, and most of all happy to be with her—so unlike her husband. These thoughts have grown so strong that she has knowingly begun flirting with him, hoping that he might catch the hint and return her advances. Then this wife is confronted with 1 Corinthians 6:18, "Run from sexual immorality! 'Every sin a person can commit is outside the body.' On the contrary, the person who is sexually immoral sins against his own body." How does she find the confidence and courage to obey God in Christ and come clean with her husband, her Christian community, and ultimately God?

Or, suppose a middle-aged couple lives a comfortable life, with a nice wage and a nice house. Then this couple trusts in Jesus as their Lord and Savior. They are immediately confronted with Jesus' words in Matthew 8:19–20: "A scribe approached Him and said, 'Teacher, I will follow You wherever You go!' Jesus told him, 'Foxes have dens and birds of the sky have nests, but the Son of Man has no place to lay His head.'" Reading this passage, they feel prompted by the Holy Spirit to downsize, give significantly to the kingdom, and to find a way to leverage their influence publicly for the cause of Christ. They know that doing any of these things means inconveniences, awkward conversations with their colleagues, perhaps professional embarrassment, and daily sacrifices. How do they find the confidence and courage to obey Christ's leadership?

Finally, suppose that you or I find ourselves sharing the jail cell of Pastor Saeed Abedini.

The Answer to the WHY Is WHO

Saeed Abedini is an Iranian American Christian pastor who was imprisoned in Iran in September 2012. He was charged and sentenced to eight years in torturous Iranian prisons for his ministry with the church in Iran. He is routinely subjected to physical and psychological torture, not only from the prison officials but also from the other inmates. In early 2013, it became known that Pastor Saeed was suffering from internal injuries. While he was finally granted a hospital stay, he was forced to return to his prison cell before the necessary surgeries were undertaken. Despite his isolation, torture, and inhumane conditions under this unjust sentence, Pastor Saeed remains "strengthened by the Lord and by His vast strength" (Eph. 6:10).[1]

On September 12, 2014, Pastor Saeed wrote a letter to his daughter Rebekka on the occasion of her eighth birthday. This was Rebekka's third birthday without her father. In this incredible letter, Pastor Saeed teaches his daughter that the source of his hope is not found in dwelling on the reasons for his suffering, but on the authority of Jesus Christ. Below is his letter in its entirety.[2]

My Dearest Rebekka Grace,

HAPPY 8th BIRTHDAY!

You are growing so fast and becoming more beautiful every day. I praise God for His faithfulness to me every day as I watch from a distance through the prison walls and see pictures and hear stories of how you are growing both spiritually and physically.

Oh how I long to see you.

I know that you question why you have prayed so many times for my return and yet I am not home yet. Now there is a big WHY? In your mind you are asking: WHY Jesus isn't answering your prayers and the prayers of all of the people around the world praying for my release and for me to be home with you and our family.

The answer to the WHY is WHO. WHO is in control? LORD JESUS CHRIST is in control.

I desire for you to learn important lessons during these trying times. Lessons that you carry now and for the rest of your life. The answer to the WHY is WHO. The confusion of "WHY has all of this happened?" and "WHY your prayers are not answered yet" is resolved with understanding WHO is in control . . . LORD JESUS CHRIST, our GOD!

God is in control of the whole world and everything that is happening in it is for His good purpose, for His glory, and will be worked out for our good (Romans 8:28). Jesus allows me to be kept here for His glory. He is doing something inside each of us and also outside in the world. People die and suffer for their Christian faith all over the world and some may wonder why? But you should know the answer of WHY is WHO. It is for Jesus. He is worth the price. And He has a plan to be glorified through our lives.

I want you to read the book of Habakkuk. He had the same question as you. But see that the Lord answered him in Habakkuk 2:3, "the vision comes and doesn't delay on time, wait for it." Mommy and I always had big desires to serve Jesus and had great vision to be used for His Kingdom and for His Glory. So today we pay a cost because God, who created us, called us to that.

And so I want you to know that the answer to all of your prayers is that God is in control, and He knows better than us what He is doing in our lives and all around the world.

Therefore declare as Daniel and his friends Shadrach, Meshach, and Abed-Nego did in Daniel 3:17–18! "If that is the case, our God whom we serve is able to deliver us from the burning fiery furnace, and He will deliver us from your hand, O king. But if not, let it be known to you, O king, that we do not serve your gods, nor will we worship the gold image which you have set up" (NKJV).

And learn and declare as Habakkuk did that even if we do not get the result that we are looking for, God is still good and we WILL praise His Holy Name.

Habakkuk 3:17–19, "Though the fig tree may not blossom, Nor fruit be on the vines; Though the labor of the olive may fail, And the fields yield no food; Though the flock may be cut off from the fold, And there be no herd in the stalls—Yet I will rejoice in the LORD, I will joy in the God of my salvation. The LORD God is my strength; He will make my feet like deer's feet, And He will make me walk on my high hills" (NKJV).

Then my dear beloved daughter, Rebekka Grace, I pray God will bring me back home soon. But if not, we will still sing together as Habakkuk did HALLELUJAH, either separated by prison walls or together at home.

So, let Daddy hear you sing a loud Hallelujah that I can hear all the way here in the prison!

I am so proud of you my sweet courageous daughter. Glory to God forever, Amen.

Kisses and Blessings,

Daddy

This is an incredible letter. The most loving and encouraging thing that this godly father can say to his eight-year-old daughter on her birthday is, "The answer to the WHY is WHO. WHO is in control? LORD JESUS CHRIST is in control." That is the message that propels a daughter to trust Christ.

Imagine a ship at sea that begins to take on water. The sailors run to the deck and start working to repair the damage. The wind strengthens. The sails begin to rip. The ship begins to list severely and the sailors begin to give up hope. At that moment, the most important part of the ship is the ballast. Will the ballast hold or will it give in, inevitably sinking the ship? The ballast of the ship has gone unnoticed and unspoken of so far in this sea journey, that is, until the storm strikes. Then everyone wants to know whether that ballast is strong and steady. Suffering forces us to trust in the authority, legitimacy, and strength of our ballast, the Lord Jesus. And Pastor Saeed has testified with his very life that this ballast is eternally trustworthy, even against the fiercest storms.

When unceasing storms arise
And the bruised mast tilts
The battered ship nears capsize
The sails ripped to their hilt.

Think not like common men
On such thund'rous nights
Who look into the wind
And think they've lost the fight.

Look rather to the ballast
This time in human flesh
His pow'r more than amplest
Though he looks as if he rests.

This Ballast keeps you steady
Firm and focused through the storm
With him you will be ready
For every tempest that may form.

The gates of hell will not withstand the advance of the kingdom of God, not because of the strength of the warriors, the genius of the war strategy, or superior weaponry, but because of the supreme authority of the warrior King who leads his troops. They have only to follow in the King's trail to enjoy the triumph of his victory.

He not only sends his ambassadors out today to the edges of hell to rescue his people from their slavery to the dragon devil (cf. Acts 18:10), but King Jesus rides with them. He assures his people not only of his presence, but of his accomplished work on the cross. His ambassadors know that if the work of Christ on the cross fails in any measure at all, then their mission is doomed. The hope of their mission is in the perfect completion of all that Christ intended on his cross. This hope propels them courageously against the fiercest foes in the most dangerous contexts.

Courage and Confidence in His Completed Work

The confidence and courage to obey Christ comes in the trust of his completed work on the cross. In this chapter we will consider a famous passage, Romans 8:31–39, and make connections between the cross and our courage and confidence to follow Jesus.

What then are we to say about these things? If God is for us, who is against us? He did not even spare His own Son but offered Him up for us all; how will He not also with Him grant us everything? Who can bring an accusation against God's elect? God is the One who justifies. Who is the one who condemns? Christ Jesus is the One who died, but even more, has been raised; He also is at the right hand of God and intercedes for us. Who can separate us from the love of Christ? Can affliction or anguish or persecution or famine or nakedness or danger or sword? As it is written: Because of You we are being put to death all day long;

we are counted as sheep to be slaughtered. No, in all these things we are more than victorious through Him who loved us. For I am persuaded that not even death or life, angels or rulers, things present or things to come, hostile powers, height or depth, or any other created thing will have the power to separate us from the love of God that is in Christ Jesus our Lord! (Rom. 8:31–39)

We begin with verse 31: "If God is for us, who is against us?" Notice that the text points to a present reality. It says, "if God *is* for us," not "if God *will be* for us." The nature of this kind of conditional statement presumes the truth of the premise. In fact, the verse could legitimately be translated, "*Since* God is for us, who is against us?" The ground of Paul's confidence that "God is for us" is God's justification of his people through the cross and resurrection of Jesus Christ.

Jesus was totally right with God when he went to the cross, without sin. He was morally and ceremonially perfect. And when he died, what we call the "great exchange" happened. All of the punishment for our sin was poured out on Jesus and all of his righteousness was transferred to us who believe in him. "He made the One who did not know sin to be sin for us, so that we might become the righteousness of God in Him" (2 Cor. 5:21). Our assurance that there is no condemnation for those who are in Christ is based on our faith that Jesus was totally righteous and therefore he perfectly accomplished our salvation in his death.

"God Is for Us" Because "God Is for Jesus"

If the work of Christ on the cross was perfectly complete, if his goals in dying were achieved, then we can be assured today that God is for us. In other words, when Scripture says, "God is for us," it is referring to the fact that God is for *Jesus*. This text is not talking about how God likes our personalities, or that he thinks we are just so gifted and unique and special. And yet many people use this verse to try to reassure themselves that they are the apple of God's eye. In the process, verse 31 gets flattened into an inspirational refrigerator magnet that says God just likes us for being us. But that's not what Paul is talking about! The "if God is for us" in this verse is based on the successful work of Christ on the cross. God was for Jesus, and nothing can separate the love of the Father for the Son, so we can say that just as God is for his Son, God is for us.

Importantly, verse 31 does not mean, "If God is for us, no one will be against us." Every follower of Christ knows that obedience to Christ will eventually lead to opposition from others. And if that is not enough, Satan and his army will be against us. Nor does the text mean, "If God is for us, we will never suffer at the hands of our enemies," for verse 36 speaks to the suffering of the saints: "For your sake we are being killed all the day long: we are regarded as sheep to be slaughtered" (ESV).

Instead, "If God is for us, who is against us" means that if God is for us, no one, not even the devil himself can take away the favor of God from us. No one can destroy God's plan of salvation for His people. So our confidence that God is for us is not in our personality, our ability, or all the work we might do for God. It is in knowing that God is for us because God is for his Son. And the love that the Father has for the Son is unbreakable. If we are in Christ, then, this favor of the Father has been transferred to us. We have been declared righteous with the righteousness of Jesus Christ and this declaration will never fail.

God Is for Us; Therefore, We Can Obey Christ

The following verses in Romans 8 describe how the truth of God being for us plays out in daily life.

First, he is for us because he provides for us. "He did not even spare His own Son but offered Him up for us all; how will He not also with Him grant us everything?" (v. 32). Notice that verse

32 looks backward. It looks to the work of Jesus Christ on the cross. If the death and resurrection of Jesus accomplished all that God intended, then we can have hope that God will take care of everything else for us according to his perfect plan. If there is any inferiority or compromise in Jesus' accomplishment on the cross, then we have no reason to hope that God will provide anything for us, no matter how small. Inferiority in Christ or his work on the cross breaks down the logic of verse 32 and we are then left with insecurity in our faith. But Christ's work *was* perfect in securing our salvation, if we are in Christ.

Verse 32 contrasts a greater work with a lesser work: if the greater work is accomplished, lesser works will be easily accomplished. The greatest work was God's placing his own Son on the cross; therefore, will he not also take care of us and one day deliver us to eternity and glorify us? Let me offer a few simple examples of how this logic works. If I have built a skyscraper, then building a one-story house will not be hard. If I've climbed Mount Everest, I can certainly climb a hill. If I can perform orthopedic surgery, then I am certainly able to put a bandage on my son when he scrapes his arm. If God put up his own Son to die for us, it is an "easy" thing for him to take care of us as we obey him.

I was pressed with this truth right before we moved to the Arab world in 2010. In preparation for our move, my wife and I had a long list of things to do. We were going from having a home with all kinds of stuff to moving overseas with about six suitcases. We were fairly daunted at the to-do list we had racked up, but we had committed our plans and lists to the Lord and trusted him. One thing we had to do was sell our two cars. One of them was old—180,000 miles, the air conditioning did not work, a window would not go down, the bumper had been duct-taped together, and so on. I planned to put a "for sale" sign on the car and advertise it online on a particular Tuesday, nearing our departure. But on the Monday before, I was at a prayer meeting with my teammate. During our prayer meeting, a stranger named Mario put a note on that car which said, "If you want to sell your car, I'll buy it from you with cash." That had never happened to me before! I called him, we met that day, and he bought the car the next day. I remember feeling overwhelmed with thanksgiving to God. If he did not spare his own Son for me, how much more is he able to take care of my to-do list this week?

Who Shall Bring Any Charge against God's Elect?

The second application of the truthful announcement of verse 31, "If God is for us, who is against us?" is found in verse 33: "Who can bring any accusation against God's elect? God is the One who justifies." God is for us because, at the cross, he frees us from the devil's accusations.

"Who can bring any accusation" alludes to a courtroom where a defendant sits and awaits trial. In walk the plaintiff lawyers with a big fat file of charges that they will levy against the defendant. And here the defendant sits trembling and asking himself, *What if that file is right? What if it's true?* Whether these accusations are truthful or not has no bearing on our favor with God if our dependence is in Christ. God's favor depends on his choice of us. Thus Paul says, "Who can bring any accusation against God's *elect?*" God knows all of our failures, he knows us in our brightest and darkest moments. But if we are in Christ, he has chosen us, even knowing our dark secrets. We are the elect of God if indeed we trust in Christ. The declaration of our righteousness has already gone out, and that declaration penetrated the farthest reach of hell. Therefore, no matter the veracity of the devil's accusations against us, God has chosen us and declared us righteous, making the devil's accusations null and void.

I believe that Paul is talking about Satan here as the one who brings the charges against us. Satan is, after all, called the "Accuser." And Satan lives to accuse us. He will tempt us to believe a litany of accusations against us—how we have sinned, how we have failed God and others, how unfit we are to be in God's service, and so on. He will whisper in our ear or shout in our face:

Don't you remember, dad, yelling at your son, and how that's going to scar him for the rest of his life? No Christian father treats his son that way.

Don't you remember, young man, last year with that girl? You know what you did. And now you are here pretending to be a Christian. You're not fooling anybody.

Don't you remember, young girl, how you went with that guy and followed his leadership into things that have made you weep the last three months?

Don't you remember, wife, how you've had those unloving thoughts about your husband? If he ever finds out, he'll walk out on you and never return.

Don't you remember, Christian, saying years ago with all your heart, "Jesus, I commit my life to you and surrender all?" Now look at you. He knows how much you've sinned against him.

At this very moment, the devil is lining up his accusations against us to destroy us. Against the devil's accusations, we speak back with mighty confidence in Romans 8:31–39: "God has already, once for all and perfectly, declared me righteous in Jesus Christ. He will even use my trials to bless me. Your accusations, Devil, no matter how legitimate, are rendered ineffective. I am a sinner, but my God is a great Savior and he himself foreknew me, he predestined me, he called me, he declared me righteous in Christ, and one day he will glorify me!" When you do that, the mount of accusations against you will crumble in the power of the gospel, freeing you to joyful service to God.

Who Is to Condemn?

Third, and similar to the second application of verse 31, God is for us because he frees us from the verdict of punishment. Paul says in verse 34, "Who is the one who condemns?" Because in the achievement of Christ on the cross, God frees us from the verdict as well as all accusations.

Paul knows that in a courtroom there are not only accusations levied, there is also a verdict. There's a judge and jury. There is a trial and a verdict with potential punishment. So Paul continues in verse 34, "Who is the one who condemns? Christ Jesus is the One who died, but even more, has been raised; He also is at the right hand of God and intercedes for us."

Paul is splitting the courtroom drama into two events: the trial and the verdict. And in both events, Paul declares the gospel is the power of God unto salvation for us. Because of the work of Christ on the cross, we will not have one word of accusation successfully levied against us. Nor will God himself condemn us as the final judge of our life.

The devil has been rendered *totally* ineffective and impotent because of the cross. And Jesus Christ has *totally* appeased the wrath of God for his chosen sinners. All that remains for us if we are in Christ is God's favor, the favor of a father for his child. Therefore, we have nothing to fear of the devil's paralyzing accusations. And we have nothing but gratitude for God because of his favor that he has for us because we are in Christ, his Son. That is what makes us different.

And that is why the rest of this passage is poetic rejoicing in the perfection of God's justifying work in Christ Jesus. Paul has already shown that if God is for you, you have no one to fear—not Satan, not yourself, not Jesus, and not even the Father. Jesus died and took our sin, he was raised to seal his work of redeeming us, and he is now with God interceding for us! What could be better news? Therefore, for those of us who trust in Christ, we stand *not accused* and *not guilty* in the throne room on Judgment Day.

The Strongest Rebuttal against God's Love for His Elect

But there is an objection here so strong that it has persisted through every century of human existence since the fall of Adam and Eve: If God is for us, why then do we suffer? This is one reason why Paul continues on in verses 35–36: "Who can separate us from the love of Christ? Can affliction or anguish or persecution or famine or nakedness or danger or sword? As it is written: Because of you we are being put to death all day long; we are counted as sheep to be slaughtered." Paul knows the power of suffering to convince us that God does not love us. He is actually writing this in the context of suffering. He is under house arrest for preaching the gospel. He has suffered through beatings, shipwrecks, being stoned, starvation, and poverty. And everyone who has gone through trials or suffering knows how it tempts us to forget or even deny God's love for us in Christ. But Paul knows personally the power of the gospel to lead us through suffering because of the assurance of God's love for us in Christ. "No, in all these things we are more than victorious through Him who loved us" (v. 37).

We Know God Loves Us Because He Loved Us

Notice that the passage speaks of God's love in the aorist tense, "Through Him who loved us." The Greek word for *loved* (*agapēsantos*) signifies a past, completed action with continuing effect. Of course this love is displayed in the cross of Christ. Once again, we see the cross at the center of Paul's admonition to be assured of God's love. We can walk in confidence through blessing or trial not because of a faint hope that God may or may not come through for us, but because of a solid faith that he already did come through. Our hope is not built on our future work, but on God's love displayed in the cross of Christ. And because the work of Christ on the cross is final and supremely authoritative over all powers of darkness, we are assured that nothing therefore will now separate us from God's love. "For I am sure that neither death nor life, nor angels, nor rulers, nor things present, nor things to come, nor powers, nor heights, nor depth, nor anything else in creation will be able to separate us from the love of God in Christ Jesus our Lord" (vv. 38–39 ESV).

Our Anchor, Megaphone, and Book of Promises

How does this doctrine play out into actually building our confidence and courage to submit to the authority of Christ in God in both big and small decisions?

First, the cross keeps us steady when it appears that things around us are unraveling. Imagine that you are on a roller coaster. As you tear along the track, no longer in control, your hope is in the integrity of the rails upon which you glide. In the same way, we hang on to the hope of Christ, forever true and unshakable.

Second, the work of Christ blasts like a megaphone to us that God loves us. If we are in Christ, he loves us because he loves his Son. And nothing will ever separate God's divine love for his Son. Therefore, nothing will ever separate God's love for you if you are in Christ. When you wake, when you sleep, when you work, and when you play, open your ears to the megaphone that blasts from the Bible to you.

Third, the work of Christ confirms all of God's various promises to us. God has given us a whole book of promises, glorious promises, and we can take each promise and bank our lives on them. Second Corinthians 1:20 reads, "For every one of God's promises is 'Yes' in Him." Therefore, with the promises of God affirmed to us as a "yes!" in Christ and secured forever through Christ's work on the cross, we have nothing but grace ahead of us.

As the famous missionary to Burma, Adoniram Judson, once said, "The future is as bright as the promises of God."

In my own journey with Jesus, I have faced crises of confidence in my decisions. I have three young children and a wife that God has given me to lead, protect, provide for, and love. As we have served in dangerous places, I constantly assess whether I believe that Jesus is trustworthy to achieve all that he intends in my life and in the world. Often, as I face temptations toward unbelief head-on, I fall into anxiety.

Years ago, in a season of intense temptation to fear, I knew that I would only find confidence and courage by extended meditation on the work of Jesus on the cross. So I spent four weeks working my way through the definitive text on the cross by John Owen, *The Death of Death in the Death of Christ*.[3] I took about fifty pages of single-spaced typed notes. I submersed my mind, heart, and spirit into the cross. And I came out more confident in one thing: that God had perfectly and once-and-for-all justified me in Christ through his work on the cross. And my righteousness in Christ would *never* decay, or else God himself is not just. If God fails to keep his promises to me in Christ, then it is God himself who is on trial. *Therefore*, I shall not fear hell itself.

Use This Sword against the Ailing Dragon

When you face temptations of insecurity, fear, or anxiety in following Christ totally, no matter how difficult his commands, take Romans 8:31–39 and use it like a sword. Use this passage as a sword to fight for courage on the basis of faith and you will shame the devil and grow in courage, confidence, and joy in following Christ.

When the devil says to you, "You'll be opposed and rejected!"
    Answer him back: "If God is for me, who is against me?"
(Rom. 8:31)

When the devil says to you, "But God might not come through as he promised!"

Answer him back: "He did not even spare His own Son but offered Him up for me; how will He not also with Him grant me everything?" (Rom. 8:32)

When the devil says to you, "I will show God and the world your worst sins and failures!"

Answer him back: "Who can bring an accusation against God's elect? God has justified me!" (Rom. 8:33)

When the devil says to you, "God knows you messed up, and he's going to condemn you on Judgment Day!"

Answer him back: "Who is the one who condemns? Christ Jesus is the one who died, but even more, has been raised; He also is at the right hand of God and intercedes for me!" (Rom. 8:34)

When the devil says to you, "God doesn't love you. You can't really believe his love never fails when you're suffering like this!"

Answer him back: "Who can separate us from the love of Christ? Can affliction or anguish or persecution or famine or nakedness or danger or sword? As it is written: Because of You we are being put to death all day long; we are counted as sheep to be slaughtered. No, in all these things we are more than victorious through Him who loved us. For I am persuaded that not even death or life, angels or rulers, things present or things to come, hostile powers, height or depth, or any other created thing will have the power to separate us from the love of God that is in Christ Jesus our Lord!" (Rom. 8:35–39)

Son, snuff not this heat, kindling under twigs,
That kindling will bring down a mighty fort.
Within the fort the men brag of their figs,
Let them brag while you burn their royal courts.

Despise the words of boastful men, those beasts.
Strong they seem, yet their brains consumed in meat.
Their stomachs love the liquor of the feasts.
Their liquor spreads the torment of the heat.

Bravery marks you, man, and with it hope.
The Witnesses cheer you, and I am pleased.
Be valiant, know your shame is when you grope
For "normal," the hemlock your friends call "ease."

Your charge is to reject passivity.
Beware of modern thought and pansy lore.
They will say when widows burn, "let it be!"
But sit not still, rise up! And make your war.

You are a warrior, son, a knight of steel.
I do not know which dragons wait for you.
They sleep now, but when your approach they feel,
Ten thousand years of hatred they will brew.

And when they do, don't tarry, grasp your sword.
Swiftly, shrewdly, strike and shame your foe.
Plunge at the beast, his fat head your reward.
With faith in king David's King, be not slow!

And when you win, bow there and make a toast.
Submit your strength in praise to him who reigns.
The Ruler's Throne yields not to men who boast,
Save that from him their rights they have obtained.

—— Chapter 7 ——

"I Give You Authority"

WHEN WE THINK ABOUT THE AUTHORITY OF JESUS, WE TEND TO think about how to *use* that authority in our lives. As I began to tell people about the topic of this book, the most common response was, "Oh, so you are writing about our authority in Christ?" I carefully would respond, "No, I'm writing primarily about the authority of Christ himself. If we do not understand and appreciate *his* authority, we will not understand the meaning of *our* authority in him."

Naturally, we tend to be more concerned with *our* authority than we are with *Christ's* authority.[1] And yet the Bible is much more concerned about the nature of Christ's authority than our authority, since the latter flows from the former. But there is huge money and ample platform for preachers when they write and talk about our spiritual authority. Myriads of books and sermons are produced to tell people how to leverage this authority for triumph in the various struggles of their lives. The problem is that we are so concerned with how to *use* his authority that we forget it is not our authority to begin with. When we focus more on how to use this authority than on the source of this authority, Jesus Christ, we inevitably become enslaved to a lust for power cloaked in religious

language. In this book, I want to recalculate our main focus
from practical authority itself to The Authority himself. We can
use Christ's authority most effectively inasmuch as we know and
abide in him. That said, it is important to understand the nature
of Christ's delegation of authority to his followers. For this delegation is critical for the accomplishment of the Great Commission.

What Do We Have Authority to Do?

Just as the Father sent Jesus, so Jesus sends us (John 20:21).
He not only authorizes us to minister in his name, he has given us
his very authority and power to do that work of ministry. What,
then, do we have the authority from him to do?

Most often we associate the topic of the authority in Christ
with that of spiritual warfare. So we will begin with that. As
Christ's soldiers, we have the authority to war against evil. *Satan*
simply means "adversary." He is the great adversary of God and of
all things of God. He hates God, his world, his people, and all of
his work. While we stray from images of physically going to war in
the name of Christ, we are in a spiritual war against Satan and his
forces. To resist him, we must know his strategies.

The Five Strategies of Satan

Richard Lovelace helpfully summarizes the five characteristic
strategies of Satan against God's people: temptation, deception,
accusation, possession, and physical attack.[2] Satan's first and foundational strategy is *temptation* to sin. Satan is called "the tempter"
(Matt. 4:3). Sin not only draws a person away from Christ, it also
damages our witness of Christ to the world. All demonic influence begins and is amplified by temptation and sin. Satan is smart.
He knows the pervasive and destructive power of sin. Simple
sins against God yield much more destructive consequences than
demonic possession, manifestations, and physical attack. While the

devil may possess an individual, sin rapidly destroys communities. Where sin takes root, death and destruction are certain. So temptation is the devil's most pervasive and powerful weapon against us.

Second, Satan is the king of *deception*. As the leader of the "domain of darkness" (Col. 1:13), supplied with an army of demons who are called the "powers of this darkness" (Eph. 6:12), Satan exists in the dark. As the "god of this age," Satan ultimately aims to pull a veil of darkness over the glory of Christ (2 Cor. 4:4). Never is he happier than when people are blinded to Christ's glory. This is why no amount of persuasion can lead an unbeliever to faith in Christ. I have shared the gospel so clearly, so persuasively with some friends, only to receive blank stares in return. The ultimate key that unlocks the door of faith is not persuasion, but only the choice of God. Someone believes in Christ only when God shines "in our hearts to give the light of the knowledge of God's glory in the face of Jesus Christ" (2 Cor. 4:6). In fact, when God shines into a heart, that person does not merely gain an option to believe, he or she *will* believe. And that is the doctrinal ground on which we stake our lives as ambassadors of Christ to some of the hardest places. When God shines, people believe. And shine he will!

Third, the devil employs *accusation* to destroy us. He is the "accuser of our brothers" (Rev. 12:10). He accuses us of our failures and sin, and he leads us to accuse others, causing division. If not countered, his accusations produce unbearable guilt, leading to depression, anxiety, violence, and death. Guilt paralyzes us. Our energy to live on mission with God will evaporate completely under the heat of guilt. This is one of the reasons that the gospel must be central to all mission mobilization. Only those who feel their freedom from all condemnation before God will gladly risk everything for God and his mission. Consider my friend Tanner. Tanner is a passionate follower of Christ who struggles every day against the accusation from the devil that since he has a propensity toward homosexual attraction, he is of no use to God and the nations. Some ministries even affirm that accusation against him. But on the contrary! Homosexuality is rampant in the Muslim world. The LGBT advocacy group Stonewall estimates there are 1.9 million LGBT Arabs in Saudi Arabia alone![3] Tanner is very competent to go to places like this and minister to others with similar struggles as himself.

The fourth strategy of Satan is the most sensational. This strategy is *possession*, or demonization. The Bible is clear that humans may become victims of the extraordinary influence of the devil through possession.

Consider this story from my parents' ministry in the Dominican Republic in the early 1980s, as retold by my father:

> One Sunday, during the music segment of the worship service, a man sitting in front of me fell into the floor and began to writhe around—like a snake. He was hissing, knocking over chairs. The service was dismissed and the man was carried to a back room and laid on a table. I sent my wife and children home, and said I would walk home after this was over.
>
> I assumed it was an epileptic seizure, but the church leaders knew the man, knew of his warped affection for a married woman, and his desire to possess her, at any cost.
>
> Present in the room were three or four Dominican church leaders, myself, and another Baptist missionary like myself.
>
> I had always assumed that it takes just one command and demons would leave. But it took us four hours to exorcise these demons from the man. At one point, four of us were on the man—each one of us restraining an extremity. He raised us all up as if we weighed nothing. Yet, at the command to lie still, he laid back down.

The man laughed, made faces, spoke with deep guttural sounds, cackled like a chicken, and asked, "Who is Jesus?!" At one point, in desperation, I asked the demon's name. It replied, "Legion!" To it I replied, "No, 'Legion' was cast into the Abyss" (Mark 5:9–13). The creature laughed and said, "You'll never have him! You'll never have him!"

About mid-afternoon, the Dominicans got together in one side of the room and began to sing songs about the blood of Jesus. The man snapped his head to see them and cried out, "Stop that! Stop that!" At that point, all of us began to sing!

Not long after that, the man sat up. His eyes were clear, and he spoke in a quiet voice, asking what happened. We urged him to trust Christ, which he refused to do. We warned him about seven more demons returning to his swept house.

He left around 4:00. Several months later, one of the brothers told me that he had seen him in the street, hair matted, acting crazy, talking to himself.[4]

Once when I was in high school, my sisters repeatedly heard someone walking in the attic above their room. They grew very frightened. My father and I decided to resist this potential manifestation of demonic forces through prayer and Scripture reading. We walked through our attic praying, reading Scripture, and speaking out that our house was submitted to God Almighty and to his Lamb. After that, there were no more footstep noises. The darkness flees when the light invades.

Lastly, the devil often *physically attacks* both unbelievers and believers. He is called a "murderer" and "the destroyer" (John 8:44; Rev. 9:11). He hopes for nothing less than our death, both physically and spiritually. It is not uncommon for missionaries among the unreached to face considerable health challenges that appear immediately before leaving for the field, or during their first term. Before we left for the field, I developed two very strange and painful abnormalities in my chest and in my abdominal area. The devil often attacks the health of our children also, knowing that we might forebear personal health problems, but we can hardly stand to see our children suffer!

The devil attacks our beloved unbelieving friends as well. My teammates are friends with an elderly lady in their former city in the Arab world. Her husband died of cancer. Her children died from a car wreck and suicide. After that, she went mentally insane. Now she spends her days meandering the streets hopelessly sweeping the dust off the street. She has survived two gun attacks against her. The devil has been attacking this poor woman for years now and most likely no one except my teammates have prayed for her. We must take the devil seriously, and be alert, for he is like a lion seeking to devour us (1 Pet. 5:8).

Our Counter Strategy: R.E.S.I.S.T.

In the face of satanic attack, we have a clear command from God's Word: "But resist the Devil, and he will flee from you" (James 4:7). Our counter strategy to defeat the devil boils down to one word: *resist*. The acrostic below helps us to remember exactly how to resist the devil.

R: REMEMBER who you are in Christ (1 John 5:20)

E: EQUIP yourself with the armor of God (Eph. 6:13)

S: SUBMIT to God (James 4:7)

I: IDENTIFY the source of the attack (1 Thess. 5:22)

S: STAND firm (1 Pet. 5:8–9)

T: TRUST the Bible (Heb. 4:12)

R: REMEMBER who you are in Christ: "We are in the true One—that is, in His Son Jesus Christ. He is the true God and eternal life" (1 John 5:20). The first thing to do when faced with temptation, deception, accusation, possession, or physical attack of the devil is to remember who you are in Christ. You are no longer a child of the devil, but you are in Christ and adopted as a child of God! When you are tempted, remember: "I have been crucified with Christ and I no longer live, but Christ lives in me. The life I now live in the body, I live by faith in the Son of God, who loved me and gave Himself for me" (Gal. 2:19–20). When you sense that Satan is trying to deceive you into thinking that God has not forgiven you, remember, "Therefore, no condemnation now exists for those in Christ Jesus, because the Spirit's law of life in Christ Jesus has set you free from the law of sin and of death" (Rom. 8:1–2). We must learn to direct our minds to remember what the Word of God says about who we are *in Christ*. Remembering is one of the most powerful tactics for defeating the devil in the theater of the mind and for preparing to help others fight as well.

E: EQUIP yourself with the armor of God. "This is why you must take up the full armor of God, so that you may be able to resist in the evil day" (Eph. 6:13). While we need the whole armor to stand against the devil, each of the five strategies of Satan—temptation, deception, accusation, possession, and physical attack—call for a tactical focus on one of the different pieces of the armor of God. When the devil tempts us, we have the shield of faith to protect us from the fiery darts of temptation that the devil lobs at us every day. Also when the devil tempts us, we have the breastplate of righteousness that keeps us standing upright. Our hearts are protected when the devil pulls his dagger on us with the breastplate of righteousness. When the devil deceives, we have a belt of truth that keeps us free from any idea that hinders us and ensures us that we are clothed in the truth of Christ. How do we "keep our heads about us" when the devil assaults us with accusations, many of them very true? We rely on the helmet of our salvation. We preach the gospel to ourselves every day: "God did not appoint us to wrath, but to obtain salvation through our Lord Jesus Christ, who died for us, so that whether we are awake or asleep we will live together with Him" (1 Thess. 5:9–10). The weapon that we have to fight the devil and deliver people from demonic possession is the "sword of the Spirit, which is the word of God" (Eph. 6:17 ESV). So when we face demons head-on, we take the Sword of the Word and speak it, shout it, and sing it out.

Satan is anti-Christ. Satan tempts, but Christ will never tempt anyone (James 1:13). Satan deceives, but in Christ there is "no deceit" (1 Pet. 2:22). Satan accuses, but Jesus is our advocate before the Father (1 John 2:1). Satan attacks us to take our life, but Jesus gave his own life for us (John 10:11). So as we abide in Christ, we begin to take on characteristics exactly opposite to Satan. With the ever-strengthening character of Christ, symbolized by this armor, we are ever more able to resist the devil and stand despite his fury.

S: SUBMIT to God. "Therefore, submit to God. But resist the Devil, and he will flee from you" (James 4:7). If we are to stand against the devil (resist), we must bow to God (submit). Practically, this means that when facing the affront of the devil, we need to evaluate whether we ourselves have submitted our hearts and lives to God. The degree to which we are submitting ourselves to God is directly related to the degree to which we are resisting the devil.

I: IDENTIFY the source of the attack. "Stay away from *every kind* of evil" (1 Thess. 5:22, italics added). Spiritual discernment is critical in resisting the devil and his works. There are three types of adversaries that we must resist as Christians: the devil himself, the flesh, and the world. Each adversary calls for slightly different responses.

When the devil tempts, deceives, accuses, possesses, or attacks, *resistance* is the protocol and the devil will flee. On the other hand, when the flesh, or immorality, shows its ungodly face, the Bible commands us to *flee* and put immorality to death (1 Cor. 6:18 ESV; Col. 3:5). This means that we run away from immorality, not try to exorcise it. When I'm walking through the airport bookstore, I do not try to exorcise the demons from the pornographic magazines! I get out of the magazine section as quickly as possible.

The adversary of the "world" refers to structures, systems, ideologies, and cultures that are opposed to Christ and the gospel. When we counter the world in this sense, the command to us is to overcome by love, faith in the blood of the Lamb, and our confession of the glory of Christ (John 16:33; 1 John 5:4; Rev. 12:11). We cannot flee from Islam, Communism, greedy capitalism, secular humanism, radical feminism, and atheism. Nor can we exorcise their demons all at once. Rather, these evil ideologies and systems demand of us a daily affront of faith, hope, love, and verbal witness of the glory of Christ. In that way, we will overcome them.

S: STAND firm. "Resist [the devil] and be firm in the faith, knowing that the same sufferings are being experienced by your fellow believers throughout the world" (1 Pet. 5:9). *Resist* literally means "stand against." The idea of "standing against" or "resisting" is to never back down to the devil, no matter what (James 4:7; Eph. 6:13; 1 Pet. 5:8–9). Persevere! Keep on keeping on and do not let him get you sidetracked. Resist the devil by resting in Christ. Affront the devil by abiding in Christ.

When you abide in Christ and live on mission with him, one thing is for sure: the devil will tempt you to sin and discouragement. My close friends Parker and Trisha served among an unreached people group in Senegal. Once, in their first days getting settled, they were sitting in their host father's hut. A man they had never seen walked in and was begging for money. He turned at them and said to them in perfect English (which was obviously quite strange since they lived in a remote village), "You want to be like them, but you will never be like them. Go home!" This was obviously an attempt of the devil to discourage them. To this, Trisha replied, "In the name of Jesus get out of here!" And he left.

The man had a point, if you think about it. Parker and Trisha will never become total insiders in that unreached people group. But what this man, and the devil that influenced him, did not know is that God uses precisely our weaknesses to magnify the power of the gospel. Parker and Trisha stood firm in their faith and they continue to minister fruitfully among the unreached.

Along with a few other leaders, we launched a prayer campaign for a certain country in North Africa and raised up hundreds of people around the world to pray and fast for the first ninety days of 2013. We were praying for the destruction of spiritual strongholds, for the gospel to be magnified in the society, and for spiritual breakthrough. Little did we realize at the time but we had found ourselves in the middle of a very real spiritual war for this country.

During the second month of this prayer campaign, we were celebrating the opening of our new business. We had raised up an Arab team to move to the country and lead the business. We spent tens of thousands of our dollars investing in the business and renovating a training center. I had spent lots of money and time investing in the Arab Christian leader of the business. After a year and a half, we finally had our grand opening.

Almost precisely halfway through these ninety days it was like the spiritual realm opened up and swallowed us in the fight. A week after the grand opening of our business, on the forty-second day of our prayer campaign, five of our Christian colleagues were rounded up and thrown in jail for the possession of a large amount of Christian literature. One of these was the sole employee at our training center. Two of the others were my friends and spiritual brothers. A couple of months into their imprisonment, one of these brothers died in prison, leaving a grieving widow with few earthly possessions and two teenage children. Not long before his imprisonment, I had been in his home hearing him and his wife chat about how much they loved life in this country, and their open doors for ministry. Now he was dead. His wife was distraught, and his children were confused, angry, and very sad.

Because of the imprisonment, we had to close the business. Our landlord took all of our assets. And our Arab partner and his wife fled the country to safety. We lost all that we had invested for a year and a half. We lost a brother to death. We lost our business. But we did not lose hope. We stood firm. The death of our brother, and the imprisonment of the others, was a clarion call to us to continue to pray and minister the authority of Jesus Christ. Almost every night, my family brings this country in prayer to the Lord. My five-year-old and three-year-old boys intercede nightly, "God, help there to be no bad guys. Help them to love God and love each other." With our boys, we talk about how, one day, Jesus will come riding on his white horse from the heavens, and with his "harsh, great, and strong sword, [he] will bring judgment on Leviathan, the fleeing serpent—Leviathan, the twisting serpent. He will slay the monster that is in the sea" (Isa. 27:1).

T: TRUST the Bible. "For the word of God is living and effective and sharper than any double-edged sword, penetrating as far as the separation of soul and spirit, joints and marrow. It is able to judge the ideas and thoughts of the heart" (Heb. 4:12). We teach our three young sons that the Bible is not a household decoration, it's a sword—a serious weapon. Although a good sword is a thing of beauty, it is not meant to sit untouched on the shelf. People of the resistance know their Bible, quote their Bible, and obey their Bible. With it, they both attack and defend. The Word is battle-tested and trustworthy. This means that in the moment of satanic attack we should not come up with our own protocol or verbal shenanigans. Rather, we use the Word. Do not let the Word just sit on your bookcase while you create some strategy of your own to defeat the devil. Use the Word to resist the devil!

Shelly lives and ministers among the unreached in China. She tells how she recently helped someone be delivered from demonic possession:

> We have a student in our discipleship program named Lucy from a minority group in China. She is the first of her people to believe in Jesus. As we got to know her and her story more, she began to share how she would often have nightmares. They were always the same kind. Four or five dark men would come into her room and try to strangle her. She would always wake up from these nightmares terrified and in cold sweat. This had been happening once or twice a week, only after she began to believe in Jesus.
>
> We decided to pray for deliverance for her. So, off I went in faith to do some deliverance in Mandarin!
>
> After explaining the basic principles of spiritual strongholds to Lucy, we asked about her personal and family history to see whether there was any idolatry or witchcraft. She shared about offerings to Confucianism, Ancestor Worship, and different forms of Animism in her family and in her past. We then had her name these things one by one, and in Jesus' name, renounce them and break their power. Afterwards we prayed for her breaking these things off, one by one, in the mighty name and authority of Jesus.
>
> She had very strong physical reactions to these prayers as her spirit was being set free. She even needed to cough and spit as the spirits left her, but afterward, as we prayed for the Holy Spirit to come in and fill and cleanse her mind and body, she was beaming so full of joy, and said, "I feel so relaxed and light now!"

The next few nights she had no nightmares of these men and on the fourth day after our prayer time she came to class and said she had another dream.

We all listened intently as she shared how one man opened the door and entered the room, he came close to her bed with his hands out and then gently pulled the blanket up and tucked her in. She then woke up and felt safe and protected and warm; she knew that it was Jesus.

She is continuing on her journey of getting to know God, and now has a strong, solid faith in Christ's authority over the enemy, demons, and spiritual darkness. Praise God!

This story illustrates how sin can permeate families. It also illustrates how one mere person looking to Christ and trusting him may stop the curse of sin. In helping Lucy be delivered, Shelly used the only weapon that she had, the proclamation of the authority of Christ from the Bible. And this spiritual weapon is "powerful through God for the demolition of strongholds" (2 Cor. 10:4).

Destroying Strongholds

Different cultures have different spiritual strongholds that day by day restrict people from experiencing fullness of life in Christ. For the sake of simplicity, I define "stronghold" as something that has unusual grasp on a culture or person. In the Arab world, one of these strongholds is hatred and unforgiveness. Sent out by Christ, we attack and destroy these strongholds with spiritual weapons. "For though we live in the body, we do not wage war in an unspiritual way, since the weapons of our warfare are not worldly, but are powerful through God for the demolition of strongholds. We demolish arguments and every high-minded thing that is raised up against the knowledge of God, taking every thought captive to obey Christ" (2 Cor. 10:3–5). When the people resist the gospel, we do not barrage them with tanks and Kalashnikovs, but with prayer, fasting, good works, and gospel proclamation.

I have a friend in North Africa whose name is Islam. One day he fervently questioned me about whether I support the Jews. I told him that I support love and am against violence, so I support love to the Palestinians *and* love to the Jews.

He got angry at me and said, "You know why you said that you support 'love'?! Because you've never had Jews come into your house and shoot your wife and children. That's what they are doing!" I was frustrated. He was accusing me of supporting love while being ignorant of the realities of violence.

I became angry. I told him furiously, "Don't tell me that I don't know about violence." I told him of my knifing incident in India and how I spilled my own blood there. My clothes were soaked in blood at the hand of violent thugs!

I told him, "Do you know what I did to those guys after they knifed me? I forgave them."

He said, "No! No! No!"

"Yes. Yes." I said, "I forgave them."

He continued, "No! Here, do you know what we do?"

"Revenge," I said.

"Revenge!" He exclaimed. "If they come and cut our face, we wait and then later we go back and cut his throat."

At this point, I knew that I had an opportunity to attack the stronghold of hate and magnify the gospel in this conversation. "Islam, do you know why I forgave them?"

"No."

"Because I was once very bad just like them. I was a bad person, a thug, just like them. And then God forgave me. So now, I can forgive them."

In that moment, Islam was shocked. The devil was shamed. Hatred was rebuked. And I was thrilled that God had used me to magnify the gospel to my friend.

"To My Husband's Attackers: I Love You and Forgive You"

One of our Austin Stone colleagues, Ronnie Smith, was shot and killed by Islamic terrorists in Libya. After he was shot and killed, we grew very mad at Satan. He had killed our brother and friend. The only weapon we had at that point against him was the gospel. With Ronnie's wife, Anita, we began to think about how to channel our energy and take advantage of the international media's attention on Ronnie's death to magnify the gospel of Jesus. So Anita decided to write an open letter to Libya, expressing the love and forgiveness that she had for her husband's killers:

To his attackers: I love you and I forgive you.

How could I not? For Jesus taught us to "Love our enemies"—not to kill them or seek revenge. Jesus sacrificed his life out of love for the very people who killed him, as well as for us today. His death and resurrection opened the door for us to walk on the straight path to God in peace and forgiveness. Jesus did not come only to take us to paradise when we die, but also to bring peace and healing on this earth. Ronnie loved you because God loves you. Ronnie loved you because God loved *him*—not because Ronnie was so great, but because God is so great.

To the Libyan people: I always expected that God would give us a heart to love you, but I never expected you to love us so much. We came to bless you, but you have blessed us much more. Thank you. Thank you for your support and love for Ronnie and our son Hosea and me. Since Ronnie's death, my love for you has increased in ways that I never imagined. I feel closer to you now than ever before.

I hear people speaking with hate, anger, and blame over Ronnie's death, but that's not what Ronnie would want. Ronnie would want his death to be an opportunity for us to show one another love and forgiveness, because that's what God has shown us.

I want all of you—all of the people of Libya—to know I am praying for the peace and prosperity of Libya. May Ronnie's blood, shed on Libyan soil, encourage peace and reconciliation between the Libyan people and God.

Anita's letter went viral all over the world.[5] The Libyan people began to personally hand out her letter. Newspapers all over the world ran the story of Anita's letter in many languages. Anita began to take interviews with the global media. She clearly articulated the gospel to a stunned Anderson Cooper on prime-time CNN. She spoke on the top two Arabic networks, Al-Jazeera and Al-Arabiya. These two major networks broadcast to every corner of the Arab world. As the media from all over the Muslim world covered the story, we realized that we succeeded. We shamed the devil. With the authority of Jesus delegated to us, and through the message of the gospel, we looked square into the face of the devil and declared, "Get away, Satan, we RESIST you. Now flee from us!"

Our Authority in Christ Is Broader Than "Spiritual Warfare"

The authority of Christ delegated to us has definite applications in spiritual warfare against the devil. But the applications are broader yet than just "spiritual warfare." Here are examples and stories of how the authority of Christ in us gives us the right to minister to the nations, to steward the flock of God, to relate to God in prayer, and to serve as an ambassador of Christ.

As Ministers of the Gospel, We Have the Authority to Serve the Nations

Is it presumptuous of us to raise the money, sell our possessions, and move to the other side of the world to preach the gospel and call people to faith and repentance? What motivates us to move to the nations? And what right do we have to tell the nations that they must repent and trust in Christ to be right with God?

In the heat of the 2014 Ebola epidemic, conservative commentator Ann Coulter mocked Dr. Kent Brantly and his fellow evangelical Christians who move to the ends of the earth to serve in the name of Christ. Dr. Brantly was working for Samaritan's Purse in Liberia when he contracted Ebola while serving Ebola patients. In an online article, Coulter mocks Brantly for turning a blind eye to the grave problems in America and foolishly risking his life by traveling to Africa to serve the poor. She rants that Christians are tired of fighting culture wars in America, so in a narcissistic search of praise, they retreat to "Third World hellholes" to serve the poor and garner the praise of humanitarians worldwide. "Evangelize in Liberia, and the Times' Nicholas Kristof will be totally impressed. Which explains why American Christians go on 'mission trips' to disease-ridden cesspools." While we are rightly shocked at Coulter's tone, she is merely repeating the age-old response to Christians who serve the nations at their own expense: "These Christians have an alternate agenda." Otherwise, why would they be so foolish as to move their families to these "Third World hellholes?"[6]

Coulter is right in one major regard. With respect to this world, followers of Christ are "foolish" to make such sacrifices. But with respect to eternity, followers of Christ are the most reasonable society in the world. We trade this world's comforts for an eternity of glory. We have been commissioned by our Lord to go to the nations at the cost of our very lives. We are not narcissists who seek our own praise. But we do seek joy. And we know that true joy is found only in following Jesus as Lord and Savior. We are flagrant joy seekers in following our Savior to the nations and proclaiming a joy that is for all peoples (Luke 2:10).

Motivated by joy in the gospel, what right do we have to tell another person, and another nation of peoples for that matter, that they must repent and believe in Christ to be made right with God? Once, during a graduate seminar, word got out that I was a missionary. People looked at me in utter shock, "You . . . uh . . . were . . . uh . . . a missionary? Really?" When the professor heard the chatter, he turned to me and exclaimed, "You were a missionary?! Do you know the ethical problems with being a missionary?!" Thankfully, I was able to stay calm, knowing that God gave me the right to call people to repentance.

As Stewards of the Gospel, We Have the Authority to Shepherd the People to God

"I solemnly charge you before God and Christ Jesus . . . Proclaim the message; persist in it whether convenient or not; rebuke, correct, and encourage with great patience and teaching" (2 Tim. 4:1–2). A steward is merely an appointed manager of someone else's property. In this case, we are stewards of the truth of the gospel and of the church of God. We have the God-given authority to contend for the gospel and for God's bride. The world does not know what to make of the church. We are no mere network of like-minded people. We are eternal brothers and sisters united under the Lord Jesus Christ. And our Lord has appointed overseers for us, to watch over us and care for us (Acts 20:28).

When we demonstrate and declare the gospel, we open the door to supernatural transformation. Two of our Austin Stone single men, Adam and Athan, lived and served refugees in Turkey. By God's grace, they led eight Afghan and Iranian refugee men to Christ and studied Bible with them regularly. One of the main ways that God is opening doors among these refugees is through dreams. Recently, one woman dreamt about snakes and a big red dragon attempting to kill her children when all of a sudden, Jesus came into the picture and spoke to the snakes and dragon with authority, commanding them to leave the family. This led to sharing the good news with this family. On another occasion, a refugee woman found herself standing at the bottom of a narrow staircase. To her amazement, heaven was waiting for her at the top of the staircase, twenty-one steps away. In her desire to reach the top, she began to climb the staircase but was met by a man on the seventh step. This man was the only thing that stood between her and the realities of heaven. The man told her that she had to pass through him in order to get to the top of the staircase. And out of love, he gave her his hand in order to help her pass through him. She then told me that she knew this man was Jesus Christ. When we minister in the authority of Christ, Christ reveals himself to the unreached and draws them to God.

As Children of God in Christ, We Have the Authority to Approach God in Prayer and Worship

Muslims often think that Christians are too casual and insincere in prayer. That much is often true. But many Muslims do not understand that we can speak to God without formalities. We can come before him as we are because we have already been accepted as his children. I do not ask my three sons to wash their hands before they give me a high five, and God does not make us get all dressed up with religiosity to come to him. It is an offense to many Muslims to tell them that as followers of Christ, we *have the right* to come before God. Because he adopted us through the blood of Christ, we have the right to approach him without hindrances or shame. "In Him we have boldness and confident access through faith in Him" (Eph. 3:12). "Therefore let us approach the throne of grace with boldness, so that we may receive mercy and find grace to help us at the proper time" (Heb. 4:16). "Therefore, brothers, since we have boldness to enter the sanctuary through the blood of Jesus . . . let us draw near with a true heart in full assurance of faith, our hearts sprinkled clean from an evil conscience and our bodies washed in pure water" (Heb. 10:19, 22).

As Ambassadors of Christ, We Have the Authority to Represent Him

"Therefore, we are ambassadors for Christ, certain that God is appealing through us. We plead on Christ's behalf, 'Be reconciled to God'" (2 Cor. 5:20). An ambassador is one who is sent by one country to another as its official representative. I like the literal Hindi translation of ambassador: "messenger of the king." The ambassador has the right to speak and work on behalf of his or her country and government. Their authority is not their own to use for their own agenda, but for their government's agenda. As Christ's ambassadors, he has authorized us to act as his representatives to this world, as well as to call upon his authority for the accomplishment of his agenda.

Ambassadors have the right to speak in the name of the leader. Ambassadors have the duty to speak in a clear and accessible way to their host nation. As Christ's ambassadors, we have the duty to understand this world and communicate the message of Christ in a way that is understandable to the world. When we move to another people group or country, we learn how to communicate most effectively. For this reason, we ought to be avid learners of culture; for the gospel is transmitted across peoples within various cultural frameworks.

I have a friend who was living and serving Christ in a Hindu context in New Delhi. Because Hindus consider cows sacred, there is little beef to be found in the Hindu parts of the city. Out of desperation for a good slab of beef, one day my friend went to the US Embassy Commissary located on official grounds in New Delhi, where he knew he could find Dr. Pepper and fresh beef! The guards told him that civilian American citizens were not allowed inside, but then they asked, "Are you a diplomat?" Shrewdly and desperately, my friend quickly replied, "Yes . . . of sorts." And so he entered, bought lots of meat, and shared the fajitas all around! Now of course my missionary friend was being cunning beyond the bounds of what I would call "truth," but his quickness to reply challenges us: Do we really understand and take seriously our appointment as Christ's ambassadors?

One of the main accusations of the enemies of Christ against us is that we do not have the right to say the things that we do. My Muslim friends often get angry when I tell them the things that I believe. "How can you say that God is like a Father?!" they cry out. "You have no right to speak on behalf of God and explain who he is." Well, in fact, as a witness to the glory of Christ and his transforming power, I *do* have the right to implore others on behalf of Christ to be reconciled to God (2 Cor. 5:20)!

When others snort at our gospel presentations with, "Who gives you the right to talk to me about religion?!" Our humble response is, "Well, Jesus Christ gives me the right, in fact. God is making his appeal to you through me right now. Be reconciled to God." I am saddened by the retreat of some so-called Christians from the proclamation of the gospel. Without proclamation, we cease to be ambassadors. We are not just communicators of information; we are Christ's ambassadors through whom our sovereign God makes his appeal to the world.

Being an ambassador for Christ may get you killed for him. John the Baptist was fatefully arrested because he spoke up against the sins of Herod. The Jews hated and finally killed Jesus "because He made Himself the Son of God" (John 19:7). Stephen was killed because he just would not shut up in his accusations against the Jewish leaders! And it continues to this day.

Morning Headlines

Truth
5 fascinating dog facts you don't know
I am the Lord
9 celebrity tweets you missed today
I will be their God
Guess who's back in skinny jeans?
I will destroys the idols
Do astronauts clean their undies?
I will seek out my sheep
Proven ways to meet women
I will lay your cities waste
Update: Obamas go organic
I will put my Spirit within you
When pretty stars go gritty
I will take you from the nations
Billionaires' top secrets
I said to you in your blood, "Live!"
Game of Thrones
I am the Lord, I have spoken, I will do it.
American Idol
I will vindicate the holiness of my great name
Vanity

---- Chapter 8 ----

"You Will Receive Power"

JESUS NOT ONLY GIVES HIS AUTHORITY TO US, HE ALSO GIVES HIS power. Authority is simply the right to use power, and power is simply the ability to use authority. Because authority and power are so closely linked, and often used together in Scripture, it is fitting that we examine the power that Christ gives us through his Holy Spirit.

When someone is reborn in Christ, at that very moment they are given access to the power of Christ in them as well as the authority to use that power. How they understand and use this authority and power is the source of dispute between many Christian denominations. There are a number of reasons for these disputes. At the center of these reasons are questions like, "How much authority and power are delegated?" and "When and by what means are they accessed?" Much of the application of the authority and power of Christ falls into the realm of mere experience. As a result, disputes are often about the precise techniques used to exercise Christ's authority in power.

People frequently give undue influence to personal experience. They approach the Scripture from the vantage point of their own experience. We should aim for just the opposite; namely, to understand our experiences from the vantage point of Scripture. That is why, before getting to the practical business of using the power of Christ, we need to trace the theological relationship between our authority and power in Christ.

Tracing the Theological Relationship between Authority and Power

Authority and Adoption

When we trust in Christ, we are adopted into the family of God as sons and daughters in Christ (John 1:12–13). To do anything in the Middle East requires obtaining official "stamps." For example, to get my second son's birth certificate from the Arab country we were living in, I had to receive over a dozen stamps of approval on our paperwork from government authorities. Each stamp bears with it the authority of that government agency. In the same way, when we are adopted, we are "stamped" as adopted children belonging to God.[1]

With this adoption comes all the legal rights of children to their parents. If we are God's children, we become "heirs of God and coheirs with Christ" (Rom. 8:17). As his adopted children, we now share the "badge" of his family. And this badge represents the authority of God in Christ. Just as a policeman has authority in the state, we have authority *in Christ*.

The legal right, or authority, to exercise spiritual power is part of the package of our adoption. The devil cannot take away our status as children, or the legitimate privileges that come with that. This means that our authority in Christ does not grow or diminish. Our authority in Christ is not contingent on our merit, our vocation, our feelings, or our personality. Inasmuch as we are adopted by grace through faith, we are given the authority of Christ as a son or daughter of God. Since our adoption is once and for all time, our authority in Christ is constant. We all have the same amount of spiritual authority, because we who are in Christ are all equally sons and daughters.

Adoption and Anointing

God does not just give us the *authority* to exercise power, but the *ability* to as well. This ability is given in the anointing of the Holy Spirit. Just as the Father anointed Christ with the Holy Spirit for the work of ministry, God anoints us who are in Christ with the Holy Spirit for the work of ministry at the very moment of our adoption (1 John 2:20–27).

Unlike the anointing on the prophets, priests, and kings of the Old Testament, which was given to a select few for select tasks, we have *all* been anointed by Christ with the Holy Spirit. We are called "Christians," which means the anointed followers of the Anointed One! This is why we say the Holy Spirit has been poured out (Acts 2:17). He is poured out like oil on Christ's people, not on our heads, as was the tradition of old, but in our hearts (Rom. 5:5). "Now it is God who strengthens us, with you, in Christ and has anointed us" (2 Cor. 1:21). "But you have an anointing from the Holy One, and all of you have knowledge" (1 John 2:20). "The anointing you received from Him remains in you, and you don't need anyone to teach you. Instead, His anointing teaches you about all things and is true and is not a lie; just as He has taught you, remain in Him" (1 John 2:27).

Anointing and Power

God anoints us with the Holy Spirit at the very moment of adoption. With this anointing he gives us access to the power of Christ within us. But that power must be accessed and utilized through prayer and fasting in the context of an abiding relationship with Christ. When we say that someone has the "anointing of the Holy Spirit," we mean that he or she is exhibiting the power of the Holy Spirit; that is, he or she is exercising the authority of Christ to witness and to overcome evil.

When the Holy Spirit is poured out on people, they become witnesses to the power of Christ. This means that they begin to demonstrate and declare the supreme authority of Christ in their lives and ministry. Most immediately, they exercise this spiritual power against sin. As Christians grow in Christ, they grow in their ability to wage war on sin and the devil through greater declarations and demonstrations of the glory of Christ.

Our Authority in Christ Is Constant; Our Power in Christ Changes

While authority and power are dependent on a relationship with Christ, they differ in one very important matter. Whereas our right to exercise power as children of God in Christ remains the same, as it is contingent on our adoption in Christ, our *ability* to exercise this power against evil is dependent on our daily relationship with Christ. In other words, our authority in Christ is constant, but our power in Christ can change. This explains why some people have more spiritual power against evil than others. It is not that they are any more of a child of God than another, but they have a more abiding relationship with Christ. Our spiritual power rises and falls on the basis of our daily relationship with Jesus Christ.

Why Do We Have Spiritual Power?

God gives power for the purpose of *witness*. The point of power is mission, which is plain to see in Matthew 28:18–20. The agenda of Jesus for his people is very clear throughout Scripture: "You will be My witnesses in Jerusalem, in all Judea and Samaria, and to the ends of the earth" (Acts 1:8).

We access the power of Christ when we join with Christ in the Father's agenda. Remember that God *gives* power. It is not ours to use at our own disposal, but his to give and use through us. We might think of spiritual power like electric power: when we plug into the right outlet, we get power. All too often, though, we try to get spiritual power through a host of tactics or techniques that really do not center on a relationship with the living Christ.

We must check our motivations for desiring the power of God. If we are honest with ourselves, we often want God's power to increase our comfort, approval from others, control over people and circumstances, or our ability to influence others.[2] In other words, we try to exploit God's power for our gain. But God does not pour out his power so that we can attain our selfish ambitions.

All too often we desire to access the authority of Christ for our own agendas. This is the origin of the prosperity gospel movement, which aims to get God to make us healthy, wealthy, and prosperous. We cannot merely "claim" his authority for our agendas. Jesus was given the authority of the Father for the accomplishment of the exact works given by the Father (John 17:4). So inasmuch as we join God in his agenda, we have access to the authority of Christ in God.

To know God's agenda puts us squarely back into the discussion of doctrine, since biblical doctrine centers on "Who is God and what does he do?" For this reason, it is altogether strange and tragic that teaching on spiritual warfare is often doctrinally wimpy. We assume that spiritual warfare is for the feelers, and theology is for the thinkers. But no, spiritual warfare exists in the context of a relationship with the living Christ, and the infrastructure of that relationship is doctrine.

The apostles met a man who was focused more on the power that comes from Christ than on Christ himself. His name was Simon. And, tellingly, he was a magician. As a magician, he made money and gained influence through amazing people with his trickery. Simon must have been a good magician, for the people "all paid attention to him, from the least of them to the greatest, and they said, 'This man is called the Great Power of God!'" (Acts 8:10). While the people were fascinated with Simon, Simon was fascinated with power. When he saw Philip preaching and doing miracles, he was instantly hooked and believed. When, later, the Holy Spirit moved in power through the disciples, Simon the magician could hold his tongue no longer. "Give me this power too, so that anyone I lay hands on may receive the Holy Spirit" (Acts 8:19). Peter was aghast at this man who claimed to believe in Christ, yet whose heart was "not right before God" (Acts 8:21). The sin of Simon finally exposed itself. Peter rebuked him of wickedness, saying that he was "poisoned by bitterness and bound by iniquity" (Acts 8:23). So what was Simon's sin? In his heart he worshiped the idol of power.

Like Simon, we too become mere magicians when our agenda for using the power of Christ differs from the agenda of Christ. We may trick the world into thinking that we have access to the power of Christ, but God knows that our hearts are not right before him and he will expose us as fakes in the end.

As our relationship with Christ deepens, our understanding of God's agenda increases. And, therefore, we are empowered by his supernatural authority against evil in accord with his agenda. The problem is that we are experts in spiritual rationalization. But before God, our rationalizations are just the intellectual face of our spiritual idolatries.

Does not the history of the church show this to be true? How many times have we relied on the strength of our programs, the influence of our leaders, the platform of our church, or the energy of our people over and above the engagement of the Holy Spirit in the task of making disciples among the lost? Is it not true that we often spend much less time in prayer than in strategizing on our programs? Are not our ministry strategies often more influenced by pragmatism than by faith in God's promises?

How Do We Access That Power?

We receive and access Christ's power on the basis of a saving and growing relationship with Jesus Christ. Just as the Father delegates authority and power to his Son in the context of a loving relationship, so the Son delegates his authority and power to us. We receive Christ's authority in full in our adoption, and we access his power in full in our relationship with him. Without the adoption as God's child in Christ, a person has no authority, or legitimacy, to exercise spiritual power against evil. And without a thriving relationship with Christ, a person has no power to bear witness to Christ.

Abide in Christ

Jesus says, "I am the vine; you are the branches. Whoever abides in me and I in him, he it is that bears much fruit, for apart from me you can do nothing" (John 15:5 ESV). To *abide* simply means to "stay" or "remain," which is why the HCSB helpfully translates John 15:5, "The one who remains in Me." One might think about the image of staying within a house. Jesus uses the illustration of a vine remaining connected to the branches. With this illustration, he amplifies the meaning of *abide* beyond merely remaining in a place or in a relationship. He emphasizes dependence on this connection for the empowerment to live and bear fruit.

Cut the branch from the vine, and the branch dies. Not long ago my wife was teaching our five-year-old son this very concept. Together they looked at a tree and how it grows. They discussed how the tree grows, specifically how leaves of the tree are dependent on the tree for their existence. At the beginning of the week they took one leaf off of the tree and compared that leaf to the other leaves. They were all green and rich with life. At the end of the week, they compared the separated leaf with the leaves still on the tree. The separated leaf had withered, became crunchy, and obviously lost its texture of life. The other leaves continued green and rich with life. What was the point? My wife explained that the withered leaf wanted to be its own boss, so it separated itself from the tree. But because leaves depend entirely on the tree for their life, the separated leaf died all alone.

I thought that this was a fantastic illustration of the principle of John 15:4: "Remain in Me, and I in you. Just as a branch is unable to produce fruit by itself unless it remains on the vine, so neither can you unless you remain in Me." Take away an abiding relationship with Christ and we are left utterly powerless in life and ministry. We will simply lose power to survive against the force of temptation and sin if we separate from Christ because—like the dying leaf in our kitchen—we want to be our own boss.

In John 15:5, abiding in Christ refers to a person's daily relationship with Christ. Consider Colossians 2:6: "Therefore, as you have received Christ Jesus the Lord, walk in Him." We received the Lord Jesus once and for all time in the moment of our salvation, but we must daily seek to walk in him. This is why we talk about having a "close" or "distant" relationship with Christ. In real terms, we do increase and decrease in the richness of our relationship with Christ.

How to Abide in Christ?

The simple answer to how to abide more in Christ is to begin to develop a relationship with Christ. That means fulfilling the universal requirements of a relationship: awareness, time, and communication. Relationships require awareness of the other. Two fish may swim near each other but have no relationship if they are not aware that each other exists. Since we cannot "see" the Spirit of Christ with our physical eyes, we need to develop spiritual eyes to remain aware of Christ in all of life. This is what the seventeenth-century monk Brother Lawrence meant when he wrote about "practicing the presence of God."[3] Most of us do not have the luxury of a monk's lifestyle. So how do we develop greater awareness of Christ's presence?

The answer is found in the next requirement of a relationship: time. The more time we spend intentionally with Christ, the more we become aware of his presence throughout all of life. This requires discipline from us to find ways to spend more time with Christ. While there are countless methods on how to spend a "quiet time" with Christ, the best ones have two basic elements: meditation on the Bible and prayer. I simply cannot accept that a person has a growing relationship with Christ if he spends less and less time in Bible meditation and prayer. On the other hand, it is difficult to not grow in a relationship with Christ if one grows in the practice of Bible meditation and prayer. When Bible meditation and prayer are combined with various other spiritual disciplines, such as solitude, Sabbath, fasting, silence, service, fellowship with Christian community, and Bible memorization (to give merely a sample), a person will grow in his or her relationship with Christ.

The more aware we are of Christ's presence, the more we become able to communicate with him. While much needs to be said about this, and much has been said, I simply want to point out that communication in relationship with Christ goes both ways. We talk with him, and he talks with us. Prayer facilitates a relationship connection with the living Christ. Often we pray with no expectation of relationship. But God is alive and he hears us! When we pray, we need to listen for the voice of God in Christ through his Spirit speaking back to us. That voice speaks in perfect unity with his Word, the Bible.

I think about a friend who is a busy stay-at-home mom of four young children. She is aware of the presence of Christ, and so she finds ways to connect with him throughout the day. One of her habits is to look out the window of her house and pray about whatever she sees. If she sees a neighbor walking, she prays for the neighbor. If she sees children playing, she prays for them. All the while, in prayer she consistently connects with the living Christ who lives in her (John 17:23).

Prayer is like gasoline for the engine of our relationship with Christ. Prayer is not a lever to pull with Christ. Prayer is a way for our own souls to break from the world and unite with Christ in relationship. When prayer and fasting are united in a relationship with Christ, they yield power.

I am learning from one of the world's most fruitful church-planting movement leaders today, David Watson. Along with a local partner, Watson catalyzed and led a church-planting movement among the Bhojpuri people of northern India, formerly one of India's most religiously hardened people groups. In more than twelve years, they launched forty thousand churches and claim over a million baptisms![4] Watson attributes the power of these leaders to one singular variable: their prayer lives.

I recently sat in a room with the top Bhojpuri church planters. Each of these church planters and their teams planted at least 50 churches per year. One team planted 500 churches the year before. A resource group, engaged to verify our numbers, wondered about possible common threads in what they saw in church planting among the Bhojpuri. They started asking questions to see if they could discover common elements present among church planters. They asked, "How much time do you spend in prayer?" As they went around the room reporting, my jaw dropped. Team leaders spent an average of three hours a day in personal prayer. After that, they spent another three hours praying with their teams everyday. One day a week the leaders fasted and prayed. Their teams spent one weekend a month fasting and praying. Many of these leaders maintained secular jobs while engaged in their church planting. They got up to pray at 4 A.M. and were at work by 10 A.M.[5]

The spiritual power of each of these church planters is not their intelligence, their will, their influence, or the richness of their pedigree. Their spiritual power is from their anointing by the Holy Spirit applied through their spiritual gifts. Abiding in Christ is their strategy for bearing fruit.

There is another element of a person's relationship with Christ that is critical for growing in abiding in Christ—namely, surrender. Christ demands that all who have a relationship with him surrender to his authority. Surrender, then, is the important connection between abiding in Christ and cherishing his authority. Without surrender, there is no relationship. Where there is a relationship, one will cherish surrender more and more as the fruits of surrender become more apparent over time.

Surrender to God in Christ takes the form of obedience to his commandments. "If you keep My commands you will remain in My love ["abide in my love" ESV], just as I have kept My Father's commands and remain in His love" (John 15:10). "The one who keeps His commands remains in Him ["abides in God" ESV], and He in him. And the way we know that He remains in us is from the Spirit He has given us" (1 John 3:24). The best barometer of a person's relationship with Christ is not one's stated feelings about Christ, or one's words about Christ but whether one obeys Christ.

As one obeys him in relationship, one will bear the fruit of greater affections for Christ and greater witness to Christ. In this way, obedience to Christ's commands is not only the requirement of a growing relationship with him; it is the fruit of a growing relationship with him.

Part of the fruit referenced in John 15:5 is more power to obey Christ's commands. A relationship with Christ will, by nature, insist on growth. A lack of impulse to grow in Christ in a person may indicate the lack of any genuine relationship with Christ at all. Christ is ever so patient with us. He is our Shepherd who gently and kindly leads us, even when we rebel against his authority and stubbornly refuse to listen to him. But a lifestyle of rebellion, or of a stagnant relationship with Christ, is indicative of deeper problems. Vines insist on growing. There is no such thing as a vine that voluntarily ceases to grow.[6]

What Is This Fruit?

According to John 15:5, only those who abide in Christ bear good and lasting fruit. The fruit of the vine of Christ is first faith. Faith then buds the famed "fruits of the Spirit": "But the fruit of the Spirit is love, joy, peace, patience, kindness, goodness, faith, gentleness, self-control. Against such things there is no law" (Gal. 5:22–23). The greatest of these fruits is love. Thus, Jesus says, "This is My command: Love one another as I have loved you" (John 15:12).

One of the indistinguishable marks of a vine, and of its fruit, is that it reproduces. I know of one disciple-making movement leader who will only call a group of people a "church" when they plant another church. He has a point. By nature, fruit reproduces itself with the spreading of the seeds. This is one reason why the fruits of the Spirit, as well as the fruits of disciple making, are eternal: they reproduce themselves into eternity.

The Fruit Comes from the Vine, Not the Branches

Abiding means "staying" and only by "staying" with Christ in relationship do we have any hope of bearing disciple-making fruit among all peoples, as we have been commissioned by Christ to do. We are totally insane when we wake and work and busy ourselves with ministry outside of an abiding relationship with Christ, for what are we working for if not for lasting fruit? Disciple making among the nations is not an envious job if in vain!

I am reminded of a powerful video and children's book written and produced by Francis Chan called *The Big Red Tractor and the Little Village.*[7] This story centers on a little farming village and a big red tractor. Each year during plowing season, all the citizens of the village would gather to start the tractor. Not knowing how to properly operate the tractor, all the people would push and pull the tractor across the fields. With all the effort of all the people, they were able to move the tractor twenty or thirty feet. "They had been doing it this way for many generations." Then, one day, farmer Dave found the owner's manual for the tractor. Reading it, he realized that the tractor has an engine and, when operated properly, could plow a whole field in one day! After farmer Dave showed the people how the tractor actually works, the people rejoiced and harvested enough food to give to other villages. "The big red tractor and his little village soon became famous throughout the land. They became known as the most generous and life-giving people in the whole wide world." This is a parable, of course, of the church. Not realizing that we have a supernatural anointing of the Holy Spirit, we toil and labor day and night in ministry and reap ever so very little. We do it this way because that is "how it has always been done." And so we rise early, sleep late, burn out from work—all for very little fruit. All the while, if we would just return to an abiding relationship with Christ, we might have access to the full power of Christ.

Could it be that the church today bears so little fruit proportional to our size, resources, and the energy put forward because we abide in Christ so little and access his power so rarely? It is jaw-dropping to consider the vast impact of the early church with regard to their incredibly small pool of resources. Where did the apostles get their spiritual power? Where did the early church get their momentum? It came from none other than the Holy Spirit that was poured out on them at Pentecost. We are able to draw upon the power of Christ to use in ministry inasmuch as we abide in Christ in a loving relationship with him.

When we do bear fruit out of an abiding relationship with Christ, then it is fitting for us to point back to Christ as the fruit bearer. There is just no room in Christian ministry for arrogance or self-congratulation. If it is indeed lasting fruit, then it is from Christ. He deserves, therefore, the full glory for that fruit. It is fitting for us in the moment of fruit bearing to remember that we have been given the gift of adoption in Christ. When we bear fruit, and when the evil powers of this earth submit to us, we do not pat ourselves on the back; but we should go back to our adoption and "rejoice that [our] names are written in heaven" (Luke 10:20). We remember that the ink with which our names are inscribed in the Book of Life is the supremely perfect blood of the authoritative Lamb.

"Have You Ever Heard of the Holy Spirit?"

I believe that a lack of active discussion of and engagement with the Holy Spirit is a critical dysfunction among evangelical disciple makers today. God has given us the Holy Spirit to empower us for the work of disciple making. Without the filling and power of the Holy Spirit, we are doomed to merely spin our wheels in ministry. Furthermore, we are doomed to discouragement if we do not engage the Holy Spirit in relationship.

My father often relates the story of his lunchtime conversation with Dr. Bill Bright. Dr. Bright was the founder and longtime chairman of Campus Crusade for Christ. He was arguably one of the most influential global disciple makers of the twentieth century. Campus Crusade was one of the most widespread evangelistic associations in the world. At the time of this lunch meeting with my father in the early 1990s, Dr. Bright was at the peak of his global influence. My father, a busy pastor of an urban church, was obviously very excited to learn all that he could from

Dr. Bright. So at lunch my father asked him, "Dr. Bright, how do you maintain health and internal peace while overseeing such an enormous organization with such incredible worldwide influence?" Dr. Bright shrewdly answered, "Sam, have you ever heard of the Holy Spirit?" At that, my father was floored, and a bit embarrassed. Dr. Bright had put his finger on the most important element in surviving the trials and weight of global ministry: living in the empowerment of the Holy Spirit. Dr. Bright then went on to tell my father that when he became a follower of Christ, he got on his knees and wrote out a covenant with God. He wrote, "Yours is to guide and provide and protect me. Mine is to obey and trust you." He signed it, "Bill Bright, a slave of Jesus Christ." My father returned to his office, got on his knees, and made the same covenant. Dr. Bright knew that submission to the authority of Jesus Christ led to effective ministry in the power of the Holy Spirit.

It is often said, "The local church is the hope of the world." I would like to upgrade that to, "The Spirit-filled local church is the hope of the world." It is not mere adherence to discipleship tactics that leads to disciple-making fruit. It is the presence and power of the Holy Spirit. In fact, in his brilliant book *Pentecost and Missions*, Harry Boer points out that the apostles and the early church were evidently not motivated by duty to obey the Great Commission in Matthew 28:18–20. Rather, they were propelled in mission by the coming of the Spirit at Pentecost and the continual filling of the Spirit among the believing Jews and Gentiles.[8] I think this is a very healthy balancing point to the widespread emphasis on obedience to the Great Commission in our day. Our hope is not in our obedience to the Great Commission but in the empowerment and saving power of God through the Holy Spirit.

We have absolutely *no chance* of fulfilling the Great Commission without the presence and power of the Holy Spirit. We often forget that a mere gospel presentation does not lead to someone following Jesus. People are dead in sin. Who among us has the power to tell a dead man to get up and walk? Indeed, it is arrogance on a cosmic scale to try to make disciples without actively engaging the Holy Spirit in relationship. Early in my ministry to Arabs, I had the idea that if I could just get a number of Arabs in the room and explain the gospel to them in full and without interruption that they would be convinced to follow Jesus Christ. Though I did pray and ask for God to come in power, my confidence in my own persuasive ability was not matched with equal trust and engagement with the Holy Spirit. So I became impatient and cocky in my friendship with these Arabs. I was trying to pull an iceberg with a canoe. My own ability was just not good enough to draw these Arab men to Christ. Instead of loving them and patiently persevering with them—as God my Father has done with me so many times—I became frustrated with them and their stubborn adherence to Islam. I nearly forgot that it is not mine but the job of the Holy Spirit to convict people of sin (John 16:8).

How Do We Use This Power?

Christ's power is accessed by means of a personal relationship with him and applied most effectively through the use of spiritual gifts (Rom. 12:6–8; 1 Cor. 12:4–11, 28–31; 1 Pet. 4:10–11). God designed us to have certain ways that each of us display the power of Christ most naturally, and those ways are called spiritual gifts. This does not mean that we are constrained to the use of these gifts, but that these gifts seem to come most naturally to each one of us. God created us different from each other in order to magnify his "varied" grace (1 Pet. 4:10). When spiritual gifts are in operation, spiritual power amplifies our witness of the gospel. As we abide in Christ, we grow in our ability to exercise our authority in works of power through our spiritual gifts. When this happens, the church grows (Eph. 4:16). This is why it is so important to know and function within your spiritual gifts.

Do Not Trust the Words; Trust the Word

Even if somebody uses the very name of Christ, but does not have a relationship with him, he or she will be exposed as a fake. While there is power in the name of Jesus, the name of Jesus is not a charm that we wear around our neck to ward off evil. Rather, simple faith in Christ is more powerful than trained use of "the name of Christ" without faith. The Holy Spirit moves in power through those who aim to exalt the name of Jesus rather than exploit the name of Jesus.

A scene in the ministry of Paul in Ephesus depicts this very point. God was doing extraordinary miracles through Paul. Some Jewish itinerant exorcists, the sons of a Jewish high priest named Sceva, observed the incredible power flowing through Paul, a follower of Jesus. They were so impressed that they decided to exploit the name of Christ for their personal gain. They "attempted to pronounce the name of the Lord Jesus over those who had evil spirits, saying, 'I command you by the Jesus that Paul preaches!'" (Acts 19:13). We might assume that invoking the name of Jesus would be enough to defeat these evil spirits. But even the demons know the name of Jesus! So the evil spirit answered and exposed the Sons of Sceva saying, "I know Jesus, and I recognize Paul—but who are you?" (Acts 19:15). After that, the evil spirit jumped on them, overpowered them, and sent them fleeing wounded and naked. Even though they called upon the name of Christ, they did not call upon their Lord and Savior Christ. The Sons of Sceva trusted the words, they did not trust the Word.

Not long ago, a man in one of our sending churches was diagnosed with cancer. The cancer had progressed rapidly in his body. The doctors gave him only a few months to live. As the man spent his final days in his hospital bed, his wife became frantically absorbed in thinking that she, "in the power of Christ," could out-trick her husband's illness and restore him to life. She refused to let anybody near her husband who might say any negative word around him, including the word *cancer*. She believed negative words would curse him. She plastered his hospital room with Scripture verses. She denied that he was sick, rebuked the very mention of cancer, and believed that if she merely claimed his health, then he would be healed. Unfortunately, he died very soon after his diagnosis. His wife was so consumed by the idea that mere words would manifest Christ's power that she missed the opportunity to joyfully and submissively draw near with her husband to their Savior who was calling him home. She trusted in the words, not the Word.

Once my wife and I, along with our two-year-old son, were driving at seventy miles per hour on an extended highway bridge. We had just picked up some food to eat on the road. As we drove, I looked down at my food for a moment. When I looked up, we had veered into the highway shoulder and there was a stalled car about fifty feet ahead of us, partially in our driving lane. I had a mere second to respond. I jerked the car in the other direction, but I overcorrected and nearly flipped the car. I pulled the wheel back the other way, toward the edge of the highway. It was a crowded high-way, and after two or three more times of swerving back and forth, nearly flipping over the bridge to our death, I cried out, "Jesus!" And at the very moment that I cried out to my Savior, the car abruptly steadied itself back in the correct driving lane as if nothing had happened. My wife was crying, my son was yelling "weeee!" and I was in shock. In that moment, we knew that Jesus had saved us. Our deliverance was not in the mere word, "Jesus," but in the very Person who bears that name. How silly it would have been for me to speak to the car, "Car, I rebuke you!" No, in our desperation in the face of death, we cry out to Christ, our hope of glory.

How silly it would have been for Peter when he was sinking in the violent ocean to try to bind the wind and sea when he could

cry out to Jesus himself! When we face the powers of darkness as
we live out the mission of God, where do we turn? Do we rely on
a set of spoken words, a kind of hocus-pocus that binds away evil
by putting up a force field of authority around us? Or do we trust
an authoritative Christ who will work in power through his Spirit
in us as he pleases, according to his agenda?

We should evaluate spiritual power primarily in terms of a
growing ability to declare and demonstrate the gospel through
our individual spiritual gifts. If there is no declaration or demonstration of the gospel, spiritual power is absent. This is true even
if someone grows mightily in his or her influence in the church or
in the world. God gives power for the exaltation of Christ, not the
exploitation of Christ for personal gain. Where the fruits of the
Spirit are combined with demonstrating and declaring the gospel
in the context of an abiding relationship with Christ, disciple-
making power is released!

Though danger at my side,
The Rock is my abide.
When fate's right arm he wills,
His presence there is still.

Chapter 9

"I Am with You Always"

AFTER DECLARING HIS SUPREME AUTHORITY (MATT. 28:18) AND GIVING the command to make disciples among all peoples (Matt. 28:19–20), Jesus gave a clear promise to his followers: "And remember, I am with you always, to the end of the age"(v. 20). Did he keep that promise with his apostles and the early church? Is he keeping that promise with us today? Those are the questions that we will answer in this chapter.

We must ask these questions for the simple reason that Jesus is not physically present with us. He ascended to heaven. Unlike the apostles, we do not walk with him, fish with him, eat dinner with him, and so on. Just this past week my five-year-old son was reading his "life verse," Joshua 1:9, ". . . for the LORD your God is with you wherever you go." He looked up at my wife, Krystal, and said, "Mom, this isn't true! Jesus is not with us here!" In fact, my son has a point! He is not physically with us. My wife was keen to respond, "Son, can you see your lungs?" "No," he replied. "But they are there, aren't they? In the same way, you can't see Jesus, but he is with us." Jesus finished his earthly ministry and ascended to heaven, but he is not gone. He is with us and continues his ministry, now from the right hand of the Father.

My wife and I heard from two Irish women a few years ago
that were working in a dangerous country in the Arab world.
These two women were each other's only friends in this country,
at that time under a terrorizing despotic regime. They told us
about how they used to walk the same streets every day to go to
work. Try to imagine these two young single girls walking the
streets in one of the most dangerous Muslim countries on earth.
But because they felt that the Lord had called them there to serve,
they were confident. One day, they were at a laundromat, and
one of the women was talking to a local Arab man. The other
woman walked up. The man asked where the third woman was.
They said, "There are only two of us . . ." They then asked about
this mysterious third woman. The man answered that the third
woman always walked in between them and that she was very tall,
and always wearing bright white.

These girls walked out of that laundromat so confident and
pumped up that they were ready for a direct war against Satan!
The Lord Christ had not only called them to this country, he was
leading them, and even sent his angel to walk with them to the
laundromat!

Even in the deepest, darkest, and nastiest corners on earth,
Jesus is still present and actively working for the accomplishment
of his redemptive purposes. A number of years ago, my sister was
trekking through the Himalayas in northern India. While in the
biggest city in the region, she visited a little shop, befriended the
shop owner, and left him a small Gideon New Testament. She
heard nothing from that shop owner afterwards. Two years later,
my father was visiting that same village. Not knowing about my
sister's experience in that local shop, he began wandering around
the town. He happened to wander into that same shop and began
to share the gospel with the shop owner. The shop owner pulled
out the little New Testament and shared that two years before a
foreign girl (my sister!) had left him this book and that he had been

reading it. My dad opened the New Testament and there was my sister's name written inside of it! My dad was stunned. Jesus was at work even while his people were not present.

The good news is that Jesus is not only keeping his promise to be with us, he is keeping that promise from the authoritative throne of heaven where he rules in all glory and power and honor and wisdom. Jesus kept his Matthew 28:20 promise to the apostles and the early church. He is keeping it with us today, and he will keep it with us forevermore.

Did Jesus Keep His Promise to the Apostles and the Early Church?

Jesus' ascension to heaven was not the end of his ministry but the continuation of it. Just as Jesus physically led his disciples during his earthly ministry, he continues to spiritually lead his disciples during his heavenly ministry. On earth he led his disciples from Palestine. In heaven now he leads his disciples from his royal throne. Jesus intercedes for his disciples from the right hand of the Father, Jesus encourages them through suffering, Jesus leads and pastors them, and Jesus appoints and directs his leaders.

As the book of Acts is the inspired narrative of the early church, it is important that we see how its inspired author, Luke, argues that the continuing ministry of Jesus is central to the life and growth of the early church.

What Is the Title of "Acts," After All?

Bible readers have no doubt encountered several titles for the book of Acts. Interestingly, the name of this book has a long and diverse history. Historically, nearly all titles of the book refer to "acts" in some form or fashion. The difference is who accomplishes these "acts" and by what means. Since the second century, the traditional title for the book has been "The Acts of the Apostles" or "Acts of Apostles." The fourth-century Codex Sinaiticus calls the book simply *praxeis*, or "Acts."[1]

The Gospel of John splits the Gospel of Luke and the book of Acts in our modern Bibles. But Luke's Gospel and his early church narrative should be considered as two volumes of the same work. Some have argued that whereas the gospel according to Luke is a treatise on the acts of Jesus Christ, his second volume should be called the "Acts of the Holy Spirit." In the United States, we take a more diplomatic approach and just refer to "the book of Acts."[2] Since the book should be read in coherence with the gospel of Luke, perhaps we should just call it "Second Luke."

When read as the second volume of the account of Luke, we begin to see that the book of Acts is really an account of the acts of Jesus. The main character in *both* the gospel of Luke and the book of Acts is Jesus Christ. And the main argument of both books is that God is keeping all of his promises through the earthly and heavenly ministry of Jesus Christ.

Luke tells us at the very beginning why he writes: "I wrote the first narrative, Theophilus, about all that Jesus began to do and teach" (Acts 1:1). If the Gospel of Luke was about what Jesus *began* to do and teach, then by natural inference, the following account is about what Jesus *continues* to do and teach. From the very first sentence, Luke establishes that this book is about the continuing ministry of Jesus. Thus, Alan Thompson's proposed title of the book is probably the most appropriate, "The acts of the Lord Jesus, through his people, by the Holy Spirit, for the accomplishment of God's purposes."[3]

How then did Jesus lead his disciples in the "book of Acts"? There are at least three ways.

Jesus Reigns from Heaven

When Jesus ascended, he ascended to heaven. And in heaven he rules supreme. Luke ends his Gospel narrative saying that Jesus was "carried up into heaven" (Luke 24:51) and begins the book of Acts with the "day He was taken up" (1:2). Setting the stage for a book full of miracles, surprises, and remarkable growth in the early church, Luke establishes that Jesus continues to lead the church and minister to the nations from his place in heaven.[4]

The ascension is the climax of the Gospel of Luke and the foundation of the book of Acts. Why is the ascension so critical for this first book of church history? One of the many reasons is that the ascension establishes the major transition for the ongoing ministry of Jesus: from earth to heaven. Having inaugurated his kingdom on earth, he returned back to the Father in bodily form to sit and rule forever. If the Gospels are about the glory of his earthly presence, then Acts is about the glory of his heavenly presence as seen in the ministry of his church to the nations.

Luke emphasizes Jesus' current heavenly position in order to emphasize his authority. He is no longer a mere carpenter. He is "both Lord and Christ" (Acts 2:36 ESV) who sits on the throne in heaven. From his throne, he pours out the Spirit on the church so that they may fulfill God's mission among the nations. The ascension of Christ signifies that his work is complete, and it sets the stage for the coming of the Holy Spirit, the seal of our assurance. The ascension marks the supreme victory of Jesus over death and the supreme hope of the church even in death. So the focus of the book of Acts is not that Christ has finished his job, left earth, and is now inactive, but rather that Jesus rules from heaven over earth through his Spirit. The focus is the place from which Jesus rules.

The ascension of Jesus signifies his completed earthly ministry and his inaugurated heavenly ministry. It may sound strange to consider that Jesus' ministry is not complete. He, as Luke wrote, "began" his ministry on earth, and now he continues to minister. Consider how his continuing ministry separates Jesus from all of the Hebrew prophets and the founders of all other religions. Others "regard their founder as having completed his ministry during his lifetime. Luke says Jesus only began his. True, he finished the work of atonement yet that end was also a beginning . . . this then is the kind of Jesus we believe in: he is both the historical Jesus who lived and the contemporary Jesus who lives."[5] The Hebrew prophets died and are gone. Muhammad died and is gone. Siddhartha Gautama died and is gone. Jesus lives in heaven and is present with us today in the Holy Spirit.

Jesus Pours Out the Holy Spirit at Pentecost

Jesus' ascension sets the stage for Pentecost. At Pentecost, God was keeping his promises to pour out his Spirit on the earth (Acts 2:17–18). The kingdom of God was inaugurated in the earthly ministry, death, and resurrection of Jesus and now God was continuing to keep his promises by calling the nations to repentance. God had "sworn an oath to [David] to seat one of his descendants on his throne" (Acts 2:30). God had kept his oath by raising Jesus from the dead. At Pentecost, God kept his promise to pour out his Spirit. But surprisingly, in his Pentecost sermon, Peter said that it is the exalted Lord Jesus who poured out his Spirit at Pentecost: "God has resurrected this Jesus. We are all witnesses of this. Therefore, since He has been exalted to the right hand of God and has received from the Father the promised Holy Spirit, He has poured out what you both see and hear" (Acts 2:32–33). In other words, as Jesus poured out the Holy Spirit at Pentecost, God was fulfilling his promises. Peter finishes his Pentecost sermon with a call to faith in Jesus who is both "Lord and Christ" (Acts 2:36 ESV). So God promised to pour out his Spirit and Jesus executed and fulfilled that promise. In Pentecost, we see Jesus ruling from heaven authoritatively.

Jesus Builds His Church

Jesus promises that *he* will build his church and will delegate authority to Peter and the apostles to lead the church. "And I also say to you that you are Peter, and on this rock I will build

My church, and the forces of Hades will not overpower it" (Matt. 16:18). In the book of Acts we see Jesus fulfilling those promises. After Pentecost, the "*Lord* added to them those who were being saved" (Acts 2:47, italics added).[6] Jesus builds his church through granting repentance and faith to God's chosen people: "God exalted this man to His right hand as ruler and Savior, to grant repentance to Israel, and forgiveness of sins" (Acts 5:31). Still today, it is Jesus who plants new churches and builds them up.

During suffering and even death Jesus is in control in the book of Acts. As Stephen was dying at the hands of young Saul (the future apostle) he "gazed into heaven. He saw God's glory, with Jesus standing at the right hand of God" (Acts 7:55). Stephen then prayed to this standing, ruling Lord with his dying breath, "Lord Jesus, receive my spirit! . . . Lord, do not charge them with this sin!" (Acts 7:59–60). And thus Stephen "fell sleep" and joined his Lord Jesus in heaven.

Jesus revealed himself directly to Paul on the Damascus road and personally commissioned him for ministry to the nations. Paul is the "chosen instrument" of Jesus (Acts 9:15). Jesus reveals himself to Ananias and tells him to go and pray for Saul (Paul) to regain sight.

As the gospel message reaches into Europe for the first time, we see Jesus himself guiding his apostles in their disciple-making ministry. As Paul and his traveling team aim at going into Bithynia (northern Turkey), "the Spirit of Jesus did not allow them" (Acts 16:7). After a vision from God, they decided instead to cross the Aegean Sea and enter Europe. Upon reaching Philippi, they met and led Lydia. "The Lord," a reference to Jesus, "opened her heart to pay attention to what was spoken by Paul" (Acts 16:14), and thus was born the church in Europe.

Jesus encourages his saints through trial. Jesus appeared to Paul one night to prepare him for the "united attack" of the Jews on him: "Don't be afraid, but keep on speaking and don't be silent. For I am with you, and no one will lay a hand on you to hurt you, because I have many people in this city" (Acts 18:9–11). The compassionate Lord Jesus, who once walked on earth and encountered a similar, but fiercer, united attack of the Jews, knew the potential discouragement of Paul during ministry in Corinth. Jesus knew how much an encouraging and direct word from him would encourage Paul through the ensuing trials. Jesus affirmed his promise given in the Great Commission—"I am with you always" (Matt. 28:20)—and promised to Paul that he has his people in Corinth.

At the beginning of Paul's hardest years of suffering, the Lord Jesus appears to him again to encourage him: "The following night, the Lord stood by him and said, 'Have courage! For as you have testified about Me in Jerusalem, so you must also testify in Rome'" (Acts 23:11). If "anxiety in a man's heart weighs it down, but a good word cheers it up" (Prov. 12:25), this encouraging word directly from the Lord Jesus was powerful to propel Paul through the following years of difficult suffering! Alan Thompson sums this up, "Thus, the subsequent events where Paul is rescued from a plot to take his life (Acts 23:12–35), sent to Caesar in the midst of false charges and corrupt rulers (Acts 24:1—26:32), marvelously protected through storm, shipwreck and snakebite (Acts 27:1—28:10) and arrives safely in Rome (28:11–16) are all meant to be read in the light of this promise from the Lord Jesus in [Acts] 23:11."[7] The lesson for Paul, and for us, is that even in the darkest of cities during the hardest of trials at the hands of the fiercest foe, Jesus reigns.

Jesus worked through Paul to make disciples among the nations. "For I would not dare say anything except what *Christ has accomplished through me* to make the Gentiles obedient by word and deed, by the power of miraculous signs and wonders, and by the power of God's Spirit" (Rom. 15:18–19, italics added). By means of Paul and his disciple-making ministry, *Jesus himself* made disciples of the unreached Gentiles.

Is Jesus Keeping His Promise to Us Today?

Jesus is no longer physically with us. He ascended to heaven long ago. How can that be good news? The ascension is good news because it reminds us that Jesus has not "called it quits" with humanity. In fact, Jesus ascended with, and still has, his resurrected *human* body. He has not forsaken humanity in the theater of heaven. Rather, his everlasting, resurrected human body symbolizes his enduring love for his people.[8]

It is good news to us because we have not been left as orphans or friendless. At Pentecost, Jesus sent the Holy Spirit to us. Surprisingly, Jesus said that it is to our advantage that he leave and send the Holy Spirit. How can that be? Should we not have sorrow with the disciples that Jesus left (John 16:6)? How can we rejoice that the physical Jesus has left us here on earth (John 14:28)?

We rejoice because though Jesus left the earth physically, he has most certainly not left the earth spiritually. He is very present with us through the Holy Spirit. The presence of the Holy Spirit is the very confirmation that Jesus is keeping his promises to be with us "to the end of the age" (Matt. 28:20). The Holy Spirit lives inside of us, teaches us truth, empowers us to do good works, and testifies through us of the glory of Jesus Christ. When we pray, we pray with the help and intercession of the Holy Spirit (Rom. 8:26–27).

Four Ways That Jesus Pastors His Church Today

Jesus Christ is the church's senior pastor. While that may sound trite to say, it is no less true. He is the "chief Shepherd" (1 Pet. 5:4) who leads the sub-shepherds (elders) and he is the "Shepherd and Guardian" (1 Pet. 2:25) of his sheep. It is healthy for a local church to publicly acknowledge that Jesus himself is their leader, for this acknowledgment keeps the issue before the staff, elders, and the body. Jesus is the *"great* Shepherd" (Heb. 13:20, italics added) who is greater in power and honor and glory, and more authoritative than other human shepherds of God's people such as Moses, Joshua, and David. As the Shepherd of the church, he not only cares for the church, he rules the church. Thus, Matthew 2:6 quotes the prophecy in Micah 5:2 about Bethlehem, "And you, Bethlehem, in the land of Judah, are by no means least among the leaders of Judah: because out of you will come a *leader who will shepherd My people Israel"* (italics added).

There are at least four ways that Jesus pastors his church today. First, Jesus leads his church by means of the *spiritual community of the local and global church.* Consider how God led Paul and his team away from Asia and Bithynia and to Macedonia in Acts 16:6–8. First the Holy Spirit says "no" to speaking the word in Asia (v. 6), then the spirit of Jesus said "no" to going north to the banks of the Black Sea in Bithynia (v. 7). So they went to the Aegean port of Troas (v. 8). At Troas, Paul had a vision calling them to the European region of Macedonia. "During the night a vision appeared to Paul: A Macedonian man was standing and pleading with him, 'Cross over to Macedonia and help us!' After he had seen the vision, we immediately made efforts to set out for Macedonia, concluding that God had called us to evangelize them" (Acts 16:9–10). In the end, they concluded that God had called them to go to Macedonia.[9]

There are many applications from Acts 16:6–10 for the church today on how to make decisions under God's leadership. Paul's spiritual community was integral to the process of Paul hearing from God.[10] Paul had the vision, but the team discussed and "concluded" (Acts 16:10) that the vision was from God. The verb *sumbibazo* ("concluded") connotes "to bring about an agreement," "to compare" and make an inference, to put minds together. The KJV translates this as "assuredly gathering that the Lord had called us." Being a maverick is not a virtue in the body of Christ. God in Christ leads his people in the context of spiritual community. Beware, therefore, when someone claims to hear from God individually but the people in their biblical community express their doubt.

Second, Jesus leads us through our *local church leadership*. A critical part of the spiritual community within the global and local church is the leadership of the church. Jesus is the chief Shepherd over the council of church shepherds (elders). The connection between the chief Shepherd Jesus and church elders is that of oversight (1 Pet. 5:2). Church elders have the authority of a shepherd over his sheep in their loving and joyful oversight of the sheep. This is why "you younger men" are commanded to be "subject [be obedient] to the elders" (1 Pet. 5:5).

Third, Jesus meets with us and leads us through the *ordinances of baptism and the Lord's Supper*. In my context in the Muslim world, I have learned that one of the most important things for a new believer in Christ to do is to be baptized and participate in the Lord's Supper with a community of believers. These ordinances connect us to the living Christ in a mysterious way.

Lastly, Jesus leads us through *supernatural means*. Just as Jesus appeared to Paul in Corinth and said, "Don't be afraid, but keep on speaking and don't be silent" (Acts 18:9), he continues to reveal himself supernaturally. Once while Paul feared for his life in Jerusalem, the Lord Jesus "stood by him" (Acts 23:11). The Lord Jesus assured Paul that he would live to make it to Rome. Those who dispute that Jesus continues to reveal himself to his people and to the lost whom he is drawing to himself must reckon with the near countless stories of evidence coming from all ends of the earth throughout the last two thousand years.

He Is with Us *for* the Nations

As the "senior pastor" of the church, Jesus has an agenda. He is working with purpose and with an end in mind. We must always remember the promise of Jesus to be with us "to the end of the age" in Matthew 28:20 in light of his commandment to go and make disciples among all peoples. Without the mandate, the promise is merely personal. Without the promise, the mandate is impossible. The mandate and the promise together are the very job of the world's hope: the local church. So the promise of Matthew 28:20 comforts us and strengthens us to move forward to complete the mandate of Matthew 28:19. When asked what had sustained him through his endless trials in Africa, David Livingstone answered by quoting Matthew 28:20. "It is said that, when his wife died in Africa, he helped prepare her body for burial, helped make the coffin, helped lower it into the grave, and helped cover it with earth, then opened his New Testament and read this text, whereupon he said to his African associates, 'Jesus Christ is too much of a Gentleman not to keep His word; let us get on with the task.'"[11]

King Jesus Sits and He Stands

In 1979 my father and mother felt called to make disciples in the Dominican Republic. The calling grew more and more firm in their hearts. But my mother still had some reservations about moving, especially with small children, to a Third World country which at that time was rife with violence and political instability. Of immense comfort and confirmation to her during those moments of internal deliberation was Acts 7:55–56, "But Stephen, filled by the Holy Spirit, gazed into heaven. He saw God's glory, with Jesus standing at the right hand of God, and he said, 'Look! I see the heavens opened and the Son of Man standing at the right hand of God!'"

The Holy Spirit prompted her heart: if Jesus was standing for Stephen, then perhaps he might stand for her. The very thought of

Jesus standing in honor of a fallen saint so deeply comforted her that she resolved with peace and joy to move overseas.

Jesus stands to honor his fallen saints and to symbolize that he is preparing for the end of the age when he will mount his war horse, rend the heavens, render his judgment, and complete his victory over all evil. Jesus stands for Stephen who is "completing . . . what is lacking in Christ's afflictions" (Col. 1:24)—namely, the demonstration of the supreme value of his name over life itself to all peoples.

But Jesus also sits because his redemption-securing work is complete. "After making purification for sins, He sat down at the right hand of the Majesty on high" (Heb 1:3). After a long day of manual labor, we sit and rest. And after securing the faith and redemption of all of his people, Jesus now sits at the Father's right hand, since all is indeed "finished" (John 19:30). Jesus sits and waits for the appointed day of his return (Ps. 110:1).

In both his sitting and his standing Jesus signifies that he is the authority over all things. He sits because his work on earth is final and complete. His blood is perfectly powerful to secure all of his children. Jesus stands because he is the Son of Man who rules in an everlasting kingdom.[12]

"At Your Word" Disciples

I love the tapestry "The Miraculous Draught of Fishes" by Raphael Sanzio, currently in the Victoria and Albert Museum in London. Raphael painted a collection of tapestries like this one to be ceremonially hung on the lower walls of the Sistine Chapel. The work is quintessential Raphael in style: the huge figures, the horizontal array of the scene that made it adept to sculpting, the dramatic scenery. The painting is also intriguing: for instance, Jesus is raising his left hand in the painting. This is taboo in classical depictions of Jesus. But since the tapestry was woven from behind, it is a reverse picture of the painting, and so in the actual tapestry Jesus is raising his right hand. I love this painting because it captures the moment when Jesus changed Simon, James, and John from fishermen to fishers of men.

The painting depicts Luke 5:1–10 where Jesus finds Simon and his friends fishing on the lake of Gennesaret. After teaching a crowd on the shore from the boat, Jesus turns to Simon and tells him to put his boat out into deep water and let down his nets for a catch. Simon objected that they had fished all night and caught nothing. "But at Your word," Simon says to Jesus, he would let down the net and try again (v. 5). As they did, the net began to sink with the weight of the fish filling it. The nets begin to break as they pull them in the boat! The fisherman signaled to others and received help. There were so many fish that the boat itself began to sink! The fishermen were all astonished. When Simon Peter saw all this, he immediately fell at Jesus' knees, saying, "Go away from me, because I'm a sinful man, Lord!" Jesus responded to Simon, "Do not be afraid, from now on you will be catching people" (Luke 5:8, 10).

The result of the miracle on Lake Gennesaret was that Simon, James, and John left everything and followed Jesus. Jesus commanded them, "Do not be afraid; from now on you will be catching men" (Luke 5:11 ESV). So, in that moment, they obeyed. Jesus would send them out in "deep waters" again, this time to the ends of the earth. And just as Jesus commanded the fish to be gathered into the nets, he would command the souls of men to be gathered into the gospel nets of these apostles.

The critical moment in this story is Simon's faith-filled response to Jesus, "But at Your word" (v. 5). They all became "at Your word" disciples who were ready to do whatever Jesus, their Lord, told them to do. Likewise, when Jesus gives his commands today, he expects us to submit with faith and become "at Your word" disciples. When Jesus gives the command, we must obey, even if he is calling us out into unknown deep waters where we will face risk.

We Are Not Alone

It is not hard to feel alone when we face risk in the cause of Christ. A few years ago, I was deeply discouraged, tired, and afraid of my own incompetence. At that time, I was charged with the following responsibilities, each of which I felt were near impossible: leading a team of twelve adults to start a church-planting movement in one of the most dangerous countries on earth, learning one of the hardest languages in the world, starting and building two new businesses with very few resources in an immature and immensely volatile Third World economy, mobilizing ten thousand people to pray for our focus people group, and raising the financial support to cover start-up funds, all while being a husband and father to two (at that time) rowdy boys ages two and six months. My only relief from the stress was remembering that Jesus sits on the throne and that he is with me.

Since I was a little boy, I have had a deep fear of abandonment. This fear of abandonment creeps into my relationship with God and paralyzes me in ministry. I have to remind myself constantly of the promise of God: "He will not leave you or forsake you" (Deut. 31:6). "For the LORD your God is with you wherever you go" (Josh. 1:9). "I am with you always, to the end of the age" (Matt. 28:20). I remember standing at the beachside colonnade once in Turkey asking myself, *How in the world are we ever going to reach a nation of eighty million Turks with the gospel?* I am reminded that we are not alone in this task. Jesus rules over Turkey and he is present in every dark corner of Turkey. All the pride and resources of the Turkish people do not compare with even one jewel on the crown of our Lord Jesus.

We do not face a lost world alone. We are never alone. There is nowhere on earth or in all existence where we might find ourselves alone. And there is no time now or in the future when we will be alone. Jesus is with us to the end of the age. And with him is all authority.

Son, hold it in your heart if it is gold.
The rubber and the wood just throw away.
You have to fight for things that will not mold.
Beware the dust and moths will have their way.

Go give away your treasures, don't withhold,
For loss of them gains greater revenues.
He is no fool who gives what he can't hold
To gain eternal treasures he can't lose.

Like slaves your classmates they will cling to stuff.
Consumption, their disease, will never please.
May hope of the new earth be now enough
To wash your soul in joy in our great King.

The world will stroke you as its precious pearl.
They'll call you names that make you feel so big.
The prizes, houses, cars, fast jets, and girls,
All empty, empty pits that dead men dig.

Do not forsake the passion of your soul
For pleasure, yes, embrace that deep desire.
But don't believe the smoke from the world's coals.
That smoke will burn you with eternal fire.

—— Chapter 10 ——

The Redemption of Authority

WE HAVE BEEN ASSUMING SOMETHING EXTREMELY IMPORTANT; namely, that Matthew 28:18 is *good news*. I recently watched a baptism testimony video of a middle-aged husband and wife. In this video, they explained how they finally surrendered to Jesus and committed to follow him as the authority of their life. They cried with tears of joy as they talked about his authority over their lives. As I watched, I realized much of the world would find this couple completely crazy. They are rejoicing with tears that they have surrendered their personal autonomy over to someone who claims to have absolute authority over their lives! And yet, as a follower of Christ, I know exactly the peace and joy of surrendering to my *Lord*.

Barriers to Receiving Matthew 28:18 as Good News

But, of course, many people do not rejoice in this truth, for countless reasons. At the center of rebellion against God is unbelief, and the roots of unbelief descend all the way into hell. Unbelief produces manifold structures that prevent people from cherishing Jesus. These barriers are philosophical, religious, sociological, empirical, and personal. It would require another book to exhaust these barriers, so I have chosen only a few as representative samples that draw out structural dynamics that revolt against the good news of the supreme authority of Jesus.

Philosophical Barriers

At the top of the list in the West is postmodernism. Skepticism, or doubt, is the philosophical heartbeat of postmodernism. The only certainty in postmodernism is uncertainty. As a movement, postmodernism aims to destabilize "concepts such as presence, identity, historical progress, epistemic certainty, and the univocity of meaning."[1] As such, postmodernism is extremely suspicious of reason, authority, and power.[2]

Catapulted by technology and an unrivaled pursuit of instant gratification, we are moving further and further into isolation from each other. Shunning any hint of universal ethics, we look to our community of allies—our tribe—for justification, vindication, and authorization. If they do not provide those things, we turn even further inward. Our in-the-moment feelings determine the veracity of our thoughts and the morality of our actions. In the end, public discourse lacks any central stability. Relationships drift like trash on ocean waves, and individuals pass their lives pursuing temporary gratifications or envying those who achieve them. As this degeneration progresses, so does rage over anything absolute. Any institution, idea, or person claiming to be absolute is almost immediately disregarded or denigrated. "The center cannot hold" ceases to be adequate; rather, a postmodern would say, "Only fools believe that the 'center' actually exists."

When Christians affirm that "all authority" has been given to Jesus, they strike two central nerves at the very heart of postmodernism. The first nerve is repulsion toward absolutes. Jesus makes no compromise about his authority. It is absolute authority that does not permit skepticism. By "all authority," he means that his right to exert sovereign power extends over all existence. His authority is as real as day and night, the sun and moon. The integrity of his authority is independent of humanity's acceptance of it. The second nerve is postmodern skepticism of authority. By "all authority" Jesus also means that there is no authority higher than his. He is not a "team player" who lets other spiritual leaders have their say. He is the King and every knee will bow to him without exception.

But postmodernism crumbles in the human desperation for authority. We are desperate to know who is in control, and that is most evident in crisis and suffering. We want authority in crisis. We want leadership in turmoil. Otherwise, why were churches packed at unprecedented levels for months after September 11, 2001? Postmodernism limps into obscurity in moments of great tragedy. Death, after all, is absolute. The philosophical crux of postmodernism—rejection of absolutes—smashed into the World Trade Center as American Airlines Flight 11 and United Airlines Flight 75.

Consider how postmodern vilification of authority sank with the South Korean ferry *Sewol*. On April 16, 2014, it tragically sank, killing 294 people, many of them students. The world raged—and rightly so—at the captain and some members of the crew when it was discovered that some drank beer during the capsizing and that the captain, chief engineer, and second mates were the first to be rescued. The captain was sentenced to thirty-six years in prison for gross negligence. While postmoderns may scoff at the notion of absolutes, they join the global rage of the Koreans at the captain. Deeper than vain philosophy in the human heart are the ethics of leadership and authority, because these ethics derive from the nature of the triune God.

The second philosophical barrier most prominent in the West is rationalism. Rationalism regards reason as "the chief source and test of knowledge."[3] Rationalism disregards the supernatural as mere fancy. Thus, Jesus was a moral and influential teacher, perhaps, but he certainly was not the Son of God who rose from the dead and who will return in great glory. Rationalism smacks a stubborn and obnoxious "doubtful" against the absolute assertion of Jesus that "all authority" has been given to Jesus in heaven and on earth. For there is no "proof"! And if there is no "proof" for his authority, then all pursuits toward fulfilling the Great Commission are unreasonable wastes of human energy.

Like postmodernism, rationalism inevitably breaks down with simple human experience, such as the experience of joy. The brilliant rationalist C. S. Lewis was surprised by the unearthly, supernatural longings and, finally, joy that he experienced in Christ drawing him near.[4]

Of his conversion, C. S. Lewis wrote:

> Doubtless, by definition, God was Reason itself. But would He also be "reasonable" in that other, more comfortable sense? Not the slightest assurance on that score was offered me. Total surrender, the absolute leap in the dark, were demanded. The reality with which no treaty can be made was upon me. The demand was not even "All or nothing." I think that stage had been passed, on the bus top when I unbuckled my armor and the snowman started to melt. Now, the demand was simply "All."[5]

Jesus smashed the idol of rationalism when he stood in front of his disciples and said, "All authority." He is the standard of truth. As the Word of God, he defines what makes sense in this world. Could it be that the evangelical church in the West defers to reason, culture, and precedent over the very commandments of Jesus to "Go, therefore, and make disciples of all nations" (v. 19)? We work around the Great Commission with excuses like, "There are still problems here, why go over there?" Or, "When God's ready to save them, he will open the door for us to walk through without such difficulty." Or, "We'll engage when we are ready and able." Through endless rationalizations, we scramble to find shade from the blazing sword of Jesus under a dying tree.

Religious Barriers

Structural attacks come not only from certain philosophies, but from other religions. At the center of all religions is the issue of authority. Humanity must answer, after all, two important questions, "Who is God?" and "What does the answer to that question mean for my life?" Inevitably, different religions have different authority structures. These authority structures are derivatives of their unique histories, geographies, and faith systems.

For instance, Islam promotes a kind of "divine fascism." The god of Islam is akin to a radical authoritarian who rules by means of fate over the affairs of fear-stricken men. In its infancy, Islam encouraged a tribal grab for political power. Islam was never envisioned to thrive outside of the domain of political power. As Islam grew, it inevitably secured political power along with the hearts of its subjects. Much of the breakdown of Islamic society, particularly Arab society in the late twentieth and twenty-first century, may be attributed to a nostalgia for power and a confused regret for having lost it.

Buddhism promotes a much more communistic structure of "divine" authority. In terms of religious authority structures, Buddhism rejects the idea of a sovereign authority over all existence. Instead, it promotes the end to the suffering of mankind through escape to the state of nirvana—the liberation of a being from a cycle of suffering into the permanent extinguishment of desire and illusion. As a result, as in communism, the notion of a sovereign God ruling over the affairs of mankind is a mere illusion contrived by earthly elites.

The theological center of Hinduism is pluralism. There are an uncountable number of deities, each of them exercising proportionate authority and power in accord with their diverse agendas. Jesus, for many Hindus that become aware of him, is simply stacked in line with the series of gods and goddesses that should be revered.

In light of all other gods, Jesus stands alone. Jesus does not accommodate being one among many. He is the God-Man who has all authority. When he says, "Anyone who does not honor the Son does not honor the Father who sent Him" (John 5:23), he means that *he* is the single criterion for establishing a person's standing before God Almighty.

Liberal Christianity and religious pluralism are bedfellows when it comes to perceptions on the authority of the Bible and of the Lord Jesus. It is no surprise that many people of status comfortably find their seats on Sunday in liberal Christian churches. For in those sanctuaries, it is rare for pluralism and humanism to be demolished by the exclusive authority of Jesus Christ.

Sociological Barriers

The 2014 shooting of Michael Brown in Ferguson, Missouri, once again unleashed the dragons of classism, racism, and ethnocentrism. No matter what the facts of the case are, one thing is certain: how one thinks and feels about the shooting of a black male by a white police officer is inevitably affected by his or her economic class, culture, or race. This difference of perspectives is not surprising, as a single authority may be viewed very differently by people on different sides of the railroad tracks or different floors of a manufacturing company.

For instance, I used to work in one of the poorest neighborhoods in Austin, Texas. Despite the beauty and dignity of many people of diverse ethnic backgrounds in that neighborhood, race and class determined friendships and trust in the neighborhood. In the 1980s and early 1990s, African-Americans were the majority, comprising eighty percent of the neighborhood, with the remaining twenty percent being Latino. Thus, an African-American police officer was seen as part of the community. A Latino police officer was commonly met with distrust. The neighborhood went through a demographic transition in the 1990s and 2000s and now the neighborhood is eighty percent Latino and twenty percent African-America. Now Latino police officers have much more community trust, and African-American police officers have to work to maintain trust. White police officers are generally treated with suspicion by both Latinos and African-Americans.

Our economic class, race, and cultural background greatly influence our perception of authority. This has definite ramifications for the ability of churches to reach different races and economic classes. There is a reason that High Church Anglicans in the U.K., along with megachurches in America, struggle to reach the poor. When a church staff, committees, and boards are stacked with middle and upper classes, the poor find it harder to trust leadership.

But Jesus rises above all cultural, ethnic, and racial barriers. The rich testimony of history is that people and peoples from all ethnic, racial, and economic varieties come to love and follow this God-Man, Jesus Christ. When he says that he has all authority, he means that he rules over and above all sociological influences too.

Jesus not only rises above, he also enters among us, he lives with us, and walks with us by his Spirit in the context of our cultural, ethnic, and racial communities. Through these contexts, he reveals diverse aspects of his glory. This is why we need to promote diversity regularly within our local and global church contexts. One of the glories of Jesus is that he appeals to peoples from the most diverse cultures, backgrounds, languages, colors, and economic classes. From the executive ballroom in New York City to the mud slums of Kolkata, one Person draws the nations to joyful surrender. This Person, this Lord Jesus, is magnified above all in both his transcendence and his immanence. The profound effect of spiritual rebirth in Christ is that what was once a barrier, such as race, becomes a structural catalyst for cherishing the diverse glories of Christ.

Empirical Barriers

As a result of the fall of man, human authority is inherently corrupted, leaving no one unexposed to the sad effects of corrupted authority. There is no authority in human relations that is unstained by corruption, deception, politicization, and in the end, oppression. Nearly everyone has stories of being oppressed by a person or institution in authority over him or her. We are constantly asking ourselves about the authorities in our lives, "Will they use their power against us? Will they exploit us to gain more power for themselves? Will they lead us unjustly? Will they make bad decisions?" Even in the cleanest democracy, there are still rampant abuses of authority.

Our experiences shape our perceptions about reality. There is a young girl in my city who regularly watches a different man slide out of her mother's bedroom and out the back door. Since her mother's divorce, this young girl has counted eighteen men. Every one of those males, as well as this girl's own parents, have perverted her view of sexuality and authority. Children grow up intently observing their parents, and when their parents abuse their authority, or avoid using it at all, the child's perception of God inevitably shifts. This is tragic, for the institution of parenthood is a gift from God designed to model the character of God to children.

It is in this context that the doctrine of the authority of Jesus Christ shines even brighter as a hope for all humanity. Whereas mere human authority always comes with corruption, deception, and oppression between humans, Jesus rules in perfect holiness and for the good of his people.

Personal Barriers

Tim Keller tells the story of a lady who was visiting his church in New York City. As she was grappling with the scope of unmerited free grace, she said, "If I was saved by my good works—then there would be a limit to what God could ask of me or put me through. . . . But if it is really true that I am a sinner saved by sheer grace—at God's infinite cost—then there's nothing he cannot ask of me."[6] She was astoundingly correct. The greatest structural barrier keeping us from cherishing the authority of Christ is not philosophical, religious, sociological, or empirical. It is much more personal. It is the human heart.

John Calvin said that the human mind and heart is "a perpetual forge of idols."[7] Idols are anything that receives the worship due to God alone. Idols produce rebellion against the authority of God. Rebellion is a refusal to submit to the authority of God while submitting to the authority of another. That "another" is called an idol.

When Jesus says, "All authority," he directly challenges every idol of the human heart. These idols are inherently hostile to God. They will never cease to war against God, because idolatry is evil. "For the mind-set of the flesh is hostile to God because it does not submit itself to God's law, for it is unable to do so. Those who are in the flesh cannot please God" (Rom. 8:7–8). Thus, at the foundation of all of these structural barriers—philosophical, sociological, empirical, and personal—is the work of the world, the flesh, and the devil. These are tireless promoters of endless idolatries of the heart, for the "flesh desires what is against the Spirit, and the Spirit desires what is against the flesh; these are opposed to each other, so that you don't do what you want" (Gal. 5:17).

The Gospel of Christ's Authority Redeems
Authority in Human Relations

How authority works itself out to be good news for all peoples is illustrated in the life and ministry of Jesus.

Illustrated in the Life of the Trinity

Jesus was given authority from the Father because the Father loves the Son with infinite and eternal love. While the Son works in step with the Father, the Father also works in step with the Son. The three Persons of the Trinity have different roles, but they are equal in worth, holiness, and glory.

The delegation of authority from the Father to the Son does not denigrate the Son. The Father gives authority to the Son, "that all people will honor the Son just as they honor the Father" (John 5:23). Mutual honor is the purpose of the authority structure within the Trinity. In this way, authority is the critical joint between the three Persons of the Trinity. Submission within the Trinity highlights the unity of the Trinity and the mutual effort to exalt the one name of God above all. That is why when every knee bows to Jesus and every mouth confesses that "Jesus Christ is Lord" it will be "to the glory of God the Father" (Phil. 2:11). So the authority of the Father to send, the authority of Jesus to come to earth, and the authority of the Spirit to breathe life into the womb of Mary, all contribute to the exaltation of the one triune God.

Illustrated in the Coming of Jesus

The gospel is the fruit of the submission of Christ to his Father and his humility to come to earth in the likeness of man. Because Jesus "humbled Himself by becoming obedient to the point of death—even to death on a cross," God exalted him with the name that is above all names. So, in the end, every knee will bow to

Jesus and every tongue will finally recognize his supreme authority when they confess, "Jesus Christ is Lord" (Phil. 2:6–11).

Jesus is not only exalted as a result of the incarnation, but also in the very act of the incarnation. God made sure to make that clear when he glorified his Son by sending angels to fill the skies and sing to the shepherds; when the shepherds came to visit the baby Jesus and worshiped him; and when the wise men came from across the earth, "falling to their knees, they worshiped Him" (Matt. 2:11). In a beautiful way, God intends to show that the point of peaceful convergence between the pauper (shepherds) and the king (wise men) is at the feet of the baby Jesus.

Illustrated in the Ministry of Jesus

The ministry of Jesus exemplifies how a proper view of the authority of the Son blesses human relationships. Consider the illustration in John 13:3–5 of Jesus washing the disciples' feet the night before he was crucified: "Jesus knew that the Father had given everything into His hands, that He had come from God, and that He was going back to God. So He got up from supper, laid aside His robe, took a towel, and tied it around Himself. Next, He poured water into a basin and began to wash His disciples' feet and to dry them with the towel tied around Him." Pay attention to the connection between what Jesus *knew* and what he *did*. Knowing that he had all authority from his Father, Jesus got on his knees and washed the dirty feet of the disciples. If there were ever a moment in Jesus' earthly ministry where he might have been tempted to ask the disciples to serve him, and to claim his rightful role as the one who should be served, it was now. For he knew that the disciples were about to forsake him and he would be crucified alone. How then could the very Son of Man find the humility, strength, and love to get down and wash their feet?

Because Jesus knew that he has authority and that he comes from the Father. He had nothing to prove to anybody. There is an insecurity rooted in pride that keeps us from serving others, because we ourselves might just get dirty with their sickness, their poverty, their bad sanitation, their bad medical systems, their strange culture, and so on. But Jesus was not insecure in his role. He knew why he had come to earth as a man. He "did not come to be served, but to serve, and to give His life—a ransom for many" (Matt. 20:28). Operating in full authority over all things, Jesus chooses to serve humbly.

What he *knew* about his authority grounded what he *did* for the disciples in serving. This same connection between knowing Jesus' authority and doing the work of a servant is made in the Great Commission. Matthew 28:18 speaks to what we know about Jesus' authority; Matthew 28:19 tells us now, "therefore," what to do. Following his example, it is when we submit to the full authority of Jesus that we find the confidence to serve others.

Illustrated in the Cross and Intercession of Jesus

The work of Jesus might be divided into two parts: his offering of himself on the cross, and his continuing intercession for the saints.[8] These two works have the same end of "bringing many sons to glory" (Heb. 2:10). In both of these works, the authority of Christ is central to the work's accomplishment and effect. Without his delegated authority from the Father, Jesus would have no right to propitiate for the sins of his people. Propitiation demanded not a set of steps, as if God were pleased by some kind of checklist, but it required the right Person to die in the right way. Jesus alone is that Person. Notice in 1 John 2:2 that Jesus did not merely do the necessary "tasks" that propitiated for our sins. Rather, he presented the necessary person, "He himself," who is the propitiation for our sins.

Jesus would be an insufficient intercessor for us if he lacked the authority to sit at the Father's right hand. Without supreme authority in Jesus, there is no comfort for the saints from Romans

8:34, "Who is the one who condemns? Christ Jesus is the One who died, but even more, has been raised; He also is at the right hand of God and intercedes for us." Only Jesus has the right to intercede for the saints from the right hand of the Father. Not only is Jesus supremely sufficient, everybody else lacks supreme authority.

Illustrated in the Last Day

Authority is part of the design of creation. In the beginning, Adam and Eve received commands from God to obey and were authorized to subdue the earth. On the last day of this present creation, Jesus will finally destroy death completely and be subject to the Father.

Authority is integral to human affairs because it is integral to the nature of God himself. The scene at the last day highlights the relationship between the Father and the Son. According to 1 Corinthians 15:20–28, the end will be a magnificent display of authority and submission by the Father and the Son. With supreme authority, the Son "abolishes all rule and all authority and power" (v. 24). He reigns until he "puts all His enemies under His feet. The last enemy to be abolished is death" (vv. 25–26). But Christ is not a rogue power who happens to triumph in the end. For God the Father gave this authority to Christ and so, in that sense, the Father "put everything under His feet" (v. 27). But lest we invert authority roles within the Trinity, Paul clarifies, "But when it says 'everything' is put under Him, it is obvious that He who puts everything under Him is the exception. And when everything is subject to Christ, then the Son Himself will also be subject to the One who subjected everything to Him" (vv. 27–28).

This magnificent display of authority and submission on the last day magnifies the glory of God, "so that God may be all in all" (v. 28). When authority is properly executed in power in human relationships, the end result is a magnificent display of the glory of God.

Illustrated within Human Relationships

How then does authority within human relationships become good news that magnifies the gospel of Christ? Keeping with our topic of the authority of Jesus, I will provide a few illustrations that point to how the authority of Christ enhances our human relationships so that they produce the fruits of joy and love.

Illustrated in Family

Consider the context of families. God delegates authority within families. Husbands have chief authority within their families. This includes authority over their wives.[9] They are accountable for their families before God, who calls them to lead with confident humility in their homes as shepherds and servants. But every family is broken. And these breaks often happen along the fault lines of authority. Authority is often leveraged to abuse the family. Unfortunately, these kinds of stories are everywhere.

Often churches struggle to motivate parents to take authority in the lives of their children. It is all too common for youth to live in rebellion against God while their so-called Christian parents essentially ignore their children's lifestyle. What motivates parents to take action in the life of their rebelling child? The knowledge that Jesus has all authority and that their children will not be happier than when they surrender to Jesus as Lord.

In the home it is critical to remember that every person in the family is a sinner and that the institution of the family as a whole has been stained by sin. For instance, part of God's judgment of Adam and Eve was on their marriage: "Your desire will be for your husband, yet he will rule over you" (Gen. 3:16). While in the Trinity authority magnifies the infinite love between the three

Persons, abused authority in a sin-stained marriage magnifies individual, and even familial, idolatries.

For instance, consider how a control idol turns a loving parent into an authoritarian tyrant toward his or her children. When a child does not perform in school in a manner that is fitting with the family name or the expectations of the parent, it is ever so easy to leverage God-given parental authority to abuse or oppress the child. When this happens, the authority of the parents ceases to be securing and comforting to the child, but instead becomes repulsive.

How we react to the authority of Christ will determine how we react to authority in human relationships. It would not be difficult for most of us to imagine a marriage where authority is leveraged for self-serving ends. When a husband and wife individually surrender to Christ as Lord, mutual surrender to each other is made possible in the context of their roles. Authority within the marriage and family relationship provides the structural support for a family to thrive in the midst of a dark world.

Illustrated in Work

Employers and employees are both subject to the authority of God. To authorities, God says, "And masters, treat your slaves the same way, without threatening them, because you know that both their Master and yours is in heaven, and there is no favoritism with Him" (Eph. 6:9). To subordinates, God says, "Slaves, obey your human masters with fear and trembling, in the sincerity of your heart, as to Christ. Don't work only while being watched, in order to please men, but as slaves of Christ, do God's will from your heart. Serve with a good attitude, as to the Lord and not to men, knowing that whatever good each one does, slave or free, he will receive this back from the Lord" (Eph. 6:5–8). Organization charts tend to communicate worth in addition to roles, but as Christians workers, we submit to the authority of God in Christ.

Our worth is found in God's adoption of us as his children. We are *freed* to bless our employees and employers.

Illustrated in the Church

God institutes the authority of church leaders for the blessing of the church. But because authority has been universally stained by sin, no church is absent of abuses of authority by its leaders. The potential for authority to destroy or bring life within the church is most pronounced in the leadership of the elders.[10] When elders cease to leverage their authority for that good, the people suffer.

The biblical image of an elder with authority is a shepherd (1 Pet. 5:2–3). Shepherds have stewardship, and thus authority, over their sheep. They are responsible to take care of the sheep and lead them well. When shepherds abuse authority, the sheep suffer (Ezek. 34:2–7). They should regularly confess their sins, humble themselves before each other, keep each other accountable, challenge each other to have faith in God, and lead the flock according to the will of God. When the gospel is central, and leaders apply the gospel to their own lives, shepherds lead their churches to become a revitalizing hospital for the sick and desperate, as well as a passionate army ready to storm the gates of hell.

Exemplary and Empowering Authority

The authority of Jesus is not only exemplary for us in our human relationships; it also empowers us to joyfully submit to earthly authorities. The authority of Jesus our Great Shepherd is most comforting to Christians living on mission with God. Thus, Matthew 28:18 really is good news for the world.

The gospel is not an idea, or a suggestion, but an announcement to be declared to all peoples. This announcement is that Jesus Christ is Lord. He is on the throne of heaven at the Father's right hand. He reigns.

The authority of God in Christ is not only the foundation from which we preach the gospel, it is part of the essence of the gospel. The person, ministry, sufficiency, and glory of Christ all hinge on the nature of his authority as the incarnate Son of God and the Son of Man. Take away the supreme authority of Christ, and the entire gospel crumbles into an impotent announcement for the world. The announcement of the authority of Christ is good news for the nations because it brings faith, hope, and love to human relationships.

The result of publicly cherishing the use of authority by the Lord Jesus in the contexts of family, government, church, work, and in our individual lives is the blessing of the nations. The nations are tired of new attempts to make this or that ideology succeed. There has never been a single nation that has avoided colossal breakdowns in the society to the detriment of the people. The only hope of the nations is to bow to the ruling Jesus. And that will happen when the church cherishes the doctrine of the authority of Christ to the extent that it takes seriously the command to "Go, therefore, and make disciples of all nations" (Matt. 28:19).

There is absolutely no action more loving, more humanitarian, or more practically beneficial to the nations than declaring and demonstrating that Jesus is Lord. "How beautiful on the mountains are the feet of the herald, who proclaims peace, who brings news of good things, who proclaims salvation, who says to Zion, 'Your God reigns!'" (Isa. 52:7).

My Lord, I can smell the feast
And hear the laughter and chatter,
And jokes—every one new and brilliant—
Down the long tables—longer than hope—
Of the family—one family made up of many.
Each day they sit and feast like it's their first
After the war, and after the safe return of their warrior.
The warrior enters the room.
He remembers the smell from his dream
That warmed his body when it was submerged in fresh blood.
The dream came when he hit the pavement
With six new jewels—each one 7.62 X 39mm—added to his chest.
Beside the feast—there on the right—is the Lamb.
This first look between them would never end
This look was the key to unlocking the ballroom door
And opening the throne room of the King.
They both smile and laugh, then fall over laughing
And crying, and laughing. And then the snorting begins.
They can not catch their breath
As if under the relentless tickling of their Father
They laugh. The families start as well.
"Dear boy catch your breath and take a bite!
It's been cooking two thousand years you see,
You'd think it's ready!" And they laugh.
The Lamb pulls back the seat
And the families quiet in sober wonder.
The warrior approaches and gasps.
His name is engraved across the chair
And the palm of the Lamb.
When he sits, the feast renews.
And the roar of laughter sends out again that familiar scent
Across the worlds and into
The dreams of the saints.

——— Conclusion ———

Abiding in the Authoritative Christ

IN THIS BOOK I HAVE TRIED TO CAREFULLY ARTICULATE THE DOC-
trine of the authority of Jesus Christ. Jesus makes the clearest
statement of all about his authority, "All authority has been given
to Me in heaven and on earth" (Matt. 28:18). He gives this self-
declaration as the prelude to the "Great Commission" of Matthew
28:19–20, "Go, therefore, and make disciples of all nations,
baptizing them in the name of the Father and of the Son and of
the Holy Spirit, teaching them to observe everything I have commanded you. And remember, I am with you always, to the end of
the age."

I believe that Matthew 28:18 comes before Matthew 28:19 for
a reason. Jesus knew that the only hope that we have for fulfilling
Matthew 28:19–20 is the doctrine declared in verse 18. In other
words, the doctrinal foundation upon which we make disciples of
all nations is the authority of Jesus Christ. If he is not in control,
then we are fools to go to the ends of the earth.

But if Matthew 28:18 is true, then that incredible truth of his
authority not only propels us to the ends of the earth in risk-taking

mission, it is actually central to the very message that we proclaim. At the very heart of the good news are three simple words, "Jesus is Lord." "Jesus is Lord" is the greatest news ever spoken on planet earth. Those three words are worth giving an entire life to proclaim, even among the most unreached peoples on earth. The first thing a new missionary among the nations should learn to say in a local language is, "Jesus is Lord"; for our whole *gospel* rests on the foundation of those three words. When we pray, "Your kingdom come" (Matt. 6:10), we mean most principally that people would submit to the King of the kingdom.

There is nothing more loving for us to do than call people to submission to Christ, for we are saved by him when we submit to him as Lord. If submission to the authoritative Christ does not happen during a lifetime, then it will happen at the end of time at judgment. Every knee will bow to him. Some will bow to Christ with unspeakable joy and love and as they have been for many years on earth, and many will bow in terror as they realize that they have resisted the very King of kings.

Jesus is not merely one Lord among many. He is "the King of kings and Lord of lords" (1 Tim. 6:15; Rev. 19:16) because he has "all authority . . . in heaven and on earth" (Matt. 28:18). His authority is supreme because it is innate, foretold, real, founding, unimpeded, empowered, exclusive, and legitimate. Therefore we can stand before kings and imams and presidents and witch doctors and professors and corporate bosses and every other human authority that might wage war against the Lamb. We stand in the faith that they have temporary and limited authority only because God permits.

But we do not merely stand in confident resistance against earthly and spiritual authorities as they wage war on the Lamb. With the power of Christ delegated to us as his children, we boldly appeal to all human authorities to submit to Christ. We know that no one is beyond the power of Christ to draw them to himself. The

Spirit draws near any and all who the Father elects and Christ saves and this includes all levels of human authority.

This is why we can pray for those who resist us. I prayed for the salvation of those thugs who knifed me even as I was running from them. And as such, even as we are beaten with the rod of human authorities for our submission to Christ, we can pray with power for their salvation. When we turn the other cheek, we turn it not in bitter spite, but in love, even for our very enemies.

We gain that radical love for others when we come back to our own adoption in Christ as God's children. For we were once "helpless" and "ungodly" "sinners" (Rom. 5:6–8). But in that condition Christ died for us and saved us to become the children of God. As fully, finally, and legitimately adopted children of God, we throw off our insecurities. We no longer *need* the approval of others, the comforts of the world, control over our own affairs, or power over others. We do not even need power over our enemies. When they strike us, we are so secure as children of God that we can actually turn our other cheek without any compromise of our identity or worth. We are not defined by our strength against evil, but by his triumph over evil. We have nothing to prove to the world, to ourselves, or to God. We are already adopted and our status will never change. We are once and for all time *his*.

Being confidently his we can begin to redeem authority in our human relationships. No longer do we have to prove that we are "men" by being abusive to women; rather, in unshakeable confidence in our adoption, we uplift women to their rightful place of equality in being. No longer must we prove our worth to our coworkers; rather, we labor for God, and thereby ask others under us to labor honestly and joyfully in the roles to which they have been given. In our churches, we have no need to prove our authority, for we all submit to the Chief Shepherd who leads us all.

As children, we not only have the right to act in the authority of God in Christ, we also have his power. We have full access to this power inasmuch as we are in an abiding relationship with the risen Christ. This is why we often grow weak in our ability to exercise Christ's authority. When we are not walking in a practical, daily relationship with Christ, we are left weak against spiritual powers.

When we are weak, it is not because Christ has left us as orphans. For even though Christ ascended to heaven, he sent his Spirit to be with us. As such, he sits at the Father's right hand ruling. He rules over history, directing history according to his royal agenda. Christ is not like a Greek god that enters and exits the affairs of men in order to manipulate them according to his passion. He is always among us, even more present than he was in his earthly ministry, since his Spirit is everywhere. As our supreme Prophet he speaks to man with divine authority on the Father's behalf. As our Priest, he speaks with divine authority to the Father on our behalf. As our King, he rules over all things in accordance with the triune will of God.

We now abide with Christ because of his supremely authoritative and powerful work on the cross. And on the basis of this work, we will abide with him forever. One day we might face death as we submit to Christ and fulfill the Great Commission. But we do not fear death, nor the Calvary Road that leads us there. For death is our key to meeting Christ in person. Therefore, we do not simply endure the way of the Calvary road; we *embrace* the way.

But how does it work that suffering on the Calvary Road actually leads us to abiding in him? Perhaps returning to my knifing illustration will answer that question as well as bring this book to a close.

After arriving back to Austin from India, I realized that this attack was a catalyst to great spiritual and emotional growth in me. The straight razor that scarred my face has become an altar of intercession for those South Asian youth who attacked us. My face is the sacrifice that was put on this alter. I doubt if any prayers have ever been lifted to the Father for those youth, that is, until they attacked us. Almost immediately, we began praying for them. Since then, thousands of people have interceded for them. In this way, therefore, God turned their sin of unjustly attacking us into a great blessing for them.

God kept all of his promises to us, even while we were attacked. Immediately after our attack, while still seeking help from local authorities, Psalm 34:19 came to mind and comforted me in prayer: "Many adversities come to the one who is righteous, but the LORD delivers him from them all." A few days later, the Lord led me to Psalm 97:10, "He protects the lives of His godly ones; He rescues them from the power of the wicked."

Yes, the Lord preserved our lives. If the straight razor hit me a few inches lower, it would have sliced open my neck, leaving me near death. If it hit me a few inches higher, it would have taken out my left eye. The knife missed my major facial nerve by probable millimeters. If this nerve was severed, I would have been paralyzed on the left side of my face. The path of the straight razor was *perfectly* guided by my Lord to thwart away these afflictions.

The Lord brought me to Psalm 97:11 a few days after the attack: "Light is sown for the righteous, and joy for the upright in heart" (ESV). I realized that the straight razor was not only an altar of intercession for those youth, but it was also a plow, tilling the soil of my body and prepping it for sowing. The straight razor plow opened the way for the seeds of joy and compassion for those youth to be sown in the soil of my heart. My wound, therefore, is now a memorial repository of joy in God and passion for the joy of unreached peoples.

The sowing of my soil—my face—also meant uprooting some of my weeds. On the car ride to the emergency room, I distinctly remember feeling sick about my sin. I already had pride about this whole event! For a moment, I saw that the nasty roots of my sin ran deeper than I could fathom, and I was grateful.

I was blown away when I realized the sowing of seed and the sprouting of the plant have one thing in common: the breaking of the soil. The breaking of the soil is *twice* the key moment in the process of harvesting a plant. In a garden, the soil is broken with hope! In my situation, the breaking of my face at the plow of those South Asian youth was outwardly quite grotesque, but spiritually it was a natural and good gift from above, opening the way for future fruit bearing!

Suffering is a *natural part* of being sent on mission. When Jesus sent out his followers on their first mission, he told them that they were going out like "sheep among wolves" (Matt. 10:16). For Jesus, suffering at the hands of the wolves was *part of* the sending! The apostle Peter says that we have been "called" to suffer (1 Pet. 2:21). Therefore, trials are a very normal and very necessary part of our calling as followers of Jesus Christ.

I am so deeply grateful for the gift of our suffering in India because I think it has led me one step further to obeying my life verse, given me by my parents when I was an infant: "Haven't I commanded you: be strong and courageous? Do not be afraid or discouraged, for the LORD your God is with you wherever you go" (Josh. 1:9). God in Christ is keeping that promise of Joshua 1:9 to me. He keeps it to all of his children.

Therefore, on the basis of the everlasting trustworthiness of all the promises of God, including the declaration that Jesus has "all authority," let us now joyfully go and make disciples of all peoples.

Notes

Introduction: Gaze and Proclaim

1. Keith Getty, Kristyn Getty, and Paul Campbell, *In Christ Alone* (Audio CD, Getty Music, Aug. 28, 2007).

2. I am well aware that "therefore" (οὖν) may not be in the original manuscripts. But that point is inconsequential. The sequence of the text makes clear the intentional connection between Matthew 28:18 and Matthew 28:19. This is evidenced by the fact that almost every English translation puts a "therefore" in Matthew 28:19.

3. For more, see www.100peoplenetwork.org.

4. Quoted in Timothy George, *Theology of the Reformers* (Nashville, TN: B&H Academic, 2013), 61.

5. Karl Barth, *God in Action* (Edinburgh, Scotland: T&T Clark 1936), 57. Quoted in Carl E. Braaten and Robert W. Jenson, *Reclaiming the Bible for the Church* (Grand Rapids, MI: W. B. Eerdmans Pub. Co., 1995), 88.

Chapter 1: The Supremacy of the Son's Authority

1. A "Sirocco" is a dusty, miserable wind that blows regularly from the Sahara northward to the Mediterranean right through Libya's main costal cities. "Phut" or "Put" is usually understood to be ancient Libya. Before 2011, Gaddafi was commonly referred to

as the "Brother Leader" of the Libyan people. After he was killed, the rebels laid Gaddafi's bare corpse in a shopping center open for public display.

2. James R. Edwards provides the evidence of this for *exousia* as well as its Hebrew equivalences in the Septuagint and the intertestamental literature. "The Authority of Jesus in the Gospel of Mark," *The Journal of the Evangelical Theological Society* 13, No. 2 (June 1994), 218–20.

3. Ibid., 218.

4. Ibid., 219.

5. Ibid., 217–18.

6. Ibid., 229.

7. I say "direct" because each pericope from Mark 1:1–20 points to the authority of Jesus. John the Baptist's appearance and announcement of Jesus' coming fulfills ancient prophecy of the coming of the Son of God (1:1–8); the baptism of Jesus is his earthly coronation as the beloved Son of God (1:9–11); the temptation of Jesus exhibits his authority over temptation and sin (1:12–13); Jesus not only points to the future kingdom of God, he announces that the "kingdom of God is at hand"—namely, in himself (1:14–15 ESV); lastly, his calling of the disciples distinguishes Jesus as something different, something more, than the Jewish rabbis. Normally keen students would choose their teacher. But Jesus effectually and authoritatively calls forth his disciples (1:16–20).

8. It does seem that Mark 1:22 and Luke 4:32 recall a separate account than Matthew 7:29, though Matthew 7:29 is still very early in Jesus' ministry.

9. A. T. Robertson, *A Grammar of the Greek New Testament in the Light of Historical Research* (Logos Bible Software, 1919), 947.

10. Edwards, "The Authority of Jesus in the Gospel of Mark," 221.

11. This *"ame⁻n"* occurs thirty times in Matthew, thirteen times in Mark, six times in Luke, and twenty-five times in John, liturgically doubled.

12. "The point of the Amen before Jesus' own sayings is rather to show that as such they are reliable and true, and that they are so as and because Jesus Himself in His Amen acknowledges them to be His own sayings and thus makes them valid. These sayings are of varied individual content, but they all have to do with the history of the kingdom of God bound up with His person. Thus in the ἀμήν preceding the λέγω ὑμῖν of Jesus we have the whole of Christology *in nuce.* The one who accepts His word as true and certain is also the one who acknowledges and affirms it in his own life and thus causes it, as fulfilled by him, to become a demand to others." Gerhard Kittel, Geoffrey W. Bromiley, and Gerhard Friedrich, eds., *Theological Dictionary of the New Testament* (Grand Rapids, MI: Eerdmans, 1964), 338.

13. "Jesus' use of amen as an introductory formula rather than as a concluding prayer response (as was customary in Judaism) is, in the words of Jeremias, 'without any parallel in the whole of Jewish literature and the rest of the New Testament.'" Edwards, "The Authority of Jesus in the Gospel of Mark," 229, quoting J. Jeremias, *New Testament Theology* (New York, NY: Scribner's, 1971), 35–36.

14. John MacArthur, *Strength for Today: Daily Readings for a Deeper Faith* (Wheaton, IL: Crossway, 2002), 25, accessed November 30, 2014, http://goo.gl/ZEtHx7.

15. William Barclay, "Commentary on Hebrews 2:1," *William Barclay's Daily Study Bible* (1956–1959), accessed November 30, 2014, http://www.studylight.org/commentaries/dsb/view.cgi?bk=57&ch=2.

16. Mark 8 seems to be the literary center and shifting point of the book of Mark. In terms of Jesus' authority in Mark, Mark

1—8 focuses on his authority manifested in his miraculous deeds. Hence, I have focused this chart on Mark 1—8.

17. Jock Purves, *Fair Sunshine: Character Studies of the Scottish Covenanters* (London, England: Banner of Truth Trust, 1968), 68, 182; "The Covenanters in the Seventeenth Century," Ulster Historical Foundation, accessed November 30, 2014, http://www.ancestryireland.com/irish-presbyterianism/presbyterian-ancestors/origins/the-covenanters-in-the-seventeenth-century.

18. I am indebted to my faithful brother, Charlie Shaw, for guiding me in understanding this story and it's meaning.

19. Cf. Mark 8:31.

20. Staying in the gospel of Mark, see 2:8–10; 19–22; 2:25–28, 3:23–30, 8:12–13; 10:3–12; 11:29–33; 12:24–27. William Hendriksen, *Exposition of the Gospel According to Mark* (Grand Rapids, MI: Baker Book House, 1975), 466.

Chapter 2: "Has Been Given to Me"

1. *Qur'an*, Surah 112, Sahih International Translation.

2. Another topic, for example, would be truth (Rom. 15:8; John 14:6; 15:26).

3. Psalm 2:6–8; Isaiah 9:6; Luke 1:32–33.

4. I mention this to caution Bible translators who are laboring to explain divine familial terminology in Muslim contexts. No doubt followers of Christ working with Muslims must explain clearly that God did not have sexual relations with a woman in order to "birth" Jesus. But we must take great care not to lighten the impact of the term "Son" in Scripture translation, or else we will lose more than translation accuracy. We will lose out on the meaning of the authority of Christ.

5. *Qur'an*, Surah 112, Sahih International Translation.

6. Walter A. Elwell and Barry J. Beitzel, *Baker Encyclopedia of the Bible* (Grand Rapids, MI: Baker Book House, 1988), 1983.

7. For an overview of the biblical evidence for the eternality of the submission of the Son to the Father, see Wayne A. Grudem, "Biblical Evidence for the Eternal Submission of the Son to the Father," in Dennis W. Jowers and H. Wayne House, eds., *The New Evangelical Subordinationism?* (Eugene, OR: Pickwick, 2012), 223–61, accessed June 28, 2015, http://www.waynegrudem. com/wp-content/uploads/2013/04/Biblical-evidence-for-the-eternal-submission-of-the-Son-to-the-Father.pdf.

8. Wayne A. Grudem, *Systematic Theology: An Introduction to Biblical Doctrine* (Leicester, England; Grand Rapids, MI: InterVarsity Press; Zondervan, 2004), 249–50.

9. John Piper, "Jesus: Equal with God," Desiring God Foundation (Sept. 6, 2009), accessed November 30, 2014, http://www.desiringgod.org/sermons/jesus-equal-with-god.

Chapter 3: The Son's Authority as Prophet, Priest, and King

1. For instance, he predicted his suffering (Matt. 16:21; 17:22–23; 20:17–19) as well as the end times (Matt. 24—25).

2. I say "final" here because many Muslims are taught that the prophet Muhammad fulfilled Deuteronomy 18:15–19. Incidentally, many Muslims believe that Muhammad is the "helper" (Gr. *paráklētos*) prophesied by Jesus in John 14—15.

3. Cf. Acts 3:22–23; 7:37.

4. In the words of John Murray, "It is because he is a priest for ever after the order of Melchizedek that redemption in its Old Testament adumbration had saving effectiveness, that redemption in its objective accomplishment has meaning, and that redemption in its consummation will be achieved." "The Heavenly Priestly Activity of Christ," (Lecture, The Campbell Morgan Memorial Bible Lectureship, No. 10, Buckingham Gate, London S.W.1, June 18, 1958), accessed June 18, 2014, http://www.biblicalstudies. org.uk/article_christ_murray.html.

5. John R. W. Stott, *The Cross of Christ* (Downers Grove, IL: InterVarsity Press, 2006), chapter 4.

6. The Puritan John Owen first opened my eyes to the immensely important biblical connections between the offering of Christ for his people and the intercession of Christ for his people. He explains this connection near irrefragably in *The Death of Death in the Death of Christ*. This book is available online for free at http://www.ccel.org/ccel/owen/deathofdeath.html.

7. John Bunyan, *The Pilgrim's Progress from This World to That Which Is to Come: Delivered under the Similitude of a Dream*, Public Domain Books, Kindle Edition, 93.

8. Russell D. Moore, *The Kingdom of Christ: The New Evangelical Perspective* (Wheaton, IL: Crossway, Kindle Edition) Kindle Locations 126–27. This paradigm is best explained in the works of George Eldon Ladd, specifically, *The Gospel of the Kingdom: Scriptural Studies in the Kingdom of God* (Grand Rapids, MI: Eerdmans, 1959); *A Theology of the New Testament* (Grand Rapids, MI: Eerdmans, 1974); and *The Presence of the Future: The Eschatology of Biblical Realism* (Grand Rapids, MI: Eerdmans 1974).

9. In the end, a renewed focus on the kingdom is essential if evangelicals are ever going to grapple with the evangel of a crucified, resurrected, and enthroned Messiah. Russell Moore argues for the growing consensus of meaning over the kingdom of Christ especially in light of evangelical engagement in the public square (Ibid.). For an overview of the debates over the meaning of the kingdom of God, see Christopher W. Morgan and Robert A. Peterson, *The Kingdom of God* (Wheaton, IL: Crossway, 2012).

10. Scholars of old refer to these three reigns as *regnum potential, regnum gratiae,* and *regnum gloriae* respectively.

11. Anna Kay Scott, *An Autobiography of Anna Kay Scott, M.D.* (Chicago, IL: Anna Kay Scott, M.D., 1917), 39.

12. John Calvin explains this in such rich form that I am compelled to include this: "Therefore, as often as we hear that Christ is armed with eternal power, let us learn that the perpetuity of the Church is thus effectually secured; that amid the turbulent agitations by which it is constantly harassed, and the grievous and fearful commotions which threaten innumerable disasters, it still remains safe. Thus, when David derides the audacity of the enemy who attempt to throw off the yoke of God and his anointed, and says, that kings and nations rage 'in vain,' (Ps. 2:2–4) because he who sitteth in the heaven is strong enough to repel their assaults, assuring believers of the perpetual preservation of the Church, he animates them to have good hope whenever it is occasionally oppressed. So, in another place, when speaking in the person of God, he says, 'The Lord said unto my Lord, Sit thou at my right hand, until I make thine enemies thy footstool,' (Ps. 110:1 KJV) he reminds us, that however numerous and powerful the enemies who conspire to assault the Church, they are not possessed of strength sufficient to prevail against the immortal decree by which he appointed his Son eternal King. Whence it follows that the devil, with the whole power of the world, can never possibly destroy the Church, which is founded on the eternal throne of Christ. Then in regard to the special use to be made by each believer, this same eternity ought to elevate us to the hope of a blessed immortality. For we see that every thing which is earthly, and of the world, is temporary, and soon fades away. Christ, therefore, to raise our hope to the heavens, declares that his kingdom is not of this world (John 18:36). In fine, let each of us, when he hears that the kingdom of Christ is spiritual, be roused by the thought to entertain the hope of a better life, and to expect that as it is now protected by the hand of Christ, so it will be fully realised in a future life." *Institutes of the Christian Religion*, vol. 2 (Edinburgh: The Calvin Translation Society, 1845), 39.

13. For example: Psalm 2:7–9; Daniel 7:13–14; Matthew 19:28; 25:31–32; Romans 15:12; 1 Corinthians 15:25; Philippians 2:9–10; Revelation 1:5; 12:5; 17:14; 19:11–16.

14. I am indebted to John Piper for articulating the paralyzing effect of shame in ministry. "When I Fall I Will Rise!" Desiring God Foundation (July 24, 1988), accessed November 30, 2014, http://www.desiringgod.org/sermons/when-i-fall-i-will-rise; "Missions and Masturbation," Desiring God Foundation (Sept. 10, 1984), accessed November 30, 2014, http://www.desiringgod.org/articles/missions-and-masturbation.

15. William Shakespeare, *Hamlet*, 3.1, accessed November 30, 2014, http://shakespeare.mit.edu/hamlet/hamlet.3.1.html.

Chapter 4: "Go Therefore"

1. Juan Pablo Spinetto, "How Brazil's Richest Man Lost $34.5 Billion," *Bloomberg Businessweek*, Oct. 3, 2013, accessed November 30, 2014, http://www.businessweek.com/articles/2013-10-03/eike-batista-how-brazils-richest-man-lost-34-dot-5-billion; Rupert Neate, "Soaring Microsoft shares boosted Bill Gates fortune by $15.8bn in 2013," *The Guardian*, Jan. 2, 2014, accessed November 30, 2014, http://www.theguardian.com/business/2014/jan/02/bill-gates-richest-man.

2. Howard Taylor, *Borden of Yale* (Minneapolis, MN: Bethany House Publishers, 1988).

Chapter 5: "Make Disciples"

1. In this section, I am indebted to I. H. Marshall, "Disciple," ed. D. R. W. Wood et al., *New Bible Dictionary* (Leicester, England; Downers Grove, IL: InterVarsity Press, 1996), 277.

2. The context of Revelation 3:20 is clear that the verse applies to Jesus calling his church to repent so that he may fill the church again, rather than to an individual who is considering trusting in Christ.

3. For these terms and their descriptions, I rely heavily on Walter A. Elwell and Barry J. Beitzel, *Baker Encyclopedia of the Bible* (Grand Rapids, MI: Baker Book House, 1988), 433–34.

4. "No More Faith," *Clear to Venus* (Essential Records, 2001).

5. Some sects in Islam have additions to the traditional *shahada*. For instance, some Shi'ites add the phrase, "And 'Ali is the vicegerent of God."

Chapter 6: The Cross and Courageous Obedience

1. See http://savesaeed.org for more information on Pastor Saeed and how to become an advocate for his release.

2. "Pastor Saeed's Letter to His Daughter Rebekka," *Samaritan's Purse*, September 26, 2014, accessed November 30, 2014, http://www.samaritanspurse.org/article/pastor-saeeds-letter-to-his-daughter-rebekka.

3. The book is available online for free here at http://www.ccel.org/ccel/owen/deathofdeath.html.

Chapter 7: "I Give You Authority"

1. Consider the outrageous second sentence in a popular book on Christian authority, "The nature of Christians' authority is a central teaching in the New Testament." Charles H. Kraft, *I Give You Authority: Practicing the Authority Jesus Gave Us* (Minneapolis, MN: Chosen, 2012), 11.

2. In this section, I rely on Richard F. Lovelace, *Dynamics of Spiritual Life: An Evangelical Theology of Renewal* (Downers Grove, IL: InterVarsity Press 1979), 133–44.

3. "Saudi Arabia Opposes Gay Internet Domain," *BBC*, Aug. 14, 2012, accessed November 30, 2014, http://www.bbc.com/news/technology-19259422.

4. Personal letter from Sam Shaw, October 15, 2014.

5. See ronniesmithlibya.com for the full letter and media coverage.

6. "Ebola Doc's Condition Downgraded to 'Idiotic,'" *Ann Coulter*, Aug. 6, 2014, accessed November 30, 2014, http://www.anncoulter.com/columns/2014-08-06.html; "Let He Who Is Without Ebola Cast the First Stone," *Ann Coulter*, Aug. 13, 2014, accessed November 30, 2014, http://www.anncoulter.com/columns/2014-08-13.html.

Chapter 8: "You Will Receive Power"

1. Jonathan Edwards, *The Works of Jonathan Edwards*, vol. 1 (Bellingham, WA: Logos Bible Software, 2008), 273. Elliot Ritzema and Elizabeth Vince, eds., *300 Quotations for Preachers from the Puritans*, Pastorum Series (Bellingham, WA: Lexham Press, 2013).

2. These four idols—approval, comfort, control, and power—are helpfully explained in Timothy J. Keller, *Gospel in Life: Grace Changes Everything* (Grand Rapids, MI: Zondervan, 2010).

3. Lawrence and Donald Attwater, *The Practice of the Presence of God* (Springfield, IL: Templegate, 1974).

4. Ralph D. Winter and Steven C. Hawthorne, rev. ed. *Perspectives: On the World Christian Movement: A Reader* (Pasadena, CA: William Carey Library, 2009), 700.

5. Ibid., 698–99.

6. In John 15 Jesus is not immediately addressing whether a person can lose his salvation and, therefore, cease to be "in Christ." For no one can snatch the people of Christ out of God's hand (John 10:28–29). Certainly, though, a lifestyle of not abiding in Christ indicates that a person has never been reborn in Christ.

7. Francis Chan and Matt Daniels, *The Big Red Tractor and the Little Village* (Colorado Springs, CO: David C. Cook, 2010), accessed November 30, 2014, http://vimeo.com/7152556.

8. On this point, I could not more strongly recommend Harry R. Boer, *Pentecost and Missions* (Grand Rapids, MI: Eerdmans, 1961).

Chapter 9: "I Am with You Always"

1. John R. W. Stott, *The Message of Acts: The Spirit, the Church, and the World with Study Guide* (Leicester, England; Downers Grove, IL: InterVarsity Press, 1994), 32–34.

2. Ibid.

3. I am indebted in this chapter to Alan Thompson's book for his argument that Acts centers on the work of the risen Lord Jesus. *The Acts of the Risen Lord Jesus: Luke's Account of God's Unfolding Plan* (Downers Grove, IL: InterVarsity Press, 2011), 49.

4. Notice the framing of the pre-Pentecost narrative by nearly the same phrase, "until the day he was taken up" in Acts 1:2 and Acts 1:22. In Acts 1:10–11 Luke says twice that Jesus is in heaven. Luke refers four times to the fact that Jesus is in heaven in chapter 1.

5. Stott, *The Message of Acts*, 34.

6. The "Lord" must be a reference to Jesus given the overwhelming emphasis on Jesus being "the Lord" in Acts 2:21, 25–36.

7. Thompson, *The Acts of the Risen Lord Jesus*, 54.

8. For more on this point, see Gerrit Scott Dawson, *Jesus Ascended: The Meaning of Christ's Continuing Incarnation* (Phillipsburg, NJ: P&R Publishing, 2004).

9. While we do not know for sure, I believe that "God" refers to the triune God, not merely God the Father. So they summed up the direct intervention of the Holy Spirit and the Spirit of Jesus as "God" leading them.

10. Consider in Acts 13:1–3 how the apostle Paul and Barnabas were set apart and sent out on their first church-planting trip by the church at Antioch after their church leadership community heard from the Holy Spirit and confirmed this hearing by the laying on of hands.

11. Myron S. Augsburger, *The Communicator's Commentary* (Waco, TX: Word Books, 1982), 331.

12. "Son of Man" (Acts 7:56) in this scene is the only time that this term is used in the New Testament by any other person than Jesus himself. Because of that fact, and because of the context of Stephen's sermon, I believe that Jesus standing does have Danielic echoes.

Chapter 10: The Redemption of Authority

1. Gary Aylesworth, "Postmodernism," *The Stanford Encyclopedia of Philosophy* (Summer 2013 Edition), ed., Edward N. Zalta, accessed November 30, 2014, http://plato.stanford.edu/archives/sum2013/entries/postmodernism.

2. "Postmodernism," *Encyclopedia Britannica Online*, s.v., accessed November 30, 2014, http://www.britannica.com/EBchecked/topic/1077292/postmodernism.

3. "Rationalism," *Encyclopedia Britannica Online*, s.v., accessed November 30, 2014, http://www.britannica.com/EBchecked/topic/492034/rationalism.

4. C. S. Lewis, *Surprised by Joy: The Shape of My Early Life* (New York, NY: Harcourt Brace, 1987).

5. Ibid., 125.

6. Timothy J. Keller, *The Reason for God: Belief in an Age of Skepticism* (New York, NY: Riverhead Books, 2009), 189.

7. John Calvin and Henry Beveridge, *Institutes of the Christian Religion*, vol. 1 (Edinburgh: The Calvin Translation Society, 1845), 128.

8. John Owen, *The Death of Death in the Death of Christ* (Philadelphia, PA: Green and M'Laughlin, 1827), I.vi.–viii.

9. 1 Corinthians 11:3; 1 Timothy 2:12; 3:4, 12.

10. The definition of *elder* has been understood and expressed in a variety of ways throughout different ecclesiastical traditions, but that is irrelevant to the point here. No matter how a tradition organizes its governance, every church governance structure is plagued by sin.

ArtBook
Rembrandt

DORLING KINDERSLEY
London • New York • Sydney
www.dk.com

Contents

■ Page 2: Rembrandt, *Self-portrait* (detail), 1658, Frick Collection, New York.

LIFE AND WORKS

BACKGROUND

MASTERPIECES

1632–1642

1642–1657

1658–1669

The golden years

Hurtling towards disaster

Alone with his work

Index

Holland: the pride and prospects of a new nation

At the end of a long, bitter war against the Spanish Empire, the seven United Provinces of the northern Low Countries (Holland being just one of these) were finally able to secure their independence. Led initially by the brave *stadhouder* William of Orange, the protestant provinces broke away from the southern regions, which would go on to become Belgium. Within the space of just a few years, this tiny territory, now known as the Netherlands, with its flat landscape dotted with windmills along the canals, grew into one of the most powerful economies in Europe. Before long, the Dutch people were able to share a sense of national pride and found much to unite them: the Dutch language, widely promoted thanks to intensive literacy campaigns; the Calvinist religion, which welcomed Catholic and Jewish minorities in a spirit of tolerance; a regularly organized calendar in which festivals and penances were alternated; a love of family; and a widespread, unparalleled prosperity that was open to everyone. Free of ecclesiastical privileges and with no court or aristocracy as such, 17th-century Holland can be regarded as the first modern capitalist democracy.

■ Dating from about 1660, *The Linen Closet* (above) by Pieter de Hooch and *The Happy Family* (below) by Jan Steen illustrate different sides of life in "Golden-Age" Holland. In one, family life is governed by order and cleanliness, and, in the other, we see the debasement – and enjoyment – of a family in which adults set a bad example. Both works are in the Rijksmuseum, Amsterdam.

■ This popular allegorical picture from the second half of the 16th century satirizes the "Dutch cow", being ridden by the King of Spain, Philip II.

■ Gerard Houckgeest, *Funerary Monument of William the Silent at Delft*, 1651, Mauritshuis, The Hague. William of Orange (The Silent), assassinated in 1584, is considered the father of modern Holland and the hero of the rebellion against the Spanish. His monumental mausoleum, frequently visited by the Dutch people, also features in many other commemorative works.

Tulipomania

This painting by Ambrosius Bosschaert (c.1618, Mauritshuis, The Hague) shows several fancifully shaped tulip varieties in a range of different colors. Imported from Constantinople and the Levant at the end of the 16th century, these precious bulbs were the object of a trade that became increasingly widespread. From the flower beds of aristocratic gardens, tulips gained rapidly in popularity and became the focus of colossal speculative dealing. The collapse of the tulip market in 1638 had many serious repercussions, ruining dozens of small savers and putting the Dutch economy in crisis.

9

A family of craftsmen
on the banks of the Rhine

Weddesteeg is a road close to Leiden's city walls. Here, on July 15, 1606, the eighth and penultimate son of a miller – the owner of a windmill on the banks of the Rhine and thus known as "Van Rijn" (of the Rhine) – was born. Catholic in origin, the family had converted to Calvinism. The boy's parents, Harmen and Cornelia, chose the unusual name of Rembrandt for their newborn infant. They may have been hoping for a girl, whom they could have named after the maternal grandmother, Remigia. Married for 17 years at the time of the birth, Rembrandt's parents were no longer young; indeed, he always saw them as weighed down by a biblical agedness. According to tradition, the patronymic Harmenszoon ("son of Harmen") was added to the child's name, together with the surname Van Rijn. The effect was high-sounding, but the artist's origins were firmly rooted in the working class, as is evidenced by the trade plied by his brothers: the eldest was a miller, like his father, another became a baker, like his maternal grandfather, and a third a cobbler. The family was nevertheless fairly comfortably off, and could afford to educate the young Rembrandt at the Latin School in Leiden.

■ Rembrandt, *Portrait of the Artist's Mother,* c.1628, etching. Rembrandt's parents were no longer young at the time of his birth and the artist typically portrays them as elderly and grave figures, rather like biblical characters.

■ Rembrandt, *Landscape with Windmill* (detail), c.1650, Albertina, Vienna. Rembrandt's drawings often recalled his father's windmill.

■ Rembrandt, *The Artist's Father*, 1630, watercolor drawing, Ashmolean Museum, Oxford. This is the only identified portrait of Rembrandt's father, although his face appears in several of the artist's paintings.

HARMAN. GERRITS.

■ This map of Leiden, engraved by Pieter Bast and printed in 1660, shows the historical town centre surrounded by its protective walls and marked out by the Rhine flowing through it. In the area to the bottom left (circled) is the windmill that belonged to Rembrandt's family. The house where he was born was close by.

■ This 17th-century drawing, housed in Leiden's historical archive, shows the city's Latin School, where Rembrandt was educated. Although he cannot be described as an intellectual, Rembrandt nevertheless had a cursory knowledge of the classics and great respect for books and the printed word.

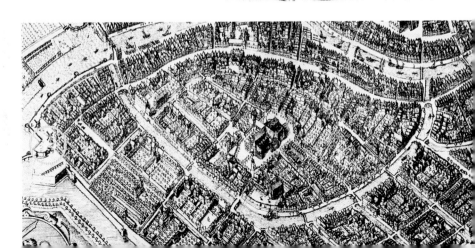

Leiden's "fine painting" and historical works

■ Rembrandt, *Anna Accused by Tobit of Stealing the Kid*, 1626, Rijksmuseum, Amsterdam. This is an early, sharply observed biblical work.

■ Rembrandt, *David Presenting Saul with the Head of Goliath*, 1625, Kunstmuseum, Basle. The splendor of Lucas van Leyden's engravings, the richness of Venetian 16th-century style, and the precious sparkle of gold all inspired Rembrandt to paint lesser-known biblical episodes and developed his taste for sumptuous narrative scenes.

The city of Leiden was one of the most important cultural centres in Holland during the "Golden Age". Roughly 40 kilometres from Amsterdam, it is held in great affection by the entire country, because of the extreme bravery with which it endured the Spanish siege in 1574. The city is criss-crossed by the canals formed by the Old Rhine, one of the two branches into which the great river divides once it reaches its intricate delta. In the early 17th century, Leiden boasted about 40,000 inhabitants and housed a dozen or so windmills, including the one belonging to the Van Rijns. The city's wealth lay mainly in its flourishing textile businesses and in the lively trade of its market, but it was above all a cultural city, with a renowned university and an impressive background in the humanities and the arts. It was in Leiden that a notable 16th-century artistic school developed, arguably the most important in Holland. Its key artist, Lucas van Leyden, was, like Rembrandt, a great painter and a skilled engraver, whose work was admired by Dürer. His elegant art, meticulous in the reproduction of detail and inspired by traditional religious themes, remained a specific point of reference for more than a century among Leiden's artists and collectors. It led to the so-called fine painting, the style adopted by the young Rembrandt.

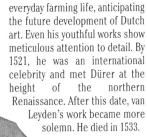

Lucas van Leyden

The main representative of the Leiden School, Lucas van Leyden was born in about 1494. A precocious engraver, it was as early as 1510 when he revealed his skill in pairing traditional sacred themes with subjects and characters drawn from contemporary, everyday farming life, anticipating the future development of Dutch art. Even his youthful works show meticulous attention to detail. By 1521, he was an international celebrity and met Dürer at the height of the northern Renaissance. After this date, van Leyden's work became more solemn. He died in 1533.

■ Lucas van Leyden, *The Adoration of the Magi*, 1513, engraving. Lucas van Leyden's Renaissance prints were widespread in Europe. Rembrandt owned a collection of them.

■ Isaac van Swanenburgh, *Aeneas in the Underworld*, Stedelijk Museum De Lakenhal, Leiden. Rembrandt's first teacher was an exponent of the local school and his style was linked to the tradition of Bosch. Besides painting, he also produced works in the applied arts, such as tapestries, and stained glass. Rembrandt's apprenticeship with Van Swanenburgh was workmanlike: he learned his craft rather than "art". It provided him with the opportunity for his first contact with Italian art, whose masterpieces he studied although he never visited the country.

■ Lucas van Leyden, *The Adoration of the Golden Calf*, central panel of a triptych, c.1530, Rijksmuseum, Amsterdam. This late work reveals an almost pre-Mannerist development in the art of the Dutch master.

A beginner's options

During the 1620s, painters throughout Europe were alerted to the news emanating from Rome: the revolutionary art of Caravaggio, who achieved astonishingly realistic effects through the use of diagonal light, corresponded with a rapid expressive development of the Baroque style and the result was a lavish tour de force of color and animation. Dutch art, too, came under the Italian influence, but the peculiarities of the local art market (which was aimed mainly at the bourgeoisie rather than the aristocracy or the Church) necessitated alternative solutions. Rembrandt's artistic training took place against this background of stimulus and debate. On the one hand, there was great historical painting, inspired by Italian models and the Antwerp school and dominated by Rubens; on the other, the singularly Dutch predilection for small, elegantly executed paintings, destined to be hung in ordinary houses and not in princely collections. Other factors were the Calvinist religion and a considerable Jewish presence, which fostered personal reflections on the Bible.

■ Jan Lievens, *Pilate Washing his Hands*, c.1625, Stedekijk Museum De Lakenhal, Leiden. Early paintings by Lievens, a close friend of the young Rembrandt, display a considerable confidence in composition, as well as a knowledge of Italian examples gleaned from the Caravaggesque Utrecht School.

■ Rembrandt, *The Martyrdom of St Stephen*, 1625, Musée des Beaux-Arts, Lyons. Dated and monogrammed "R f" (Rembrandt *fecit*), this medium-sized painting on panel is the first work that can be attributed with certainty to the artist, easily recognizable as the elegant, precious style of the Leiden School. The melodramatic gestures and the classical style of the faces, however, hark back to the period that Rembrandt spent in the workshop of Pieter Lastman.

■ Rembrandt, *Self-portrait*, c.1628, Rijksmuseum, Amsterdam. Because so many copies exist, it is difficult to establish just how many self-portraits Rembrandt produced. This is a "private" work, free in expression and consummately original in technique. To pick out the light on the the curly hair, Rembrandt dotted the canvas with the wooden tip of his paintbrush.

■ Hendrick Terbrugghen, *King David Playing the Harp*, c.1625, Muzeum Narodowe, Warsaw.

The Utrecht School

In the early decades of the 17th century, Utrecht was, perhaps, the foremost artistic centre of the United Provinces. In Calvinist Holland, it remained mostly Catholic and the city's painters drew their inspiration directly from Caravaggio. The leading figure was Gerrit van Honthorst, who promoted a taste for nocturnal scenes. Equally important artists included Hendrick Terbrugghen and Gerard Ter Borch, who applied the Caravaggesque style to their paintings of scenes drawn from everyday life.

1 6 0 6 – 1 6 2 7

The Parable of the Wealthy Simpleton

Signed and dated 1627, this small but important
early work is housed in the Staatliche Museen,
Berlin. The figure, an old, bespectacled man
examining a coin against the light of a candle,
has been interpreted in different ways.

■ A fundamental
precedent for the
realistic interpretation
of religious themes was
set by the *Calling of
St Matthew*, painted in
1600 by Caravaggio for
the church of San Luigi
dei Francesi in Rome.

■ Rembrandt, *Two Scholars Disputing St Peter and St Paul in Conversation)*, c.1628, National Gallery of Victoria, Melbourne. The books, candlestick, and light are borrowed from Caravaggio.

■ Hendrick Terbrugghen, *Calling of St Matthew* (detail), c.1620, Musée des Beaux-Arts, Le Havre. The best-known exponent of the Utrecht School, Terbrugghen introduced many Caravaggio-inspired figures into his work. Rembrandt's old man in *The Parable of the Wealthy Simpleton* has many affinities with this tax collector, in turn influenced by Caravaggio.

■ Gerrit van Honthorst, *Christ Before the High Priest*, c.1617, National Gallery, London. The candlelit scene was one of the effects most favored by early 17th-century artists and collectors throughout Europe. Gerrit van Honthorst produced some remarkable examples. Rembrandt thus cut his teeth on a difficult technique that was very much in vogue at this time.

The influence of Lastman

Rembrandt's artistic training ended in 1624 with a six-month stay in Amsterdam with the artist Pieter Lastman. The high quality of Lastman's work was in marked contrast to the artists with whom he had previously come into contact. Lastman was an established artist who was able to exercise a decisive influence on his talented pupil. Having returned to Amsterdam from Italy in 1610, Lastman was inspired by the international environment of Roman painting in the early 17th century. He was a typical historical painter, producing religious and mythological scenes destined for a public of connoisseurs. His style, which nowadays appears to be too serious and pompous, appealed to the Italianate taste of a section of the Amsterdam public. Rembrandt studied Lastman's work in detail, patiently copying his subjects and compositions. He mastered the art of precise draughtsmanship, the wide-ranging scene, and the reference to ancient models, but added to them a dynamism and feeling that Lastman's works never achieved.

■ Pieter Lastman, *The Angel and the Prophet Balaam*, 1622, Private Collection, New York. The difference between Rembrandt and Lastman can be illustrated by comparing this work by the older master (below) with the interpretation by his younger pupil (left). The main episode, with the prophet beating the ass and the animal's reaction, is very similar. In Lastman's painting, the angel remains essentially apart from the action and the light of an Italian landscape illuminates the work; in Rembrandt's version, the angel is more directly involved in the scene, making it much more dramatic.

■ Rembrandt, *The Angel and the Prophet Balaam*, 1626, Musée Cognacq-Jay, Paris.

■ Rembrandt, *Susanna Surprised by the Elders*, drawing, Kupferstichkabinett, Berlin. This drawing, executed with a confident technique, is a faithful reproduction of one of Lastman's most important works. A comparison between the master's original version and the pupil's copy reveals the detail with which Rembrandt studied Lastman's paintings. It also highlights the weakness of the original composition; Rembrandt widens the space between the figures, giving the scene a dramatic sweep that his teacher was unable to achieve.

■ Left: Pieter Lastman, *Susanna Surprised by the Elders*, 1614, Staatliche Museen, Berlin.

■ Below: Pieter Lastman, *The Baptism of the Ethiopian Eunuch*, 1623, Staatliche Museen, Karlsruhe. This unusual theme also inspired an early work of the same title by Rembrandt (right), painted in 1626 and now in the Museum Catharijne Convent, Utrecht.

19

The beginning of
a glorious career

A partnership with Jan Lievens

■ Rembrandt, *The Apostle Paul in Prison*, 1627, Staatsgalerie, Stuttgart. The sword leaning against the bed (an incongrous detail in a prison cell) is the traditional attribute that identifies St Paul.

Once he had completed his training with Lastman, Rembrandt returned to Leiden, now with professional prospects. At the age of 19, his destiny was clear. He set up a joint studio with Jan Lievens, another novice painter from Leiden, who was a year younger than Rembrandt and had also been a pupil of Lastman's. The two young artists worked closely together, their style and subject-matter almost playfully overlapping. They used the same models, painted portraits of each other, and competed in the painting of similar themes. Both introduced Italianate elements into their work (learned from Lastman and from their common admiration for the Utrecht artists), in the "fine painting" tradition of Leiden. Success, for the time being, was confined to their native city, but more widespread recognition for the pair would not be long in coming.

■ Rembrandt, *The Noble Slave*, 1632, Metropolitan Museum of Art, New York. During the years he spent in the studio shared with Lievens, Rembrandt developed a taste for the exotic, the unusual, and the picturesque. A comparison between this work and Lievens' oriental figure (left) reveals significant differences: Lievens' is composed and illustrative, while Rembrandt's is a much livelier interpretation.

■ Jan Lievens, *An Oriental*, c.1628, Sanssouci Castle, Potsdam. Lievens' work differs from Rembrandt's in its heavier volumes, which are more strongly defined by the shade.

■ Jan Lievens, *The Apostle Paul Writing the Epistle to the Thessalonians*, c.1629, Kunsthalle, Bremen. The two artists, who were themselves still very young, often painted elderly figures, expressively marked with wrinkles and with long, unkempt beards.

■ Jan Lievens, *Portrait of Rembrandt*, c.1629, Rijksmuseum, Amsterdam. The most unusual feature of the partnership between the two artists is their creation of "crossed" portraits, a game in which they swapped identities.

■ Rembrandt, *Self-portrait*, c.1629, Mauritshuis, The Hague. The piece of armor is deceptive: Rembrandt had no connection with any garrison, but the dignity of his stance reflects the pride of the young Dutch nation.

The Prophet Jeremiah Mourning over the Destruction of Jerusalem

Signed and dated 1630, this painting is housed in the Rijksmuseum, Amsterdam. The prophet Jeremiah laments the destruction and fire of Jerusalem, caused by King Nebuchadnezzar, who banished the Jews to exile in Babylonia.

■ Below: Rembrandt, *Old Man Sleeping By the Fire*, 1629, Galleria Sabauda, Turin. Rembrandt had painted this similar figure a year earlier, but this work has none of the dramatic enormity of Jeremiah's situation.

■ The face of the aged prophet presents features similar to Rembrandt's father Harmen van Rijn, who died shortly before this work was painted. There are no certain portraits of Harmen, however, although he appears in some works.

■ The painting's most unusual feature is the lavish and elaborately detailed goldwork. Rembrandt skilfully reproduces the precious metal, which glows with the reflection of what appears to be the fire ravaging the city of Jerusalem.

■ Jan Lievens, *Job on the Dungheap*, 1631, National Gallery of Canada, Ottawa.

Rembrandt's first pupil: Gerrit Dou

In February 1628, Rembrandt took on his first pupil, his fellow townsman Gerrit Dou, who was only 15 at the time. The acquiring of pupils (who paid a not inconsiderable sum to their teacher) was a clear sign of the artist's standing. Dou's arrival coincided with Rembrandt's first economic success: a painting that he transported on foot from Leiden to Amsterdam was sold in the capital for the more than respectable sum of 100 guilders. Dou remained in the workshop until Rembrandt moved to Amsterdam in 1632. He went on to become a master in his own right, and the most typical representative of the *fijnschilders* ("fine painters") of the Leiden School. He also carried out a civic role in his native city, being personally responsible for the founding of a guild of painters (1648). Born into a family of artists (his father was a glass engraver) and himself an artist of great skill and distinctive style, Dou concentrated exclusively on creating very small paintings, which he executed with a flawless technique and in minute detail. The years he spent with Rembrandt were fundamental to his artistic development, and he also painted some works in conjunction with his teacher.

■ Gerrit Dou, *Card Players by Candlelight*, Residenzgalerie, Salzburg. Dou specialized in genre paintings such as this candlelit scene.

■ Gerrit Dou, *The Young Mother*, Staatliche Museen, Berlin. Here, the realistic details are handled with a minute precision reminiscent of Flemish painting.

■ Gerrit Dou, *A Poulterer's Shop*, c.1670, National Gallery, London. Some of Dou's paintings feature exuberant, almost *trompe l'oeil* still lifes in the foreground, rendered with flourish and skill.

■ Gerrit Dou, *Self-portrait with Easel*, Private Collection.

■ Gerrit Dou, *Interior with Woman Eating Barley Broth*, c.1632, Private Collection. The model for the woman in profile in this youthful work is Rembrandt's mother, who would pose for her son's pupils.

Obsessive behaviour

According to some scholars, Dou's psychological make-up presents some interesting peculiarities. As we can see from his paintings, the artist was obsessed with cleanliness. Contemporary sources report a mania for keeping his studio austerely clean, to the point of restricting visits from outsiders to an absolute minimum. He was prone to outbursts of rage over what he saw as the "contamination" introduced by laborers or tradesmen who were less than scrupulously clean. The fear that there could be dust in his studio would make him stop work for days at a time. Unsurprisingly, his obsession meant that he could not take a wife. On the other hand, Dou would set out his palette, brushes, and other equipment with impressive care and perfect order. The object of much collector and academic interest, he painted a limited number of works, slowly, with an exasperating precision.

A turning point: the role of Constantijn Huygens

BACKGROUND

■ Above right, Jan Lievens, *Constantijn Huygens*, 1628–29, Rijksmuseum, Amsterdam.

The turning point in Rembrandt's career and that of his partner Lievens came with a visit to their studio by Constantijn Huygens in 1628. Secretary to Prince Frederick Henry of Orange and one of the most cultured and influential figures in Holland, he was an experienced diplomat and tireless traveller, and a moderately talented poet. His opinion, in matters artistic, carried considerable weight. In his autobiography, published in 1631, he describes a visit to two young painters of humble origin who were virtually unknown. The artists made a deep impression on him. Huygens found Lievens the more open-minded, and deeply inventive, of the two, whereas Rembrandt had a superior elegance of touch and was able to communicate intense emotion in his work. The young artists' destiny was mapped out by the visit. Huygens commissioned Lievens to paint his portrait and Rembrandt to paint his brother's. He followed the career of both artists for some years, assisting Lievens in his move to England and securing princely commissions for Rembrandt. For a while, he acted almost as their agent, submitting their works to international collectors. A fervent supporter of Dutch art and culture, Huygens stressed that although neither Rembrandt nor Lievens had ever been to Italy, their work stands on a par with the great masters of the past.

■ This 17th-century drawing of The Hague shows, in the foreground, Huygens' house, and the Mauritshuis, built for John Maurice, Count of Nassau-Siegen, and now the Royal Museum of Painting.

A sophisticated thinker

The United Provinces ambassador to Venice and, later, London, polyglot, scholar of astronomy, translator, and eminent man of letters, Huygens offers us a perfect example of the autonomy of 17th-century Holland. Highly skilled in recognizing and developing talent in the young, he inspired Rembrandt to focus on religious and mythological themes, such as this (below), and encouraged his own son Christiaan to study science. Christiaan Huygens went on to invent the pendulum clock, and his theories helped Newton to formulate his law of gravitation.

■ Thomas de Keyser, *Constantijn Huygens and his Clerk*, 1627, National Gallery, London. This illustrates the social prestige enjoyed by Huygens.

■ Right: *The Abduction of Proserpine* (1632, Staatliche Museen, Berlin) was painted by Rembrandt at the suggestion of Huygens.

■ Opposite: These two small portraits were painted by Rembrandt as a pair in 1632. The subjects are Constantijn's brother Maurits Huygens (above) and his friend the artist Jacob de Gheyn III (below). They are housed in the Kunsthalle, Hamburg, and the Dulwich Picture Gallery, London, respectively. They mark the beginning of the long and profitable friendship the artist shared with Huygens.

Family members as models

All his life, Rembrandt painted his relatives, choosing particular moments, poses, clothes, and hairstyles. The memorable series of paintings depicting his wife Saskia, arguably the most intense sequence of paintings ever to be devoted by an artist to his companion, was preceded and followed by countless others. Family members are usually shown as "characters", almost as though specializing in a few specific roles in a universal theatre, so works in which they feature can usually be viewed as interpretations rather than portraits. The artist's mother is an infirm, devoted old woman, his father a picturesque, gruff old man, his sister Lijsbeth a large, comely, and rather vacant-looking blonde, and his son Titus a child who discovers the beauty and wonder of the world for the first time. Saskia warrants a separate analysis. Her painted and engraved portraits tell the story of their marriage, from the joy of the early years to its dramatic conclusion.

■ Rembrandt workshop, *Young Woman with Embroidered Gown*, 1632, Pinacoteca di Brera, Milan. Recent studies have cast doubt on the attribution of this portrait, which can be identified with Rembrandt's sister Lijsbeth. In all likelihood, it is a workshop painting

■ Rembrandt, *Young Woman Holding a Fan*, 1632, Statens Konstmuseer, Stockholm. The girl portrayed is almost certainly the artist's younger sister Lijsbeth.

■ Rembrandt, *Old Woman in Prayer* (*"Portrait of the Artist's Mother"*), 1630, Rresidenzgalerie, Salzburg. Rembrandt's mother, unnaturally aged and wrinkled, acted as a model for her son on many occasions, becoming the very image of old age.

■ Rembrandt, *The Artist's Mother as the Biblical Prophetess Hannah*, 1631, Rijksmuseum, Amsterdam. The light of knowledge, reflected in the yellowing pages of the large tome, suffuses the entire picture with penetrating impact. The trepidation with which the old woman leafs through the pages of the Bible imbues the painting with a solemn awareness of the Word.

■ Rembrandt, *Old Man in a Fur Hat* (*"Portrait of the Artist's Father"*), 1630, Tiroler Landesmuseum, Innsbruck.

Portraits or character studies?

Rembrandt's repeated portrayal of his parents reveals a curious side to his role as a portraitist. These paintings are not strictly speaking portraits in the accepted sense of the term, that is, realistic images of recognizable figures, but rather character studies of a more psychological nature. Particular facial expressions, unusual features, hairstyles, exotic hats or clothing are used to echo the sitters' quirks. These character studies were called *tronijes* in Dutch and were highly sought after. Rembrandt executed a large number of these works, both painted and engraved.

Judas Returning the Thirty Pieces of Silver

In a private collection in England, this work dates from 1629. Constantijn Huygens praised its expressive power and the use of light, comparing it to the best of antiquity.

■ The contrite expression and the exaggerated pose of Judas are of clear theatrical derivation. From his earliest works, Rembrandt displayed a keen interest in the world of the theatre.

■ Rembrandt,
*Self-portraits with
Grimaces*, 1628–30.
Here, the study of
facial expressions
almost culminates
in caricature. Using
a mirror, Rembrandt
distorted his own
features in order to
achieve violent effects.

■ Rembrandt, *Concert
in Biblical Garb*,
1626, Rijksmuseum,
Amsterdam. Even in his
early works, Rembrandt
places his figures in
evocative settings, with
precious fabrics, great
tomes, carefully painted
objects, sumptuous

costumes, and a
profusion of gilded
elements. The artist
would collect assorted
objects to use as props
in his work. This taste for
opulence, which can be
traced back to the Leiden
tradition, characterized
his entire output.

■ Rembrandt, *The
Presentation in the
Temple*, c.1628,
Kunsthalle, Hamburg.
Expressive, rather
forced poses recur
throughout Rembrandt's
youthful works.

1632–1642

Rembrandt, *Saskia as Flora*, 1635, National Gallery, London.

The move to Amsterdam

H uygens' praise, the increasingly frequent visits from art lovers, his first economic successes, and his gradual detachment from the family environment after the death of his father in 1630 all combined to give Rembrandt a bold new idea. After meeting the Amsterdam art dealer Hendrick van Uylenburch, in 1631, Rembrandt invested the large sum of 1,000 florins in the trading of works of art. Van Uylenburch had many useful and influential contacts and an affluent, demanding clientele that was particularly interested in portraits. Recognizing Rembrandt's ambition, he offered him a particularly advantageous deal. The young artist left Leiden for good in July 1632 and moved to Amsterdam, the main mercantile and artistic centre in the country. Van Uylenburch offered him lodgings and a studio in an elegant part of the capital and acted as intermediary between Rembrandt and his clients. For a while, Rembrandt had to concentrate exclusively on portrait painting, in order to make his name known among the circle of collectors, art lovers, and Holland's wealthiest purchasers of works of art.

■ Rembrandt, *View of the River Amstel from the Blauwbrug, Amsterdam*, Rijksmuseum, Amsterdam. In his rare drawings of Amsterdam, Rembrandt records minor details and impressions of the city.

■ Right: Rembrandt, *Jesus and His Disciples in the Storm*, 1633, Isabella Stewart Gardner Museum, Boston. Following his move to Amsterdam, Rembrandt alternated between portraits and sought-after paintings of biblical or historical subjects. These were skilfully executed with the refined style and detailed structure of the Leiden School.

■ Rembrandt, *The Holy Family*, c.1634, Alte Pinakothek, Munich. Throughout his long career, Rembrandt painted religious works. In Calvinist Holland, such paintings were not intended for churches, but for collectors and private devotion. Rembrandt thus handles religious themes in both a grandiose, elegant manner and in a domestic, everyday context.

■ Rembrandt, *Self-portait with Wide-brimmed Hat*, 1631, engraving. Once he became successful, the artist's wardrobe became more elaborate and his pose more confident.

■ Jan van der Heyden, *The Internal Canals of Amsterdam*, Mauritshuis, The Hague. Thanks to his pioneering use of a camera obscura, van der Heyden has left us the most precise views of the Amsterdam townscape.

Merchants, customers, and intellectuals

■ Rembrandt, *Jan Uytenbogaert, the Gold Fisherman,* 1639, engraving. This prestigious figure had a clearly defined role for Rembrandt: as tax collector general, he had to pay him the fees due to him for the paintings he produced for the court at The Hague.

At the time of Rembrandt's move to Amsterdam, the city was enjoying a period of full economic, urban, and social development. The capital of an increasingly vast colonial empire (Nieuw Amsterdam was founded in 1626, subsequently ceded to the English and renamed New York), it charmed and fascinated its visitors. The thriving commercial port was packed with ships, and shops and markets sold goods from all over the world, with an opulence and choice that had no equal anywhere in Europe. The layout of the city was extended and made more regular through the creation of three wide concentric canals flowing through the old historical town centre. Studded side by side along one of these, the *Herengracht,* were beautiful stone and brick edifices, with the characteristic terraced façades, which were the comfortable dwellings of the wealthier merchants and professionals, many of whom were Rembrandt's customers. New churches, such as the Westerkerk, were built in a dignified Baroque style, as was the Stock Exchange, particularly interesting for its architectural features and at the heart of the city's commercial activity, dominated by the powerful East and West India companies.

■ Right: Cornelis de Man, *Group Portrait in the Chemist's House,* Muzeum Narodowe, Warsaw. Scientific activity abounded in Amsterdam after Descartes moved to the city in 1628.

■ Rembrandt, *Maarten Soolmans* and, right, *Oopjen Coppit*, 1634, Rothschild Bequest, Paris. Rembrandt gave the full-length portraits of the 1630s a sumptuous treatment. Men and women sport lace, bows, feathers, and puff sleeves, in works that hold their own, in terms of their finery, with the more high-flown portraits of the period, such as those by Van Dyck. The exuberance of Rembrandt's painting during this phase mirrors the success enjoyed by Frans Hals, the most popular Dutch portrait painter of this time.

■ Rembrandt, *Portrait of a Man Rising from a Chair*, 1633, The Taft Museum, Cincinnati. In some cases, Rembrandt indulges in more dynamic, intimate poses than those allowed under the rules set out for official portraiture.

The Anatomy Lesson of Dr Tulp

Housed in the Mauritshuis, The Hague, this fascinating and lively group portrait was commissioned in 1632. It was originally exhibited at the headquarters of the surgeons' guild in Amsterdam.

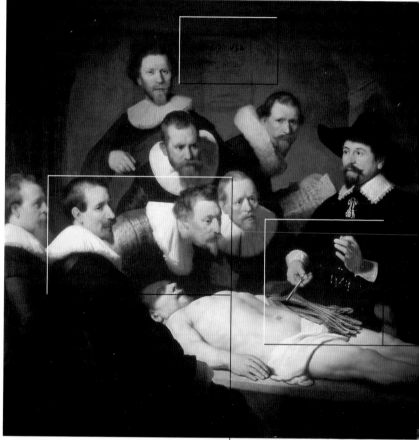

■ The seven figures gathered around the dissecting table are not medical people, but city officials. Their expressions reveal both a scientific interest and a justifiable repulsion.

■ Rembrandt's signature can be seen on the wall in the background and hints at his new-found awareness of his artistic merit. During his early years, the artist signed himself merely RHL (Rembrandt Harmenszoon of Leiden), or Rembrandt van Rijn. From 1632, however, he signed himself only with his forename, occasionally followed by the letter "f" (for the Latin *fecit*). In this way, the artist was following in the tradition of Italian masters of the 16th century, Titian, Raphael, Leonardo and Michelangelo.

■ Dr Tulp is dissecting the left arm of the corpse, exposing the tendons. With his left hand, he skilfully demonstrates the contractions and movements of the fingers. The anatomic precision indicates direct study on Rembrandt's part.

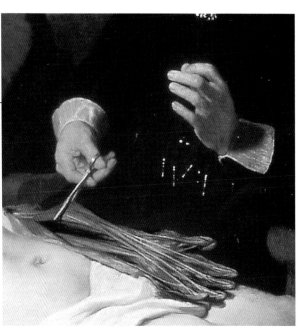

Saskia

Rembrandt met the twenty-year-old Saskia at the home of Hendrick van Uylenburch, his associate and dealer. She was a close relative of van Uylenburch. On the death of her father, who had been burgomaster of Leeuwarden, she had left the province of Friesland in order to settle in Amsterdam. A love affair developed between the young artist and the cultured, florid, and rather timid girl. Saskia and Rembrandt, defying the guarded reaction from her tutor and relatives, became officially engaged on June 5, 1633. Arrangements for the marriage were made, with Rembrandt's mother dithering for a long time before giving her consent. Finally, on July 22, 1634, Rembrandt and Saskia were married, having chosen to return to Saskia's native Friesland for the wedding. Rembrandt and Saskia enjoyed a mutually affectionate relationship, based on imagination, fun, and sensual fulfilment. For Rembrandt, the miller's son, the marriage also involved a considerable rise in his social status.

■ Rembrandt, *Saskia Wearing a Veil,* 1633, Rijksmuseum, Amsterdam. Saskia, from a considerably affluent family, brought a dowry of no less than 40,000 guilders to the marriage. Some of her relatives were envious of the large sum and would later accuse Rembrandt of squandering it.

■ Rembrandt, *Saskia in a Hat,* c.1635, Staatliche Museen, Gemäldegalerie, Kassel.

■ Rembrandt, *Heads of Three Women,* c.1634. Saskia recurs throughout Rembrandt's work, in paintings, drawings, and engravings. He often captures intimately tender expressions.

■ Rembrandt, *Saskia in a Straw Hat*, 1633, Kupferstichkabinett, Berlin. At the side of this drawing, Rembrandt wrote: "This is a portrait of my fiancée at the age of twenty-one, three days after our engagement".

■ Rembrandt, *Saskia as Flora*, 1634, State Hermitage Museum, St Petersburg. Here, the pose and clothing suggest pregnancy: in 1635 Saskia gave birth to a boy, Rombertus, who only lived two months.

A rapid ascent

Thanks to his successful marriage and the consistently high fees he earned as a painter and engraver, Rembrandt became a wealthy man almost overnight, on a par with highly respected professionals and members of high society. In 1635, at the age of 29, he was able to move out of van Uylenburch's house and take up residence in an elegant dwelling on the banks of the Amstel. At the same time, he rented a large warehouse and converted it into a studio, where he could also welcome an increasingly large number of pupils. Through his relationship with Constantijn Huygens, and their continuing correspondence, Rembrandt's name became known at the court at The Hague. He was thus able to receive many aristocratic commissions, the fees for which were, however, not always settled promptly. Shrewdly, he avoided openly endorsing any particular religious persuasion; this enabled him to paint for Catholics, Mennonites, and Jews alike in the cosmopolitan atmosphere of Amsterdam.

■ Rembrandt, *Pastor Johannes Elison*, 1634, Museum of Fine Arts, Boston. Rembrandt portrayed severe, clean-living pastors, interpreting their moral stance in a sober way.

■ Rembrandt, *Presumed Self-portrait as Standard Bearer*, 1636, Private Collection, Paris. The grandiloquent poses and showy clothes of Rembrandt's self-portraits of this period were in marked constrast to the portraits of black-clad Puritans. The happiest decade of Rembrandt's life and work is characterized above all by the sophisticated eclecticism of his models and style.

■ Rembrandt, *Artemisia or Sophonisba*, 1634, Museo Nacional del Prado, Madrid. The identity of the matronly heroine of this painting has not been identified with certainty. It may be Artemisia, wife of Mausolus, about to drink her husband's ashes mixed into a drink, or Sophonisba, Queen of Numidia, who chose to kill herself by drinking from a poisoned goblet rather than surrender to the Romans. Other suggestions have also been put forward. The model is undoubtedly Saskia.

■ Rembrandt, *Portrait of a Young Woman Holding a Fan*, 1633, Metropolitan Museum of Art, New York.

Rembrandt and women

There is no doubt that Rembrandt loved women. His all-consuming, deep love for Saskia was later replaced by stormier relationships, but his passion for women remained undimmed. Few other artists have succeeded in portraying women with the same intensity. His memorable interpretations of women's feelings and innermost secrets include portrayals of little girls, adolescents, young married women overcoming the embarrassment of coming out in society, mothers, pert servant girls, and failing old women who retained an inner wisdom.

Self-portrait with Saskia

This delightful painting is housed in Dresden's Gemäldegalerie and dates from 1635. A portrayal of utter happiness, it cheerfully expresses Rembrandt's joy in his marriage. He holds Saskia on his knee and raises a glass to us.

■ Saskia's expression betrays a certain embarrassment at the rather vulgar laughter of her husband. The scene has also been viewed as an interpretation of the parable of the prodigal son, who squandered his father's fortune on improper revelry. However, the genuine happiness expressed by the painting seems to contradict any possible intention to moralize.

■ Rembrandt, *Saskia Smiling in a Plumed Hat*, 1635; Gemäldegalerie, Dresden. In the *Self-portrait with Saskia* shown opposite, Rembrandt's wife appears polite and controlled. Here, she seems more relaxed; the plumed hat was clearly part of the collection of theatrical props that the artist kept in his studio.

■ Rembrandt, *Self-portrait with Saskia*, 1636, engraving. A different, somber atmosphere is expressed here. Rembrandt and Saskia appear to reflect on the destiny of a family struggling to establish itself: the couple's first three children (one boy and two girls) failed to live beyond two months.

47

Foreign exoticism and Calvinist sobriety

■ Rembrandt, *Head of a Man in Oriental Costume*, 1635, Rijksmuseum, Amsterdam. This is most likely a character study rather than an actual portrait of the sitter.

A love of anything new and extravagant, an inexhaustible curiosity, and the wish to possess whatever he painted are all characteristics that recur throughout Rembrandt's career. During his early years in Amsterdam, the artist experienced a daily onslaught of sights and sensations. An open, welcoming city, Amsterdam illustrates the two sides of 17th-century Holland: on the one hand, the pursuit of a sober, controlled family life that was mindful of proper behavior and respectful of the social hierarchy; on the other, an abundant cornucopia of all manner of goods that poured onto the quayside every day from foreign ports. During the 1630s, Dutch colonial expansion was at its height, with the consolidation of dominions in Brazil and the opening of emporia in various continents: Ceylon, Caracas, Pernambuco, Curaçao, Surinam, Java, the Moluccas, even faraway Tasmania. The Dutch fleet and army held their own against Spanish attempts to reconquer the country, but the true battles at this time were being fought elsewhere: Europe was ravaged by the Thirty Years War, and flourishing, wealthy Holland, which remained untouched by the conflict, came to be regarded as a kind of island of happiness.

■ Rembrandt, *Elephant*, British Museum, London. Rembrandt seized every opportunity to collect visual impressions. This drawing came about after a visit to the port at Amsterdam, where goods and natural curiosities from all over the world could be seen.

■ Rembrandt, *Portrait of Aechje Claesdr. Presser*, 1634, National Gallery, London. This old woman's expression and demeanour suggest moral and domestic virtues, and a parsimonious life.

■ Rembrandt, *Two Africans*, 1661, Mauritshuis, The Hague. Regarded as a preparatory sketch for a painting that was never executed, this shows Rembrandt's interest in different physical types. People from the Dutch overseas colonies were a common sight in Amsterdam.

■ Rembrandt, *Portrait of a Man in Polish Costume*, 1637, National Gallery of Art, Washington, DC. Fur-trimmed clothing and hats came into fashion at this time, in imitation of Polish or Hungarian models.

■ Rembrandt, *The Amsterdam Merchant Nicolaes Ruts*, 1631, The Frick Collection, New York. The pursuit of exoticism was important to Rembrandt as a necessary antithesis to the propriety of the Dutch Calvinists, whose dress deliberately reflected their morality and sobriety of attitude. Ruffs were the only permissible affectation.

The engravings

Rembrandt is without question one of the greatest engravers of all time. His graphic output is impressive for the number and variety of its subjects, his consummate knowledge of the technique, and his expressiveness. Small genre sketches alternate with large, highly elaborate compositions, produced in various versions, each with slight variations. For Rembrandt, prints fulfilled a different function to painting, but remained first and foremost a formidable field of figurative research. He only seldom translated subjects he had already treated in his paintings into engravings. It was more usual for him to study totally new themes, innovatively developing the possibilities underlying the relationship between black and white, light and shade. The skill with which Rembrandt printed the plates, the exceptional control he exercised over the chemical solutions necessary to the etching process, and the knowledge that he could produce a considerable number of copies convinced him that engravings could help him in the teaching of his craft, especially in the workshop. Much of Rembrandt's earnings came from engravings, but would later prove insufficient to save him from financial ruin.

■ Rembrandt, *The Raising of Lazarus*, engraving. Rembrandt's pupils worked on this composition, no doubt stimulated by the open theatricality of the gestures, the unusual viewpoint (from Jesus' shoulders), and by the original treatment of light and shade. An example of these exercises is the painting by Carel Fabritius (see page 63).

■ Rembrandt, *Ecce Homo*, 1636, etching. Here, Rembrandt has taken the engraving from a previous, monochrome painting (dated 1634), which is now in London's National Gallery.

■ Rembrandt, *The Hundred Guilder Print*, 1639–40, etching and dry-point. Even today, this magnificent composition continues to fetch high prices.

■ Rembrandt, *Jesus Preaching to the People* (*"Le petit tombeau"*), etching. This famous, frequently copied scene is powerful in its structure and luminosity.

■ Rembrandt, *St Jerome in an Italian Landscape*, etching and dry-point. In this work, Rembrandt reproduces a landscape he has never seen.

Italian and Flemish models

Constantijn Huygens, the first and most authoritative person to discover Rembrandt's talent, had early on noticed the particular affinity between the Leiden artist's work and the great classical artists, particularly the Italian masters and the school of Rubens at Antwerp. Rembrandt constitutes a spectacular exception in Baroque painting: he never undertook the obligatory journey to Rome and, indeed, hardly left his native Holland. Many reasons can be put forward for his decision: his profound indolence, the need to keep up an intensive working pace without "wasting time" on long journeys, the ready availability of important Italian works on the Amsterdam art market, and the widespread circulation of copies and engravings. Rembrandt was well-versed in Renaissance and Baroque art: his painting is far from self-contained or "spontaneous". On the contrary, he was constantly aware of the need to have his work endorsed at the highest level.

■ Pieter Paul Rubens, *The Descent from the Cross*, 1609–11, Courtauld Gallery, London. This oil sketch was for the great altarpiece in Antwerp Cathedral.

■ Rembrandt, *The Descent from the Cross*, 1632–33, Alte Pinakothek, Munich. Although he never went to Antwerp, Rembrandt was familiar with Rubens' altarpiece through works such as that shown far left, or through engravings or drawings. *The Descent from the Cross* is part of a group of religious paintings Rembrandt produced for the court at The Hague, a commission organized by Constantijn Huygens.

■ Above: This splendid and rare engraving of the *Madonna and Child* is an example of the care Rembrandt always took over figurative models. He used a print by Mantegna (below) as the basis for this extraordinarily luminous work, which he would certainly have had in his collection. The particularly intimate treatment of this theme is also found in the work of engravers from the previous century, such as the Italian Jacopo Francia (shown above right is a detail of a *Holy Family* by him) and the northern European Renaissance master Albrecht Dürer. The latter, a supremely gifted engraver, produced a number of versions of the *Madonna and Child*.

53

The Raising of the Cross

This is the first in a series of five paintings on Christ's Passion destined for the court of the House of Orange at The Hague. Work on the series, which is now in the Alte Pinakothek in Munich, began in about 1633.

■ *The Entombment of Christ* was completed in 1639, together with the *Resurrection*. Progress on the Passion cycle for Prince Frederick Henry of Orange was overshadowed by the delay with which the artist's fees for the commission were paid and by aesthetic changes of heart by the House of Orange.

■ *The Resurrection of Christ* (1639) is extraordinarily inventive in its luminosity and composition. The Passion paintings all share the same format – 92 x 70 cm (36 x 27 in) – and a rounded outline at the top, in the style of a small altarpiece. The skilfully rendered chiaroscuro effects echo those in Rembrandt's engravings.

■ *The Resurrection of Christ*, dating from 1636, can be placed midway between *The Raising of the Cross* and *The Descent from the Cross* (c.1633) and the two paintings executed in 1639. During this time, Gerrit van Honthorst had become court painter at

The Hague. Rembrandt later sold two further scenes: an *Adoration of the Shepherds* (now in London) and a *Circumcision*, which has been lost. The two paintings were purchased as finished works and were not commissioned.

1632–1642

Collectors, friends – and creditors

R embrandt participated actively in Amsterdam's social life. In 1632 he was already regarded as a prominent figure, even receiving the visit of a legal official who had been sent to confirm the actual existence of a hundred well-known personages following a bet waged by two high-living citizens. Commissions by Huygens and the court, his contact with Dr Tulp (twice burgomaster of Amsterdam and a widely respected physician), his partnership with an established dealer such as van Uylenburch and, of course, his marriage to Saskia placed Rembrandt in a strong, enviable position. The portraits he executed during the 1630s, both painted and engraved, are a consummate record of Amsterdam's highest social circles. It is interesting to note his more indifferent portrayal of Catholics, Jews, Calvinists and Baptists, Mennonites, and members of some other congregations. Rembrandt had many friends and admirers but some of them would, within just a few years, turn into rapacious creditors. The artist went from success to ruin in just 15 years.

■ Rembrandt, *Portrait of Nicolaes van Bambeeck, Husband of Agatha Bas*, 1641, Musées Royaux des Beaux-Arts, Brussels. This portrait was one of a pair with a portrait of the sitter's wife, Agatha Bas (opposite). A comparison between the two works reveals their differing states of repair.

■ Frans Francken and David Teniers' *Interior of a Picture Gallery* (Courtauld Gallery, London) gives us an idea of a typical Flemish art collection of about 1640. Alongside religious paintings, there are a considerable number of "bourgeois" works, such as portraits and landscapes. The paintings are stacked, or propped on furniture.

■ Reproduced opposite and left are two landscape engravings by Rembrandt: *Windmill in the Kemmerland* and the so-called *Six's Bridge*.

■ Rembrandt, *Portrait of Agatha Bas*, 1641, Royal Collection, Buckingham Palace, London. The sitter seems to look out of a window, in a skilful *trompe l'oeil* effect.

■ Rembrandt, *Jan Six*, 1647, etching. The original luminosity of this scene, with Rembrandt's friend Six reading casually by a window, was imitated many times by Dutch painters in the centuries that followed.

Jan Six

One of Rembrandt's closest friends, Jan Six occupied a special place in the artist's life. Wealthy and cultured, he wrote poetry and tragedies, had open political ambitions, shared Rembrandt's taste for collecting, and often helped him out financially. According to a highly credible anecdote, Rembrandt produced the drawing for *Six's Bridge* while enjoying a day out on his friend's estate – during a break over lunch while a servant went to fetch some mustard between courses.

The Blinding of Samson

Now in the Städelsches Kunstinstitut, Frankfurt, this, Rembrandt's most violent work, dates from 1636. Rembrandt presented it to Constantijn Huygens in gratitude for the support he had received at court.

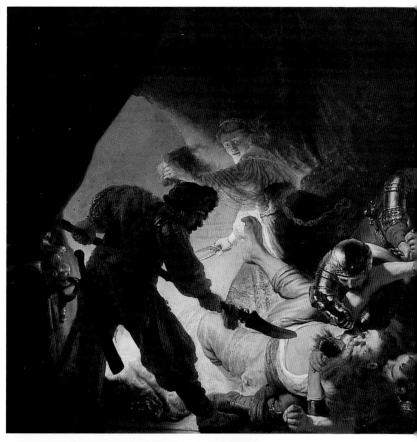

■ The dynamism and drama in the painting recall the work of Caravaggio, particularly *The Martyrdom of St Matthew* (1600–01) in the church of San Luigi dei Francesi in Rome.

■ Rembrandt, *Samson Betrayed by Delilah*, 1629–30, Staatliche Museen, Berlin. Rembrandt was clearly very interested in the story of Samson, returning to it several times in his career. This work, which captures the very moment of Samson's betrayal, is typical of Rembrandt's early period, while he was still working with Jan Lievens in his native Leiden.

■ Rembrandt, *Samson Threatening his Father-in-Law*, c.1635, Staatliche Museen, Berlin. With his characteristic adherence to the biblical text, Rembrandt explores the story of Samson in all its detail, finding minor episodes among the Scriptures that are almost genre scenes. Here, the religious meaning is overshadowed by the characterization.

■ Rembrandt, *Samson's Wedding Feast*, 1638, Gemäldegalerie, Dresden. This delicate composition reveals affinities with Leonardo's *Last Supper*.

The workshop

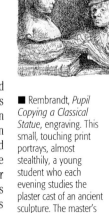

Throughout his life, Rembrandt invested much energy in his role as workshop master. Even when he was very young, at the time of his partnership with Jan Lievens in Leiden, he would take in pupils and co-workers, who were often very talented. Not only did the students boost the work carried out in the workshop, but they also paid handsome fees for the privilege of studying with the master – although Rembrandt never exploited this, spending long hours tutoring his apprentices personally. During the 1630s, his workshop's quota of pupils was so high as to put Rembrandt's organizational skills very much to the test. The artist rented a large disused warehouse and set up his workshop there, dividing the space into autonomous little rooms for his students by means of partitions and drapes. His co-artists could thus work undisturbed (although the partitions were often ribaldly dismantled to reveal the presence of a nude model) and also take group lessons, in which they were invited to reproduce life compositions and make use of Rembrandt's collection of costumes and theatrical props.

■ Rembrandt, *Pupil Copying a Classical Statue*, engraving. This small, touching print portrays, almost stealthily, a young student who each evening studies the plaster cast of an ancient sculpture. The master's observation of the pupils' struggle to come to grips with the secrets of art is both amused and affectionate.

■ Rembrandt may have executed these two engravings (with a model seated in the half-shade and another with an oustretched leg) for teaching purposes. They are typical "academy" engravings, produced with a view to studying specific postures of the male nude. Such studies were mainly carried out to instruct pupils, who had the opportunity to observe and copy the master's own work with posed models in the studio – a useful exercise in developing their craft.

■ Constantijn van Renesse, *Annunciation*, Kupferstichkabinett, Berlin. This drawing, certainly executed in Rembrandt's workshop, presents a number of vigorous corrections made by the master, showing the care he took in reviewing his pupils' work.

■ Rembrandt's relationship with his pupils is well illustrated by the *Good Samaritan* by Govaert Flinck (Wallace Collection, London, above), which is directly based on Rembrandt's engraving of the same subject (left). Flinck has omitted the embarrassing detail of the dog defecating in the foreground.

Theatre in Amsterdam

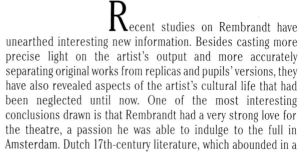

■ Govaert Flinck,
*Portrait of Rembrandt
Dressed as a Shepherd,*
c.1636, Rijksmuseum,
Amsterdam. This is one
of many examples of
how Rembrandt enjoyed
adopting different
guises for portraiture.

Recent studies on Rembrandt have unearthed interesting new information. Besides casting more precise light on the artist's output and more accurately separating original works from replicas and pupils' versions, they have also revealed aspects of the artist's cultural life that had been neglected until now. One of the most interesting conclusions drawn is that Rembrandt had a very strong love for the theatre, a passion he was able to indulge to the full in Amsterdam. Dutch 17th-century literature, which abounded in a variety of different publications, also included some notable dramatic texts. In spite of the more rigorous Calvinists viewing the excesses of the stage with suspicion, the theatre continued to thrive. Vondel, Holland's foremost 17th-century poet, was a prolific dramatist and even Rembrandt's friend, the collector Jan Six, penned a *Medea* in the classical manner. Cultured theatre alternated with travelling shows, particularly during festivals or markets: actors' poses, expressions, and costumes provided Rembrandt with a fascinating world from which he could draw inspiration.

■ Rembrandt, *The
Suicide of Lucretia,*
1664, National Gallery,
Washington, DC. Here,
the classical heroine
strikes a distinctly
theatrical pose. The
first female actress
appeared on the
stage at Amsterdam
in about 1640, creating
something of a scandal.

■ Rembrandt, *Seated Actor*, c.1635, Courtauld Gallery, London. Actors' excessive costumes and brash poses were a constant source of inspiration for Rembrandt, who is likely to have enjoyed Amsterdam's theatrical world and the many travelling shows performed in the city's theatres and streets.

■ Carel Fabritius, *The Raising of Lazarus*, c.1640, Muzeum Narodowe, Warsaw. Some of Rembrandt's own works, as well as those of his pupils, point to the performance of small but well-coordinated plays. Models and pupils would "pose" together, mimicking episodes from life or the Bible, which would then be copied by other pupils. This elegant painting is the work of one of Rembrandt's most gifted pupils, Carel Fabritius. Like his brother Barendt, Carel moved to Delft and was important in the artistic development of Jan Vermeer.

1632–1642

A house fit for a successful artist

During the first ten years Rembrandt spent in Amsterdam, he moved house frequently. From his lodgings in van Uylenburch's house he gradually progressed towards larger and more elegant dwellings. In January 1639, the artist spotted the house of his dreams, where he could settle his family and his rapidly growing collections of art and assorted objects. It was a stone and brickwork building dating from the beginning of the 17th century and located in a fairly central part of Amsterdam. Rembrandt paid the owners, Pieter Belten and Christoffel Thijssens, the handsome sum of 13,000 guilders. The artist was earning good money, and felt he could afford the house, even if the sum had to be paid in instalments. After lengthy negotiations, he took possession in May 1639, paying one-quarter of the purchase price as an advance and undertaking to pay the balance over the next five or six years.

■ Rembrandt's house in Sint Anthonisbreestrat, Amsterdam is now a museum housing some of the master's most important works. He and Saskia moved into the house in early May 1639; it was the most luxurious house the artist had ever lived in. The extremely high purchase price and running costs, however, were to bring about his financial ruin.

■ Rembrandt, *Copy after Raphael's "Portrait of Baldassare Castiglione"*, 1639, Graphische Sammlung Albertina, Vienna. Auctioned on May 9, 1639 by the dealer Lucas van Uffelen, Raphael's painting fetched 3,800 guilders. Rembrandt bid for it but was defeated by Alfonso Lopez, an art dealer and diamond merchant.

■ Rembrandt, *Self-portrait at the Age of 34*, 1640, National Gallery, London. The painting is directly inspired by Raphael's *Portrait of Baldassare Castiglione*. Evidently, having acquired the painting at auction by bidding against Rembrandt, Alfonso Lopez allowed him to study the work. The Dutch master's interpretation remains a memorable example of delicacy in its treatment of light and color.

■ Rembrandt, *Self-portrait Leaning on a Stone Sill*, 1639. Rembrandt's satisfaction at having scored a victory in a financial argument with Saskia's parents is evident.

■ Rembrandt, *Esther Preparing to Intercede with Ahasuerus*, c.1633, National Gallery of Canada, Ottawa. Rembrandt owned the precious fabrics worn by his sitters in his works.

■ Michiel Sweerts, *A Painter's Studio*, Rijksmuseum, Amsterdam. In this work, Rembrandt's pupil seems to mirror the chaotic interior of the master's workshop, with many apprentices at work among casts of ancient statues, models posing, a variety of objects, and noble clients looking on. It seems impossible that anyone would have been able to concentrate in such an environment, but some of Rembrandt's greatest masterpieces were executed in a fascinating and confused atmosphere very similar to this.

The Mennonite Minister Cornelis Anslo

A member of the Mennonite minority, Cornelis Claeszoon Anslo was one of Holland's most famous preachers. This painting, dating from 1641 and now in the Gemäldegalerie (Staatliche Museen), Berlin, shows him with his wife.

■ Positioned in the most luminous part of the composition, the book and candelabra assume a particular significance. All his life, Rembrandt continued to remember the power, light, and depth of the written word, in particular the Bible. Here, the symbolic meaning is emphasized by the relationship between books and candelabra – both sources of illumination.

■ Rembrandt, *Portrait of Cornelis Anslo*, 1640, drawing, British Museum, London.

■ Rembrandt, *Portrait of Cornelis Anslo*, 1640, drawing, British Museum, London. The contact between Rembrandt and Anslo began with this drawing. The preacher sits at his desk, with an open book on the book-stand and another large volume in his left hand.

The pose was retained for the engraved version; the face and dress remained essentially unchanged even in the painted version. However, the scene was expanded to take in his wife, which inspired Rembrandt to use the effective device of a dialogue between the couple.

■ Rembrandt, *Portrait of Cornelis Anslo*, 1641, etching. This version represents the second stage in Rembrandt's progression towards the final oil painting. The artist seems to have risen to the challenge set by the poet Vondel: "Rembrandt should paint Cornelis' voice because his outward appearance is the least of the man; the invisible can only be intuited by hearing. Whoever wants to see Anslo, must listen to him". Rembrandt, indeed, only dwells briefly on the preacher's features; the gesture that accompanies what Anslo is saying, the visibly moved expression of the woman, and the ineffable light of knowledge that illuminates the entire scene are totally in keeping with Vondel's expectations, and breathe life into one of the most intense "voice portraits" to be found in the entire history of painting.

■ Rembrandt, *The Shipbuilder and his Wife*, 1633, Royal Collection, Buckingham Palace, London. As we can see from other masterpieces, such as *The Happy Couple* and *The Jewish Bride*, Rembrandt painted several scenes of conjugal intimacy. Here, the severe engineer appears to be irritated by his wife's interruption.

The guilds

■ Right: Nicolaes Pickenoy, *The Guard of Captain Jan Vlooswijck*, 1642, Rijksmuseum, Amsterdam. Works such as this serve to highlight the exceptional novelty of Rembrandt's paintings.

■ Willem Kalf, *Still Life with the Drinking Horn of the Guild of the St Sebastian Archer's Guild*, c.1653, National Gallery, London. This lavish still life gives us an idea of the pomp that characterized the gatherings of the Dutch guilds, described in contemporary chronicles as glamorous gastronomic exploits. In the background is the symbolic horn used for libations and toasts. This magnificent 16th-century artefact is housed in Amsterdam to this day.

The history of Holland in the 17th century, the proud vindication of the United Provinces' independence, and the way in which the cities had successfully protected themselves against danger (fire, flood, crime, vagrancy): all were factors in arousing a keen sense of national and civic solidarity in the Dutch population. This was expressed through all kinds of guilds – associations of merchants or artisans formed for the mutual aid and protection of their members. Parades, commemorative ceremonies, and banquets hosted by the main guilds abounded. Like anywhere else, however, Holland was no stranger to excess, and the strictest Calvinist preachers constantly thundered against ostentation and profligacy. Without a proper, blood aristocracy, the more elevated Dutch circles established their superior position in society through their involvement with the highest professional bodies. Leading or presiding over such an organization was a recognition of prestige, and this status was often demonstrated by the commissioning of works of art and group portraits to decorate the headquarters. Rembrandt had many professional contacts with guilds, corporations, and civic bodies, which led to some of his finest masterpieces, such as the two *Anatomy Lesson* paintings, commissioned by the Guild of Surgeons, the group portrait of the Clothmakers' Guild, known as *The Syndics*, and, of course, *The Night Watch*.

■ Right: Bartholomeus van der Helst, *Banquet of the Civic Guard*, 1648, Rijksmuseum, Amsterdam. The guilds' convivial social gatherings culminated in feasts, at which legendary quantities of fine and expensive foods were consumed. Van der Helst engagingly portrays the members of the Civic Guard at table, gathered to celebrate the Peace of Westphalia.

■ Frans Hals and Pieter Codde, *The Company of Captain Reynier Reael*, 1636, Rijksmuseum, Amsterdam. Predating Rembrandt's *Night Watch* by just a few years, this large-scale painting represents the peak of official, "posed" group portraiture. Unlike Rembrandt's masterpiece, the figures here, rather stilted and self-conscious, are clearly aware of having to adopt poses and expressions that befit their status. Frans Hals' fresh brushstrokes and lively style, however, prevent any risk of monotony or repetitiveness from seeping into the work.

1632–1642

Preparing for a masterpiece

T en years after *The Anatomy Lesson of Dr Tulp*, Rembrandt began work on another group portrait: the militia company of Captain Frans Banning Cocq, the masterpiece better known by the erroneous name of *The Night Watch*. This was an extremely prestigious commission, intended to be the unquestionable apex of the master's career. In tackling this enormous painting, Rembrandt revised and re-assessed every single stage in his artistic training and in the earlier part of his output: the unsurpassed liveliness of his portraits, richly elaborate compositions, and a depth of color reminiscent of Venetian Renaissance painting. *The Night Watch* is nothing less than the perfect synthesis of Rembrandt's stylistic choices. As with *The Anatomy Lesson of Dr Tulp*, it provides a wholly original but coherent interpretation within the context of a clearly defined, typically local tradition. Perfectly integrated into Dutch customs and culture, of which he was a conscious and satisfied exponent, Rembrandt was nevertheless able to draw on foreign models when appropriate, without any reverential timidity in tone or dimension.

■ Jakob Backer, *The Company of Captain Cornelis de Graeff*, 1642, Rijksmuseum, Amsterdam. Executed in the same year as *The Night Watch*, and similar in subject-matter, this work remains faithful to the descriptive tradition.

■ Rembrandt, *Belshazzar's Feast*, c.1635, National Gallery, London. At the age of about 30, Rembrandt displayed a keen interest in strongly dramatic scenes, with great figures involved in emotional situations. The Hebrew script on the wall, reads: "God hath numbered thy kingdom, and finished it".

■ Rembrandt, *Portrait of Menasseh-ben-Israel*, 1636, etching.

■ Rembrandt, *The Last Supper, after Leonardo da Vinci*, c.1635, Kupferstichkabinett, Berlin. Leonardo's supreme model was crucial in Rembrandt's exploration and understanding of the group portrait.

Mene mene tekel: a linguistic enigma

Like Titian, whose heir he regarded himself, Rembrandt displayed a keen sense of curiosity and a tireless desire for knowledge and understanding. This led him occasionally to come across insoluble problems. A typical example is the feast of Belshazzar, who, in the middle of the banquet, sees a mysterious hand writing an illegible prophecy on the wall. To understand why Belshazzar was unable to read the divine script, Rembrandt turned to Menasseh-ben-Israel, a Jewish man of culture, who solved the arcane mystery by explaining that the characters were intended to be read vertically and not horizontally.

The Night Watch

Executed in 1642 and now in the Rijksmuseum, Amsterdam, this is Rembrandt's largest and most famous painting and one of the most important works in 17th-century European art. The title by which it is commonly known in no way reflects the scene depicted, which actually takes place in daylight. This is a portrait of the civic militia of Captain Banning Cocq. Destined for the seat of the Civic Guard in Amsterdam, the work was paid for by 16 of the sitters, in varying amounts according to their position.

■ The group of figures, all shown in motion, includes 28 adults and three youths. The presence of a fair-haired little girl, wearing a light dress with a chicken strapped to her belt, has given rise to debate. The child, who looks frightened, occupies an almost central position, to the left of Captain Cocq and below the standard bearer.

■ Contrasting with the severe, authoritative expression of the captain is the fancily dressed and rather frivolous-looking Lieutenant Willem van Ruytenburgh, the most luminous figure in the entire painting.

■ The central figure in the action is Captain Frans Banning Cocq, shown in the act of preparing the men for a parade. Defying the traditional convention of static portraits, Rembrandt opts for a moment of action and dynamism.

Hurtling towards disaster

The death of Saskia

Rembrandt's life has provided many opportunities for novels and film interpretations: the most central events – and the key to understanding the master – are those that took place in 1642. Rembrandt was at the peak of his fame and economic success thanks to a number of factors: the favourable reception of *The Night Watch* and *The Hundred Guilder Print;* the support of his many pupils; the growing requests for works of art; and the praise of art writers. Parallel to all this success, however, came a series of bereavements: having already buried both his parents, Saskia's cherished sister, and three of his children who died in infancy, Rembrandt now faced the gravest loss of all – Saskia. After giving birth to Titus (who was baptized in September 1641), the physical strain of childbirth was compounded by tuberculosis and she was unable to recover. Aged just 30, Saskia died on June 14, 1642. After a provisional burial, she was laid to rest on July 9 in the left-hand transept of the Oudekerk.

■ Rembrandt, *The Farewell of David and Jonathan*, 1642, State Hermitage Museum, St Petersburg. This biblical painting clearly reflects the personal vicissitudes undergone by the artist himself: the embrace between David and Jonathan becomes a moving farewell between Rembrandt and Saskia.

■ A memory of happier years: Saskia leans out of a window in a watercolor drawing by Rembrandt, now in the Museum Boymans van Beuningen in Rotterdam. The many pictures Rembrandt has left us of Saskia are a kind of private diary charting the course of their marriage, which was clearly rich in intensity and feeling.

■ Rembrandt, *Saskia as Flora*, 1641, Gemäldegalerie, Dresden. In this last portrait of the dying Saskia, there are circles under her eyes, she is visibly frail, and her hair is dry and faded. Rembrandt does not forget her gentle smile, however, and gives her the tender gift of a single red flower. The contrast between this moving portrait and the flourishing pictures of Saskia as Flora in earlier years, in which she is shown surrounded by a multitude of flowers, is striking. It captures the awareness of imminent death and expresses an eternally enduring declaration of love.

■ Rembrandt, *Death Appearing to a Wedded Couple*, 1639, etching.

Testament and burial

On June 5, 1642, nine days before her death, Saskia made her last will and testament. She left half of her dowry of 40,000 guilders (we do not know if the money was still available, because Rembrandt was exempted from having to draw up an inventory) to her husband and half to Titus, with the clause that the money should not be administered by the Chamber of Orphans, but by Rembrandt himself. Twenty years after Saskia's death, the artist was forced to sell the tomb in the prestigious Oudekerk, and to have her ashes moved to the Westerkerk.

Women in Dutch society

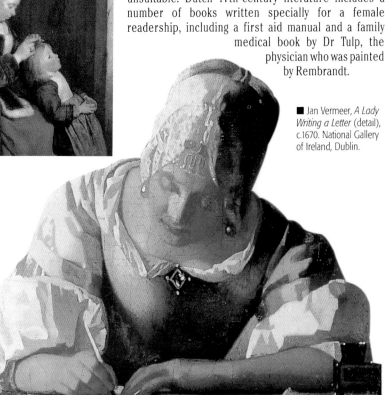

■ Gerard Ter Borch, *Looking for Head Lice*, 1653, Mauritshuis, Amsterdam. The principal role played by women in the Dutch family was to maintain order, keep a clean house, and look after the children.

Saskia's death was not just a personal tragedy for Rembrandt but also the start of a series of difficulties in the organization of his family life. Women played a key role in Dutch society, one that was essentially moral and organizational as opposed to the more "financial" role undertaken by the men. Women managed the home, cared for the children (both for the sake of the family and for the nation as a whole, as a number of widely circulated pamphlets on hygiene and housewifery admonished), and, with the assistance of a servant girl, were responsible for keeping the house impeccably clean. A medium level of schooling ensured that Dutch ladies were moderately cultured, although they were discouraged from knowing about books, authors, or subjects that were considered unsuitable. Dutch 17th-century literature includes a number of books written specially for a female readership, including a first aid manual and a family medical book by Dr Tulp, the physician who was painted by Rembrandt.

■ Jan Vermeer, *A Lady Writing a Letter* (detail), c.1670. National Gallery of Ireland, Dublin.

■ Pieter de Hooch, *The Larder*, 1658, Rijksmuseum, Amsterdam. In the Calvinist society, the mother's duty within the family was above all to teach her children how to keep house properly. Many of De Hooch's paintings show mothers instructing their daughters in matters of housewifery.

■ Jan Miense Molenaer, *The Harpsichord Player*, 1635, Rijksmuseum, Amsterdam. The woman portrayed in this picture may be Judith Leyster, Molenaer's wife and a gifted painter in her own right. Leyster is an example of a an emancipated female artist, fully aware of her role in society.

■ Gabriel Metsu, *The Sick Child*, c.1660, Rijksmuseum, Amsterdam. Dutch women were renowned throughout Europe for the affectionate way in which they cared for their children. Hugs, kisses, and the attention lavished on children were repeatedly remarked on by travellers and chroniclers.

Women and art: the case of Judith Leyster

A female artist of considerable talent features in the history of Dutch 17th-century art: Judith Leyster, a near-contemporary of Rembrandt's, is not as well known as she ought to be because, to this day, many of her paintings continue to be attributed to her first teacher, Frans Hals. Born in Haarlem in 1609, Leyster learned her craft in the workshop of the great portrait painter and fellow townsman Hals. Towards 1629, she moved to Utrecht. Her style is characterized by bold, quick brushstrokes and is rich in dense, Caravaggesque touches. After her marriage to her colleague Molenaer, Judith Leyster followed his example and took up genre painting.

A Woman in Bed

Dating from 1645 and now in the National Gallery of Scotland, Edinburgh, this painting shows a girl drawing back the drapes of her bed. It may be a biblical subject, possibly Sarah waiting for Tobias on her wedding night.

■ Rembrandt, *A Girl Leaning on a Stone Pedestal*, 1645, Dulwich Picture Gallery. Much later, works such as this were greatly admired by the Impressionists.

■ Samuel van Hoogstraten, *Young Girl Behind a Door*, The Art Institute, Chicago. Here, Rembrandt's pupil borrows elements of his teacher's style.

■ Nicolaes Maes, *Young Girl at a Window*, c.1655, Amsterdam, Rijksmuseum. For a long time wrongly attributed to Rembrandt, this is in fact the work of one of his most sensitive and original pupils.

■ Rembrandt, *Young Girl at a Window*, 1651, Statens Konstmuseer, Stockholm. In his private works, Rembrandt began to experiment with the long, separate brushstrokes that would characterize the style of his later paintings.

Titus and Geertje

Left with the nine-month-old Titus when Saskia died, Rembrandt employed Geertje Dircx as nurse and housekeeper. A widowed farmer's wife from Zeeland, she carried out her duties with energetic efficiency. Illiterate but sensible, rugged, and healthy, she was the very antithesis of Saskia. Before long, she had become the artist's mistress. Rembrandt's affections were now shared between tenderness towards his infant son and a private liaison that, more than reprehensible, was decidedly scandalous within the upright context of official Calvinist society. Rembrandt was not involved with the religious community and spent more than he earned, often on extravagant purchases. He kept exotic animals as pets (including an almost inconceivably filthy monkey that was grossly out of place in a clean Dutch home) and was conducting a blatant affair with his child's nurse. All of these things compromised his fame in his own country, although foreign art writers and collectors still took an interest in his work. His family life had meanwhile found a certain stability, but his relationship with Geertje was soon destined to turn sour.

■ Rembrandt, *A Woman in Dutch National Costume*, c.1638, British Museum, London. Titus' nurse was a rough country-woman from the northern Zeeland region.

■ Rembrandt, *Woman at a Window*, 1656–57, Staatliche Museen, Berlin. After Saskia's death, Rembrandt's love life became complicated. While Geertje was still mistress of the house, he began a liaison with Hendrickije Stoffels. She posed as model for this painting, which echoes a work by Palma the Elder.

■ Rembrandt, *The Holy Family with a Cat*, 1646, Staatliche Museen, Gemäldegalerie, Kassel. The *trompe l'oeil* of the parted curtain, in front of the figures, is cleverly executed.

■ Rembrandt, *Titus at his Desk*, 1655, Museum Boymans van Beuningen, Rotterdam.

■ Rembrandt, *Geertje Dircx (?)*, Teylers Museum, Haarlem. This painting may show Geertje seen from behind, with the young Titus barely sketched in at the side.

83

The Holy Family with Angels

Painted in 1645 and now in the State Hermitage Museum, St Petersburg, this affectionate painting is part of a large number of works devoted to the birth and early childhood of Jesus – no doubt related to Titus' early years.

■ Rembrandt, *the Holy Family at Night*, c.1645, Rijksmuseum, Amsterdam. The fragile concept provided by traditional religious iconography is discarded in favor of a scene of immediate, moving realism. The deep evening shadows, the frail light emanating from the child asleep in his crib, and the reflection on the "three ages of man" suggested by the presence of the mother and grandmother combine to make this one of Rembrandt's most touching works.

■ Rembrandt, *The Woman Taken in Adultery*, 1644, National Gallery, London. This work represents a return to the "fine painting" of Rembrandt's early years.

■ Rembrandt, *The Adoration of the Shepherds*, 1645, Alte Pinakothek, Munich. Even if we can trace elements of previous works in this painting, this is still a powerful picture. It is part of a group of canvases devoted to biblical subjects, not executed to a commission but marketed independently.

A new social order

■ Rembrandt, *The Unity of the Country*, c.1640, Museum Boymans van Beuningen, Rotterdam. This monochrome painting can be interpreted as a complex allegory on the need for union and concord among the United Provinces, in the wake of the dramatic and bewildering events of the Thirty Years' War. In terms of technique, it is a remarkable example of a deliberately "unfinished" work, with some parts merely sketched in.

The memorable Battle of the Downs in 1639 banished once and for all the threat of a Spanish reconquest of the Dutch territory. The United Provinces were, however, continually obliged to look for new allegiances among other European powers. At home, the political situation was relatively stable (only Leiden, Rembrandt's native city, displayed occasional instances of social hardship) and the Dutch people were unanimously united in upholding a few basic values: the tolerance of foreign communities and different religions, a strongly nationalistic feeling, the perfect organization of all social strata: family, neighborhood, city, state. This led to an intolerance of people who dropped out of society – tramps, gypsies, and people of no fixed abode – and promoted the constant pursuit of new guilds and business partnerships. A new generation of merchants and financiers gradually came to run the Dutch economy and, by extension, to dominate the collecting of works of art. The seat of government was at the Hague, with the *stadhouder* based in a luxurious court. The republic was changing, almost unconsciously, into the stable monarchy of the House of Orange.

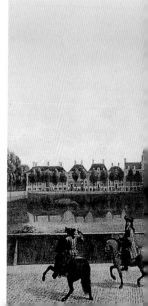

■ Govaert Flinck, *The Company of Captain Albert Bas*, 1645, Rijksmuseum, Amsterdam. After *The Night Watch*, civic guard companies requested livelier and more dynamic group portraits than had been the norm in the past. The taste for this particular type of collective picture persisted for a long time in Holland.

■ Rembrandt, *Portrait of Nicolaes Bruyningh*, 1652, Staatliche Museen, Gemäldegalerie, Kassel. The subject typifies the new, dashing type of Dutch gentleman.

■ Gerrit Berckheyde, *View of the Binnenhof at The Hague*, Mauritshuis, The Hague. This impressive, originally medieval building, which faces a romantic little lake, housed the Orange court and remains the seat of the Dutch government to this day.

87

A clash with the law: friends turn away

One of the clauses in Saskia's will stipulated that Rembrandt must not remarry or he would forfeit half his inheritance. The artist now lived through a very difficult period in his life. Patrons' tastes were changing and the morally upright Calvinists condemned his personal life as seriously improper. Rembrandt lived openly with Geertje, spent large sums of money on bizarre collector's items, and practiced no religion. Gradually, friends disowned him and some pupils left his studio. Only Jan Six remained constant in his support and also helped the artist out financially. On January 24, 1648, Geertje made her own will and testament, naming Titus as her sole heir. The jewels that had belonged to Saskia were to be part of the inheritance. A few months after this, when the relationship between Rembrandt and Hendrickije Stoffels had become evident, Geertje sued the artist for breach of promise, accusing him of reneging on a proposal of marriage. The tribunal found in favor of Rembrandt, but stipulated that he should pay a considerable annual pension to Geertje. In 1649, the master countersued Geertje for pawning Saskia's jewellery. The lengthy lawsuit ended on October 23, 1649; Geertje was detained in the women's house of correction in Gouda, but Rembrandt still had to keep up the annual pension payment of 200 guilders.

■ Rembrandt, *Homer Reciting his Verses*, 1652, Six Collection, Amsterdam. During his years of financial hardship, Rembrandt repeatedly turned to the classical literature for inspiration, particularly to Homer. The blind bard appears in many of Rembrandt's works dating from the 1650s.

■ Rembrandt, *A Woman Sleeping (Hendrickije Stoffels)*, 1655–56, British Museum, London.

■ Rembrandt, *Hendrickije Stoffels*, c.1652, Musée du Louvre, Paris. Stoffels acted as a witness for the artist in the suit brought against him by Geertje.

■ Rembrandt, *Portrait of Jan Six*, 1654, Six Collection, Amsterdam. This is one of Rembrandt's most important portraits. Six (who was also the author of the first catalogue of Rembrandt's etchings) adopts an impatient pose, pulling on his gloves. As this was a portrait destined for a friend, Rembrandt was able to apply the color loosely, with large brushstrokes, in a manner similar to Titian's late style. The painting has always remained in the Six family collection.

■ Rembrandt, *Self-portrait*, 1652, Kunsthistorisches Museum, Vienna. Here, the artist presents himself as a craftsman.

A masterpiece lost and found: Danaë

Every museum in the world wants to acquire works by Rembrandt, but detailed research carried out by the Rembrandt Research Project has led to a general reassessment of attributions, which may have been too hastily determined in earlier years. A group of extremely important works (excluding, of course, the masterpieces housed in Amsterdam's Rijksmuseum) is to be found in the State Hermitage Museum in St Petersburg. Many beautiful works that are crucial to an understanding of Rembrandt's painting, especially his mature and late period, found their way to the former capital of Tsarist Russia, founded by Peter the Great, a champion of Dutch painting and culture. Among the most prized works, *Danaë* has had a singular history. Repeatedly revised by the master, the splendid mythological figure inspired by Titian was badly damaged by a vandal, who hurled corrosive acid at the canvas. The painting was withdrawn for many years, and regarded as a lost masterpiece. It was exhibited in public again in the spring of 1998, after lengthy and successful restoration work.

■ Rembrandt, *The Abduction of Ganymede*, 1635, Gemäldegalerie, Dresden. Ganymede, wetting himself in fear, is engagingly drawn.

■ Rembrandt, *Danaë*, 1636–54, State Hermitage Museum, St Petersburg. Rembrandt touched up this work several times over the course of 18 years.

■ Rembrandt, *The Angel Stopping Abraham from Sacrificing Isaac to God*, 1635, State Hermitage Museum, St Petersburg.

■ Rembrandt, *Diana Bathing*, 1634, Wasserburg Anholt Museum, Anholt. This work, classical in feel, was most likely suggested by Constantijn Huygens, who encouraged Rembrandt to devote himself to the classical themes of mythology and ancient literature.

1642–1657

A Woman Bathing in a Stream

Regarded by some as a portrait of Hendrickije Stoffels, this painting, which used to be regarded erroneously as unfinished, dates from 1654 and is in the National Gallery, London.

■ Rembrandt,
*Bathsheba with King
David's Letter*, 1654,
Musée du Louvre, Paris.
Bathsheba has just
received David's love
letter and is perplexed,
because she is married
to Uriah. Here, too, the
model is most likely to
have been Hendrickije.

■ Rembrandt,
*Andromeda Tied to the
Cliff*, c.1629, Mauritshuis,
the Hague. Rembrandt
loved to paint heroines
of religion and literature
caught in situations
of difficulty.

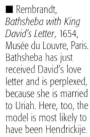

■ Cornelis van Haarlem,
Bathsheba, 1594,
Rijksmuseum, Amsterdam.
A fine example of late
Mannerism, this painting
was certainly an important
compositional source for
Rembrandt's *Bathsheba*.

Changing tastes

In 1648, the Peace of Westphalia put an end to the bloody Thirty Years' War and new political scenarios meant a redrawing of the map of Europe. The threat to Holland now came from the sea: from 1651, Dutch admirals engaged in a series of naval battles with the English. At stake was control over the commercial routes in the North Sea. After a few serious defeats, the Dutch were forced to review their colonial policies; they abandoned settlements in Brazil and concentrated on landing-places on routes to the Orient, founding Cape Town in 1652. The 1650s also saw a change in taste on the part of Dutch collectors and the general public. They purchased sumptuous paintings, luxuriant still lifes, elaborate landscapes, and works that were more courtly in tone than the descriptive, popular works that had prevailed in previous decades. The new generation, born after the hard-fought, glorious war of independence against Spain, did not share the excessive rigour of their elders, tending to favor a more exuberant, decorative style and painting that could convey the feeling of wealth acquired.

■ Below: Jan van der Heyden, *The Martelaarsgracht in Amsterdam,* Rijksmuseum, Amsterdam. Unlike Pieter Saenredam's severe views, van der Heyden's urban landscapes were immensely successful.

■ This still life by Willem Kalf (Thyssen-Bornemisza Collection, Madrid) features luxury objects such as a Chinese porcelain bowl.

94

■ Jan Steen, *The Feast of St Nicholas,* Rijksmuseum, Amsterdam. Jan Steen provides us with the most intimate, amusing scenes of Dutch private

life. Here, a group of children enjoy their Christmas gifts. The little girl is overjoyed with her doll, while the rascal next to her, who has received nothing, whines.

■ The most significant novelty in the Dutch artistic taste of the mid-17th century was the demand for lavish still lifes, triumphs of luxury, such as this one by Abraham van Beyeren in the Rijksmuseum.

■ Gérard de Lairesse, *The Emperor Augustus Patronizing the Arts,* 1667, Muzeum Narodowe, Warsaw. The paintings by De Lairesse, formerly a pupil and an imitator of Rembrandt's reflect the new, classical taste of collectors in the Netherlands in their titles and themes. A comparison with works by Rembrandt dating from the same period reveals marked similarities.

Rembrandt's genre paintings: still life and landscape

From his earliest years, Rembrandt clearly favored historical painting as a genre and produced works based on biblical, mythological, or literary stories, which may be compared with the Italian Renaissance tradition. Although he was an excellent portrait painter, and portraits progressively became the most profitable part of his painterly activity, he preferred the "great" subjects. Paintings by him that may be included in the development of the so-called genre painting popular with Flemish and Dutch collectors, therefore, are very rare. There are, however, about a dozen pure landscape paintings (generally not regarded as being among the artist's most impressive masterpieces) by Rembrandt, together with a few works that can be linked to the development of the still life. It is here that Rembrandt stands far apart from the new Dutch taste. At a time when people buying works of art wanted rich and elaborate compositions, he painted a dramatic picture, such as *The Slaughtered Ox*, a metaphor for death.

■ Rembrandt, *Girl with Dead Peacocks*, c.1639, Rijksmuseum, Amsterdam. Rembrandt uses the dead bird hanging by its legs in a strongly narrative manner, in a picture in which the girl's feelings of curiosity, fear, and compassion prevail.

■ Jan Baptist Weenix, *Dead Partridge*, c.1657, Mauritshuis, the Hague. Dutch still lifes made frequent, skilful use of the *trompe l'oeil* device.

■ Rembrandt, *Landscape with a Stone Bridge*, c.1636, Rijksmuseum, Amsterdam. This is possibly Rembrandt's most famous landscape. Equally important, and often more spontaneous and direct, are his many landscape drawings and engravings.

■ Rembrandt, *Self-portrait with Bittern*, (detail), 1639, Gemäldegalerie, Dresden. The hidden meaning of this highly unusual treatment of the self-portrait has yet to be explained.

■ Rembrandt, *The Slaughtered Ox*, 1655, Musée du Louvre, Paris. A memorable painting, frequently imitated and reinterpreted (for example, by Picasso and Bacon), this work is based on the direct observation of butchers at work. In between the sketch and the finished painting, the butchers were removed to allow the enormous carcass to take centre stage.

Emerging artists and cities: Vermeer of Delft

Halfway through the 17th century, a precious, refined painter began his artistic career: Jan Vermeer, whose surname is often qualified by the addition of his native city of Delft to avoid confusion with other artists of the same name. Today, Vermeer is regarded as one of the greatest and most intense European 17th-century painters, but he was not very successful in his day and, after his death, was quickly and almost entirely forgotten. Paintings by his own hand are undoubtedly very few but they are nevertheless sufficient to illustrate the turning point in art that they brought about. Although remaining within the Dutch tradition and taste, Vermeer did not restrict himself to an affectionate description of family and other scenes; instead, he looked for their inner meaning. Cityscapes, domestic interiors, conversations in houses are all pictures drawn from reality, with skilful light effects, but not only visible reality. What Vermeer was really interested in was the soul within his subjects.

■ Jan Vermeer, *Servant Pouring Milk*, 1658–60, Rijksmuseum, Amsterdam. This painting led to the "rediscovery" of Vermeer. Noticed by the English painter Joshua Reynolds at the end of the 18th century, the work had gone from collection to collection. Finally acquired by the Rijksmuseum, the serious, well-built girl is almost a symbol for 17th-century Holland as a whole: flourishing and parsimonious, physically heathly, and morally virtuous.

■ Jan Vermeer, *The Glass of Wine*, 1655–60, Staatliche Museen, Berlin. Not all Vermeer's paintings exalt chaste femininity. The glass of wine, consumed to the dregs, is a well-known metaphor for sexual availability.

■ Jan Vermeer, *Officer and Laughing Girl*, 1655–60, Frick Collection, New York. The expedient of showing the soldier against the light serves to bring the viewer closer to the girl.

■ Vermeer, *Sleeping Girl*, c.1657, The Metropolitan Museum of Art, New York. Vermeer's best-known paintings are immersed in an atmosphere of silence and intimacy. Here, the viewer almost feels as though he ought to tip-toe out of the room so as not to disturb the girl's slumber.

■ Jan Vermeer, *View of Delft*, 1660–61, Mauritshuis, The Hague. Proust's enthusiasm for this painting, one of the most famous literary celebrations of a painting, emphasizes the success enjoyed by Vermeer in European culture from the end of the 19th century. The Impressionists were also instrumental in contributing to a renewed interest in the Dutch master.

Italian collectors

The considerable difficulties that Rembrandt encountered in the Dutch art market of the 1650s were partly offset by the interest shown in his work by cultured people and collectors throughout Europe. Among these was the Sicilian nobleman Antonio Ruffo, who entered into a long correspondence with the artist. Besides engravings (Ruffo purchased about 200 of these), Rembrandt also sent him some of his paintings: the first and most popular was *Aristotle Contemplating the Bust of Homer*, for which Ruffo paid eight times more than the average sum charged by Italian artists. This was followed by the *Homer* that is now in The Hague, sent unfinished and returned to Rembrandt to be completed, and *Alexander the Great*. A debate arose over this last painting: Ruffo complained that it was made up of four pieces of canvas, roughly stitched together, and Rembrandt offered to take it back and paint a new, but much more expensive version. Two versions of the work exist.

■ Rembrandt, *Homer Dictating to a Scribe*, c.1660, Statens Konstmuseer, Stockholm. This drawing is a variation of the painting in The Hague. The patron, Antonio Ruffo of Messina, wanted to build up a kind of triptych: with Aristotle representing philosophy, Homer poetry, and Alexander the Great active life.

■ Rembrandt, *Homer*, 1663, Mauritshuis, the Hague. A surviving fragment from a larger composition partly destroyed in a fire.

■ Rembrandt, *The Man in Armor*, 1655, City Art Gallery, Glasgow. It is most likely that this, and not the replica housed in the Gulbenkian Foundation, Lisbon, is the painting Rembrandt sent to Antonio Ruffo.

■ Rembrandt, *Self-portrait with Chain and Pendant*, 1668, Uffizi, Florence. This was bought by Cosimo III de' Medici for the self-portrait collection in the Uffizi after meeting the master during a journey to Holland.

■ Rembrandt workshop, *Portrait of Rembrandt with Throat-Piece*, 1634, Uffizi, Florence. The master's signature is not certain. This may be a work produced in the workshop under the direct supervision of Rembrandt.

Rembrandt in the Uffizi

Three works bear Rembrandt's name in the Galleria degli Uffizi, Florence, a shrine to Italian Renaissance painting. These are a portrait of an old man in a chair (*Old Rabbi*) of 1661 and the two self-portraits shown here. The interest taken by the Medici in Rembrandt's work is the most significant evidence of the master's fame outside Holland, which had reached as far as the heart of Italy. The purchase made by the future Archduke Cosimo III during a study trip to Amsterdam was followed by Cardinal Leopoldo de'Medici's stormy choice of the youthful self-portrait (even though the attribution was doubtful), which he bought just after Rembrandt's death.

Aristotle Contemplating the Bust of Homer

Now in New York's Metropolitan Museum, this painting dates from 1653. It was painted for the Italian collector Antonio Ruffo, who asked Guercino for a painting that would complement it.

■ Rembrandt, *David Playing the Harp Before Saul*, 1656, Mauritshuis, The Hague. Here, the feeling aroused by the music is comparable to that produced by poetry in *Aristotle Contemplating the Bust of Homer.*

■ Rembrandt, *Portrait of Floris Soop as Standard Bearer*, 1654, The Metropolitan Museum of Art, New York. Portraits dating from this period reveal a similar, inner feeling: the sitters, elaborately costumed, are engrossed in their own private thoughts.

■ Rembrandt, *Moses with the Tables of the Law*, 1659, Staatliche Museen, Berlin. During his years of financial ruin, Rembrandt's solitary heroes grew in dramatic expression.

■ Rembrandt, *Portrait of an Old Man with a Gold Chain*, c.1631, The Art Institute, Chicago. Aristotle's clothes, hat, and chain recall Rembrandt's youthful character studies, such as this, but the manner in which the color is applied is radically different.

103

Ruin

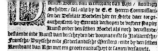

■ This notice was posted in the streets of Amsterdam to publicize the sale at auction of Rembrandt's possessions in a room of the De Keyserkroon Hotel.

Asa result, among other things, of the recession caused by the war against England, creditors began to put pressure on Rembrandt. The artist had been able to keep them at bay in 1650, thanks to an official valuation of his possessions. Now, however, the situation was grave. In 1653, he asked Jan Six and other friends for help and, putting up his own works as guarantee, he managed to cobble together the money to pay Christoffel Thijssen, the former owner of the house on Sint Anthonisbreestrat, of which Rembrandt had taken possession in 1639 with a down payment of just part of the selling price. With interest added on, he still owed 8,470 guilders. In 1654, Hendrickije gave birth to a girl, for whom Rembrandt once again chose the name Cornelia. He remained in severe financial difficulties, not least because some of his customers were rejecting works they had already bought and demanding a refund. He tried to transfer the ownership of the house to Titus, but the Institute of Orphans opposed the idea. In July 1656, an official inventory of the artist's possessions was drawn up: there were 363 items, including entire collections of drawings, engravings, and paintings by Italian and Flemish masters. Everything was sold in September 1656 for roughly 600 guilders, a derisory sum. In February 1658, the artist's house was sold at auction for 11,2118 guilders. The sale marked the end of a dismal, anguished period.

■ Rembrandt, *Clement de Jonghe,* 1651, etching. Rembrandt hoped to earn more money from the sale of engravings.

■ This late 17th-century Dutch painting, with its jumble of assorted chattels, gives us an idea of what auctions at this time were like.

■ Rembrandt, *Four Orientals under a Tree* (copy after an Indian miniature), c.1656, British Museum, London. Among the rare pieces auctioned was a group of Moghul school miniatures, studied and copied by the master.

■ Rembrandt, *Abraham Entertaining the Angels*, 1656, engraving. As this engraving also shows, Rembrandt did not collect exotic works for mere collecting purposes, but also as original sources of inspiration for his work.

■ Rembrandt, *Self-portrait*, 1657, National Gallery of Scotland, Edinburgh. Despite his economic ruin, Rembrandt's art from this period was indisputably excellent.

■ Rembrandt, *Hendrickije Stoffels*, c.1660, The Metropolitan Museum of Art, New York. Hendrickije displayed an unexpected resilience in adversity.

Jacob Blessing the Sons of Joseph

Now in the Gemäldegalerie, Kassel, this painting dates from 1656. The complex iconography is drawn in a literal manner from a passage in Genesis.

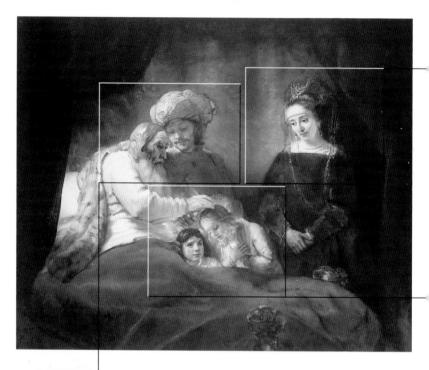

■ The dominant figures in the compositions are the aged Jacob and his son Joseph. The elderly patriarch sits up in bed with some difficulty in order to bless one of his grandsons, effectively entrusting him with the family destiny and the people of Israel. Joseph, however, rebukes his father, who has chosen not the firstborn but his younger brother.

■ Rembrandt's attention and faithfulness to the biblical text has become almost proverbial. Here, however, the artist permits himself a slight departure, inserting a person who does not figure in the text, but who is fundamental for the compositional and psychological balance of the scene: Asenet, Joseph's wife, looks on.

■ Jacob's hand rests on Ephraim's blonde hair. The child bows delicately in a gesture of humility. Next to him is his elder brother Manasse, who is smaller, darker and clearly saddened by his grandfather's incomprehensible favoring of Ephraim.

■ Rembrandt, *Portrait of a Man in a Fur Coat*, 1654–56, Museum of Fine Arts, Boston. Dating from the same period as *Jacob*, this work is similar to it in style, with wide, richly colored brushstrokes, undoubtedly inspired by Titian, to whose work Rembrandt's style grew increasingly close.

Self-portrait Holding his Palette, Brushes and Mahlstick, c.1665, Kenwood House, London.

Titus, Rembrandt's great hope

Rembrandt adored his son Titus. He was also the father of a daughter, born at the beginning of his relationship with Hendrickije Stoffels, but Titus was a living, bittersweet memory of Saskia, who had died not long after his birth. Rembrandt watched the boy grow up with love and pride. Blonde, refined, and, intelligent, Titus appeared to be delicate, however, and his early death proved dramatically that his health had never been good. The beautiful portraitsof him painted by Rembrandt express a powerful feeling of affection and protectiveness. Titus returned his father's love wholeheartedly: he was a source of comfort to Rembrandt during the dark years of penury and was also of practical help to his father (the artist signed over all his possessions to his son, to escape the claims of his creditors). It was Titus who replaced Saskia as the inspiration for some of Rembrandt's most moving masterpieces.

■ Rembrandt, *Portrait of Titus Dressed as a Monk*, c.1660, Rijksmuseum, Amsterdam. Titus harboured no monastic leanings: Rembrandt liked to paint his son dressed up in a variety of unusual costumes.

■ Rembrandt (and workshop?), *Portrait of Titus in a Hat*, c.1660, Musée du Louvre, Paris. Like other members of the family (the artist's mother, Saskia, and his sister), Titus was also painted many times by both the master and his pupils. There was such a strong mutual affection between Rembrandt and his family that it is almost inconceivable for Saskia or Titus to have posed for other colleagues. The belief that they may have done has held up the historical and critical analysis into the master's work.

■ Rembrandt, *The Artist's Son Titus*, c.1658, Wallace Collection, London. Here, the figure of Titus seems to be enveloped by his father's concern and care for him.

■ Rembrandt, *Portrait of Titus Reading*, c.1658, Kunsthistorisches Museum, Vienna. In this tender portrait of the young Titus in all his callowness, wonder, and hope, Rembrandt's feelings are clear. The painting becomes an inner diary, an avowal of fatherly affection.

The group portraits of Frans Hals

■ Frans Hals, *The Merry Drinker*, c.1635, Rijksmuseum, Amsterdam. This is one of the artist's most famous portraits, full of life and good cheer. The sitter offers us a glass with his left hand, openly inviting us to join him in a toast.

Oₙe of the most representative and important Dutch 17th-century painters was actually Belgian: Frans Hals was born in Antwerp shortly after 1580. His Flemish origins may account for the luxuriant exuberance of his work, which can be compared to the paintings of Pieter Paul Rubens. His entire artistic life, however – he began late, after the age of 30 – was spent in the beautiful, wealthy, and commercially lively city of Haarlem, in the agricultural heartland of Holland, among endless fields and canals dotted with windmills. Frans Hals introduced a note of vibrant cheer into this restful but rather dull landscape. His portraits, especially those dating from his early mature phase, display an explosive power, particularly through their obviously quick, color-laden brushstrokes. Almost exclusively a portrait painter, Hals excels in busy group scenes, crowded with figures: solemn banquets, commemorative works, parades of members of the civic guard, hospital governors. His main works are housed in the museum named after him in Haarlem. He died in 1666.

■ Frans Hals, *Officials of the Guard of St George*, 1639, Hals Museum, Haarlem. Frans Hals' group portraits are richly varied. Here, he arranges his sitters according to a complex hierarchy of importance, with the most prominent at the front.

■ Frans Hals, *Isaac Massa and his Wife*, 1622, Rijksmuseum, Amsterdam. The couple's happiness enlivens the whole painting, certainly one of the most cheerful in 17th-century Dutch art. The background recalls Haarlem's late Mannerist painting, but Hals counterbalances this with a new compositional structure that gives the scene a *plein air* effect.

■ Frans Hals, *Officers of the Civic Guard of St Hadrian at Haarlem*, 1627, Frans Hals Museum, Haarlem. The exuberant use of color is one of the characteristic features of Frans Hals' mature style, when he was fully confident in the handling of large groups on canvas.

■ Frans Hals, *The Governors of the Hospital of St Elizabeth*, 1641, Frans Hals Museum, Haarlem. In later years, Hals's figures, often in black, became more sober and severe.

113

The Syndics

In 1662, having regained favor with Amsterdam patrons, Rembrandt painted *The Portrait of the Syndics of the Clothmakers' Guild* (sometimes known as *The Syndics*), now housed in the Rijksmuseum, Amsterdam.

■ Rembrandt, *Three Members of the Clothmakers' Guild*, Kupferstichkabinett, Berlin. From the earliest sketches, at the heart of the composition is the book of cloth samples, which the members of the Clothmakers' Guild (Syndics) are studying.

■ Rembrandt, *A Member of the Clothmakers' Guild*, Rijksmuseum, Amsterdam. Rembrandt prepared the painting over a long time, producing several drawings portraying the members both individually and collectively and exploring alternative viewpoints.

■ Rembrandt, *A Member of the Clothmakers' Guild Standing*, Museum Boymans van Beuningen, Rotterdam. This drawing, lively in its immediacy, shows the figure about to stand up. The pose is a clever expedient chosen by Rembrandt in order to animate the scene, departing from the rigid structure of traditional group portraits.

■ Ferdinand Bol, *The Governors of the Amsterdam Leper Hospital*, 1649, Rijksmuseum, Amsterdam. This similar painting by one of Rembrandt's pupils shows an illustrative and narrative precision, in contrast to Rembrandt's overall inventive power.

Amsterdam's new town hall

The Dam is the nerve centre of Amsterdam. The square opens out in the dense network of streets and canals in front of one of the most imposing buildings in the city, the royal palace. The name, and its royal connection, however, are historically recent: this great building started out as a town hall. The ornamental bas-reliefs, the large *Maiden of Amsterdam* statue, and the allegory of justice on the façade are testament to this original administrative function. The building is regarded as a supreme masterpiece of Dutch architecture of the mid-17th century and is clearly inspired by stately models from Renaissance classicism. It was built by the gifted architect Jacob van Campen, who completely restored the building after it was damaged by fire in 1652. The decoration of the restored interior naturally represented a most challenging commission for Dutch artists. The style of the building, and the Italianate taste in vogue at the time did not make Rembrandt an obvious choice for involvement: indeed, the most important paintings were commissioned from Govaert Flinck. Within a few years, however, Rembrandt also became involved in the enterprise, through his grandiose painting of the Conspiracy of Julius Civilis, leader of the Batavians, the ancient inhabitants of Holland who rebelled against the Roman invaders.

■ Rembrandt, *The Ruins of the Old Town Hall after the Fire of 7 July 1652*, 1652, Rembrandt's House, Amsterdam. The fate of the old town hall is dramatically depicted.

■ This drawing of Jacob van Campen was taken from a lost painting by Frans Hals.

■ Jan van der Heyden, *The Dam at Amsterdam*, Historisch Museum, Amsterdam. The square remains the heart of the city to this day. Behind the façade of the new town hall (now the royal palace) can be seen the apse of the Gothic Nieuwe Kerk, where exhibitions are often held. This splendid painting, which must have been executed with the help of a camera obscura, emphasizes the wide, clear volumes of the town hall. The building is a supreme example of the classical style, inspired in part by works by the 16th-century Andrea Palladio, whose work had been introduced to Dutch culture by van Campen.

■ Below: Pieter Saenredam, *The Old Town Hall, Amsterdam* (detail), 1641–57, Rijksmuseum, Amsterdam. As an inscription explains, this work was first sketched out in 1641, then revised much later in order to record the by-now destroyed building.

■ Right: Jan van der Heyden, *The New Town Hall at Amsterdam*, Musée du Louvre, Paris. The painting has been partly cut on the left and has thus lost its compositional harmony. The viewpoint, different from that in the painting above, here favors the church.

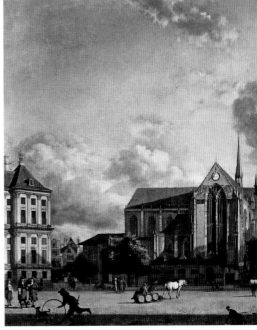

117

The Conspiracy of Julius Civilis

Executed in 1661 for Amsterdam's new town hall, this painting has had a troubled history. All that survives is the central fragment of the composition, which is badly damaged. It is housed in the Statens Konstmuseer, Stockholm.

■ Rembrandt, *Ahasuerus and Haman at the Feast of Esther*, 1660, Pushkin Museum, Moscow. Many scenes with figures set around a table recall *The Last Supper* by Leonardo. Rembrandt's expressive and compositional freedom is always balanced and tempered by a careful study of the great Renaissance prototypes.

■ Rembrandt,
Peter's Denial,
c.1660, Rijksmuseum,
Amsterdam. As in *The
Conspiracy of Julius
Civilis*, Rembrandt
exploits the nocturnal
atmosphere to make
the episode more
dramatically charged.

It is interesting to
note in this painting
the clear disproportion
of the figures' unnaturally
large hands, an effect
often employed by
Rembrandt to emphasize
gestural expressions.

■ Rembrandt,
*Preparatory Drawing for
The Conspiracy of Julius
Civilis*, 1661, Graphische
Sammlung Albertina,
Munich. The scene
illustrates the conspiracy
hatched by Julius Civilis
against the Romans: the
Batavian leaders swear
to rid themselves of the
Roman oppressor during
a banquet. The setting
was to feature grandiose
architectural elements.

Rembrandt's old age and the memory of Titian

In 1663, Rembrandt had once again to mourn the loss of a loved one: Hendrickije Stoffels, the final companion of his life, died, styling herself in her will as the artist's "wife". For a few years, Rembrandt had been living in a modest house on the Rosengracht, having surrendered the comforts of the beautiful, large house on the Breestrat. In order to minimize his problems with the public revenue and his creditors, he had worked out a complicated legal strategy: he registered himself as a man of no property, defining himself a dependant of Hendrickije and his son Titus, who gave him board and lodging in exchange for his paintings and engravings, to which the two held the exclusive rights. Prices of his paintings thus started to rise once again, and he was increasingly admired abroad. Public commissions also resumed, but the artist remained destitute and was even forced to sell Saskia's tomb. Meanwhile, his style moved even closer to the memory of Titian.

■ Below: Rembrandt, *Hendrickije as Flora*, 1657, The Metropolitan Museum of Art, New York. Here, the Titianesque model is brought up to date for the artist's new companion.

■ Rembrandt, *The Suicide of Lucretia*, 1666, Institute of Arts, Minneapolis. The model for this work was an actress, but this beautiful painting may have evoked the death of Hendrickije.

■ Rembrandt, *Juno*, c.1665, Armand Hammer Collection, Los Angeles. This quickly executed painting was produced for the collector Harmen Becker.

■ Rembrandt, *Portrait of Frederick Rihel on Horseback*, 1663, National Gallery, London. The manner of Titian is clear in this unusual commemorative portrait.

■ Titian, *Flora*, 1516, Galeria degli Uffizi, Florence. The sensual female figure is a constant model in Rembrandt's work. He adopted the spirit and style of Titian several times in his portraits of women.

Titian and the "unfinished" style

The stylistic links between Rembrandt and Titian are more obvious in the Dutch master's later work. In particular, Rembrandt systematically adopted a singular, decidedly Titianesque way of applying color: the so-called unfinished style. The late canvases of both artists may appear to be incomplete, almost sketched in. In fact, these are totally finished works, but not revised or touched up, the bare color left clearly in view, with thick, heavy brushstrokes. According to a contemporary, a portrait by Rembrandt was "so thick with color you could lift it up with your nose".

The Jewish Bride

Dating from about 1667, this masterpiece of affection and tenderness is in the Rijksmuseum, Amsterdam. The figures have never been positively identified: the work may celebrate the wedding of a Jewish poet.

■ The same intense depiction of family loves, expressed incomparably in *The Jewish Bride*, can also be seen in *Family Group* (Herzog Anton Ulrich-Museum, Brunswick), dating from the same period. This work is also similar in its threadlike golden lights on the red fabric.

■ Rembrandt, *Haman Sees His Own Death*, c.1665, State Hermitage Museum, St Petersburg. Another painting similar in style to *The Jewish Bride*, this work confirms Rembrandt's direction in his late phase: the wish to express controlled passions and emotions, rather than the explicit feelings he had favored in his youth. Inner meditation now prevails over theatricality.

■ Rembrandt, *Jacob Fighting the Angel*, c.1660, Staatliche Museen, Berlin. The embrace depicted in this work, totally different from that in *The Jewish Bride*, stresses Rembrandt's exceptional subtlety of feeling.

The pupils

Pupils, apprentices working to a contract, paying visitors to his studio: Rembrandt was always surrounded by a small retinue of assistants to whom he devoted a great deal of time and attention, more so than most of the other great masters. Even during the darkest years of his economic decline, when he was morally ostracized by the puritan circles of Amsterdam, he was always willing and able to teach the secrets of art to aspiring colleagues. His teaching success, however, poses something of a problem in retrospect. Many of his pupils imitated the master's style, to the extent of creating serious difficulties in the precise attribution of his works. Only a handful of his pupils achieved autonomous artistic fame, with a clearly recognizable, independent style. Centuries of dealing have contributed further to these problems, with forged signatures on paintings, copies, replicas, and works by other artists. The Rembrandt Research Project, formed through the initiative of some of the world's major museums, is in charge of the study and correct attribution of the artist's works, with the help of an international team of art specialists and restorers.

■ Rembrandt's circle, *Man with a Golden Helmet*, Staatliche Museen, Berlin. One of the Rembrandt Research Project's most controversial finds was the "demoting" of this painting's attribution; for a long time held to be by Rembrandt, it is now known to be the work of an unidentified pupil.

■ Rembrandt, *Gérard de Lairesse*, 1655, The Metropolitan Museum of Art, New York. Facially deformed, treatise-author De Lairesse was one of the major Dutch writers on art. A supporter of Rembrandt, he differed from the master in suggesting Dutch painting turn towards classicism.

■ Left: Nicolaes Maes, *Jacob Trip*, 1659–60, Mauritshuis, The Hague; below left: Rembrandt, *Portrait of Jacob Trip*, 1661, National Gallery, London. A comparison between these two works, which portray the same person, speaks for itself. The pupil is precise, analytical, and describes the facial features and social standing of the subject, whereas Rembrandt concentrates more on the likeness and recognizability of the sitter. He gives Jacob Trip an aura of high moral dignity, almost as if he were a biblical figure.

■ Ferdinand Bol, *The Governors of the Amsterdam Leper Hospital*, 1649, Rijksmuseum, Amsterdam. The works of Bol, one of Rembrandt's best pupils, have often been mistaken for the master's own.

A shattered family

Titus celebrated many important events in his young life. When he attained his majority, he was finally able to inherit his share of his mother's money. On February 10, 1668, he married Magdalena van Loo, the niece of Saskia's sister, and soon after the wedding, to the delight of the ageing Rembrandt, the couple announced that they were expecting a child. The last months of 1668 were a whirlwind of emotions for the artist. Titus's marriage to his second cousin brought back memories of the past, of the years he spent with Saskia, of the happiest time of his life. In September, however, tragedy struck once again: Titus died, and Rembrandt sank into the depths of solitude.

He remained alone in the sparsely decorated house on the Rosengracht with Cornelia, the daughter Hendrickije had borne him 15 years earlier. He was tired, desultorily living off bread and cheese. On March 22, in tears, he attended the baptism of his granddaughter, who was named Titia. The unfortunate child would soon lose her mother, as well. Meanwhile, her grandfather tried to keep his grief at bay by clinging to his painting.

■ Rembrandt, *Portrait of a Woman Holding a Carnation*, c.1665, Metropolitan Museum of Art, New York. Saskia's touching pose of many years before is repeated in this painting.

■ Rembrandt, *A Model in the Artist's Studio*, c.1665, Ashmolean Museum, Oxford. This drawing, executed at the time of his financial embarrassment, shows Rembrandt's studio, once full of pupils and all manner of precious objects, but now empty.

■ Rembrandt and follower, *Simeon with the Christ Child in the Temple*, 1669, Statens Konstmuseer, Stockholm. "Lord, now lettest thou thy servant depart in peace". These words are spoken by the aged preacher in one of the most poetic verses of the Bible. This was Rembrandt's last painting, in which he bared his soul yet again. Like the old man in the picture, Rembrandt was left holding an infant – his granddaughter, Titus' daughter.

■ Rembrandt, *View of the River Y from the Diemerdyke*, Devonshire Collections, Chatsworth. Rembrandt's last landscape drawings echo the way in which he reviewed his whole life, looking at it from a distant, almost secret viewpoint, no longer part of the scene but as a faraway observer.

1658–1669

The Return of the Prodigal Son

A late masterpiece, dating from 1668, this painting is now in the State Hermitage Museum, St Petersburg. It is likely that the emotional meaning behind this large canvas (the figures are life-sized) is connected with Titus' death.

■ Rembrandt had already drawn on this theme in an engraving, *The Prodigal Son,* executed 30 years before. The composition differs from that in the painting in that it is less emotional. A comparison between the two works underlines the exceptionally powerful and personal message of the painting.

■ The father is not Rembrandt himself, but rather a kind of archetypal paternal figure, who would never forsake his son. The father's pose is deeply felt: he appears to enfold his repentant son in a physical and moral embrace, isolating him from an outside world that is incapable of understanding total and unreserved love.

■ The embrace has an important precedent in Rembrandt's work. It appears in the dramatic *Farewell of David and Jonathan,* painted in 1642 on the occasion of Saskia's death. This painting is also housed in the Hermitage.

■ The father's large hands rest on the shoulders of his kneeling son. They feel the young man's weakened body through the coarse fabric of his ragged clothes. The roles are reversed: it is the frail old man who protects the young man, holding him close in a protective embrace. Rembrandt, however, can do nothing for Titus: his son can never return.

129

The last self-portraits

Aand so Rembrandt's life ended, colored by the bitterness of loss. He devoted his final paintings, the last pages in a lifetime's diary, to his own image in self-portraits in which the quality of his achievement is undiminished. Few artists can be compared with Rembrandt in the history of art; perhaps the only possible parallel can be found in Titian, who, shortly before his death, had also seen his favorite son fall victim to a fatal illness. For Titian, as for Rembrandt, death was the end of a final journey through an arid, loveless desert made bearable only by work. In the self-portrait in Kenwood House, palette and brushes form a single entity with the hand, almost becoming an extension of it. Rembrandt's death, in 1669, marked the end of an era and of the rarefied world that was Holland during the so-called Golden Age. Dutch painting and lifestyle underwent a change, moving towards an anonymous, Frenchified conformity. The artist's death went virtually unnoticed, but it was not long before his fame spread across the world.

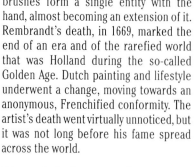

■ Rembrandt, *Self-portrait*, 1669, Mauritshuis, The Hague. This bare, but ever-dignified, picture may well be the master's final self-portrait.

■ Rembrandt, *Self-portrait Holding his Palette, Brushes and Mahlstick*, c.1665, The Iveagh Bequest, Kenwood House (English Heritage). The unresolved meaning of the two circles has been widely debated.

■ Rembrandt, *Self-portrait*, 1669, National Gallery, London. The artist's proud demeanor shines through, even in the years of his physical decline.

■ Jan van der Heyden, *View of the Westerkerk, Amsterdam*, c.1660, National Gallery, London. Rembrandt was buried here on October 8, 1669.

 Rembrandt, *Self-portrait Laughing*, 1669, Wallraf Richartz Museum, Cologne. This painting is the artist's final joke, taking his leave of us in the guise, possibly, of the Greek painter Zeuxis, who died laughing excessively at his own painting of a wizened old woman.

■ Rembrandt, *Self-portrait*, 1629, Alte Pinakothek, Munich. By the time of the artist's death, forty long years of vicissitudes had passed since this curious, eager young man faced the world. His expression of surprise and vitality became the look of resignation of a disenchanted old man.

Rembrandt, *David Playing the Harp Before Saul*, 1656, Mauritshuis, The Hague.

Index

■ The Rijksmuseum, Amsterdam.

Note

The places listed in this section refer to the current location of Rembrandt's works. Where more than one work is housed in the same **place,** *they are listed in chronological order.*

Amsterdam, Rembrandthuis,
The Ruins of the Old Town Hall after the Fire of 7 July 1652, p. 116.

Amsterdam, Six Collection,
Homer Reciting his Verses, p. 88;
Portrait of Jan Six, p. 89.

Amsterdam, Historisch Museum,
The Anatomy Lesson of Dr Johan Deyman, p. 74.

Amsterdam, Rijksmuseum,
Anna Accused by Tobit of Stealing the Kid, p.12;
Self-portrait, p. 15;
The Prophet Jeremiah Mourning over the Destruction of Jerusalem, p.24.
The Artist's Mother as the Biblical

Prophetess Hannah, p. 31;
Concert in Biblical Garb, p. 33;
View of the River Amstel from the Blauwburg, Amsterdam, p. 36;
Saskia Wearing a Veil, p. 42;
Head of a Man in Oriental Costume, p. 48;
The Night Watch, p. 72;
The Holy Family at Night, p. 85;
Girl with Dead Peacocks, p. 96;
Landscape with a Stone Bridge, p. 97; *Portrait of Titus Dressed as a Monk,* p. 110;
The Portrait of the Syndics of the Clothmakers' Guild, p. 114;
A Member of the Clothmakers' Guild, p. 115;
Peter's Denial, p. 119;
The Jewish Bride, p. 122.

Anholt, Wasserburg Anholt Museum,
Diana Bathing, p. 91.

Basle, Kunstmuseum,
David Presenting Saul with the Head of Goliath, p. 12.

Berlin, Kupferstichkabinett,
Susanna Surprised by the Elders, p. 19;

Saskia in a Straw Hat, p. 43;
The Last Supper, after Leonardo da Vinci, p. 70;
Three Members of the Clothmakers' Guild, p. 114.

Berlin, Staatliche Museen,
The Parable of the Wealthy Simpleton, p. 16;
The Abduction of Proserpine, p. 29;
Samson Betrayed by Delilah, p. 59;
Samson Threatening his Father-in-Law, p. 59;
The Mennonite Minister Cornelis Anslo, p. 66;
Young Girl at a Window, p. 81;
Moses with the Tables of the Law, p. 103;
Jacob Fighting the Angel, p. 123.

Boston, Isabella Stewart Gardner Museum,
Jesus and his Disciples in the Storm, p. 36.

Boston, Museum of Fine Arts,
The Artist in his Studio p. 6;
Pastor Johannes Elison, p. 44;
Portrait of a Man in a Fur Coat, p. 107.

■ Antoon François Heijligers, *Interior of the Rembrandt Room in the Mauritshuis,* 1884, Mauritshuis, The Hague.

■ Rembrandt, *Bust of a Man in Oriental Costume*, 1633, Alte Pinakothek, Munich.

■ Rembrandt, *Portrait of a Man Sharpening a Quill Pen*, 1632, Staatliche Museen, Gamäldegalerie, Kassel.

The Shipbuilder and his Wife, p. 67.

■ Gerrit Berckheyde, *The Spaarne at Haarlem*, c.1670, Rijksmuseum, Amsterdam.

Note

All the names mentioned here are artists, intellectuals, politicians, and businessmen who had some connection with Rembrandt, as well as painters, sculptors, and architects who were contemporaries or active in the same places as Rembrandt.

Anslo, Cornelis Claeszoon, one of Holland's best-known preachers. He was portrayed by Rembrandt together with his wife in a painting dating from 1641, now in Berlin, pp. 66–67.

Backer, Jakob Adriaenszoon (Harlingen 1608 – Amsterdam 1651), Dutch painter. A pupil and colleague of Rembrandt's, painter of historical subjects and hunting scenes, Backer is known most of all for his activity as a portrait painter, p. 71.

■ Jakob Backer, *The Angel Appearing to Cornelius, Centurion in Galilee, during Prayers and Fasting*, Bader Collection, Milwaukee.

Banning Cocq, Frans, captain of the Amsterdam civic guard portrayed in *The Night Watch*, the famous painting by Rembrandt dating from 1642, pp. 70, 72–73.

Belten, Pieter, owner, together with Christoffel Thijssens, of the house on Sint Anthonisbreestraat in Amsterdam, which Rembrandt bought in 1639 for 13,000 guilders, p. 64.

Berckheyde, Gerrit (Haarlem 1638 – 1698), Dutch painter. A pupil of Frans Hals and his brother Job, he painted mainly urban views of Amsterdam, Haarlem, and The Hague, p. 87.

Beyeren, Abraham Kendrickszoon van (The Hague c.1620 – Overschie 1690), Dutch painter of marine scenes and still lifes, van Beyeren also painted many famous meal scenes. His work is celebrated for its wide variety of subject-matter, p. 95.

Bol, Ferdinand (Dordrecht 1616 – Amsterdam 1680), Dutch painter and engraver. A pupil of Rembrandt, he enjoyed considerable success among the Amsterdam gentry through his portraits, pp. 115, 125.

Bosschaert, Ambrosius (Antwerp 1573 – Middelburg 1621), Dutch painter. He specialized in the still life genre, favoring in particular elaborate and colorful floral arrangements, p. 9.

Campen, Jacob van (Haarlem 1595 – Amersfoort 1657), Dutch architect. He was one of the main exponents of Dutch classicism inspired by the architectural works of Andrea Palladio. He rebuilt the Amsterdam Town Hall after it was destroyed by fire in 1652, pp. 116–17.

Caravaggio (Michelangelo Merisi, Milan 1571 – Porto Ercole 1610), Italian painter. His work is characterized by strong contrasts between light and shade that are able to evoke atmosphere and mould the figures by stressing their inner drama and the religious meaning of the scenes represented, pp. 14–17.

Codde, Pieter Jacobszoon (Amsterdam c.1599 – 1678), Dutch painter. He may have been

a pupil of Frans Hals and painted
interiors, portraits, and social
gatherings, p. 69.

Dircx, Geertje, farmer's widow
from Zeeland. She became
Rembrandt's mistress after the
death of the artist's wife in 1642,
pp. 82–83, 88.

Dou, Gerrit (Leiden 1613 –
1675), Dutch painter. He worked
in Rembrandt's workshop from
1628 to 1630. His elegant
paintings, of diminutive
proportions, are characterized by
their extremely precise and
detailed execution, pp. 26–27.

Dürer, Albrecht (Nuremberg
1471 – 1528), German painter,
engraver, and theorist. A
singularly gifted artist, he was
the true protagonist of central
European Renaissance art. In his
work, northern elements such as
gravity and meticulousness blend
with the monumentality and

■ Govaert Flinck,
Margaretha Tulp, 1655,
Staatliche Museen,
Gemäldegalerie, Kassel.

sense of color drawn from
Italian Renaissance models,
pp. 12–13, 53.

Fabritius, Barendt (Midden-
beemster 1624 – Amsterdam
1673), Dutch painter. A pupil of
Rembrandt and brother of Carel,
he painted costume scenes,
portraits, mythological and
biblical paintings, p. 63.

Fabritius, Carel (Midden-
beemster 1622 – Delft 1654),
Dutch painter. One of
Rembrandt's most gifted pupils,
he was in the master's workshop
from 1641 to 1643. His paintings,
softer and more luminous than
Rembrandt's, anticipate the work
of Jan Vermeer, pp. 50, 63.

Flinck, Govaert (Cleves
1615 – Amsterdam 1660), Dutch
painter. He was apprenticed in
Rembrandt's workshop from 1632
to 1636, painting mainly portraits
and religious scenes. He became
famous as a painter of historical
scenes through his large baroque
allegorical canvases, pp. 61–62,
87, 116.

Francken, Frans II (Antwerp
1581 – 1642), Flemish painter.
A prominent exponent of the
famous family of Flemish painters
active between the 16th and the

17th century, he was influenced
by the painterly style of Rubens.
He spent some time in Rome,
where he enjoyed considerable
success with his detailed genre
and mythological paintings, p. 56.

Gheyn, Jacob III de (Haarlem
c.1596 – The Hague? 1644), Dutch
engraver. He favored works of a
mythological nature, p. 29.

Haarlem, Cornelis van (1562
– 1638), Dutch painter. A refined
artist and a key figure in Dutch
late Mannerism, Cornelis van
Haarlem is regarded as the
founder of the baroque current
in Haarlem's classicism, p. 93.

Hals, Frans (Antwerp, c.1580 –
Haarlem 1666), Dutch painter.
A consummate portraitist, he
went beyond the Mannerist
conventions, restoring truth
and a spontaneity of pose and
expression to his models, thanks
to his choice of subject (women,
boys, drinkers, old men) and to

■ Carel Fabritius,
The Goldfinch, 1654,
Mauritshuis, The Hague.

■ Frans Hals, *Smiling Boy*, c.1677, Mauritshuis, The Hague.

his swift, uneven brushstrokes, pp. 39, 69, 79, 112–13, 116.

Helst, Bartholomeus van der (Haarlem 1613 – Amsterdam 1670), Dutch painter. He specialized among other things in portrait painting, portraying mainly members of the Amsterdam gentry, p. 69.

Heyden, Jan van der (Gorinchem 1637 – Amsterdam 1712), Dutch painter. During the course of his travels, he painted views of many European cities, particularly Amsterdam, pp. 37, 94, 117, 130.

Honthorst, Gerrit van, (Utrecht 1590 – 656), Dutch painter and engraver. His atmospheric candlelit scenes earned him the name of Gherardo delle Notti (Gerard of the Nocturnes) in Italy, pp. 15, 17, 55.

Hooch, Pieter de (Rotterdam 1629 – after 1648), Dutch painter. After painting genre scenes in his youth he turned mainly to paintings of bourgeois interiors, pp. 8, 79.

Hoogstraten, Samuel van (Dordrecht 1627 – 1678), Dutch painter. After spending some time in Rembrandt's workshop, van Hoogstraten moved away from the master's painterly style to specialize in paintings of interiors, although he also painted portraits, still lifes, and religious scenes, p. 81.

Houckgeest, Gerard (The Hague 1600 – Bergen Op Zoom 1661), Dutch painter famous for his architectural paintings. His paintings of the two main churches in Delft are particularly well known, p. 9.

Huygens, Christiaan (The Hague 1629 – 695), Dutch physicist, mathematician, and astronomer. The son of Constantijn, he proved the fundamental laws of optics, p. 29.

Huygens, Constantijn (The Hague 1596 – 1687), Dutch diplomat. Secretary to Frederick Henry, Prince of Orange and one of Rembrandt's greatest admirers, with a wide knowledge of the arts and sciences, pp. 22, 28–29, 32, 36, 44, 52, 56, 58, 91.

Huygens, Maurits. brother of Constantijn, he was painted by Rembrandt in 1632, p. 29.

Kalf, Willem (Rotterdam 1619 – Amsterdam 1693), Dutch painter. He enjoyed considerable success; his compositions were characterized by strong contrasts in chiaroscuro, metal dishes, and Chinese porcelain, pp. 68, 94.

Keyser, Thomas de (Amsterdam 1596 – 1667), Dutch painter and architect. A popular portrait artist, De Keyser executed many portraits in a miniature format, in which the subject portrayed is shown full-length in an interior, p. 29.

Lairesse, Gérard de (Liège 1640 – Amsterdam 1711), Walloon painter and engraver. His works, which are classical in tone and structure, mostly portray historical or mythological subjects, pp. 95, 124.

Lastman, Pieter (Amsterdam 1583 – 1633), Dutch painter. His work, influenced by Adam Elsheimer, Caravaggio, and, chiefly, by the Carracci brothers, is characterized by a theatrical style and a strong element of pathos, pp. 18–19.

Leyster, Judith (Haarlem 1609 – 1660), Dutch painter. A pupil of Frans Hals in Haarlem, she favored genre scenes and still

■ Bartholomeus van der Helst, *The Company of Captain Roelof Bicker and Lieutenant Michielsz. Blaeuw.*, 1639, Rijksmuseum, Amsterdam.

■ Pieter lastman,
The Rejection of Hagar and Ishmael, 1612,
Kunsthalle, Hamburg.

■ Pieter de Hooch,
Country House, c.1665,
Rijksmuseum,
Amsterdam.

■ Jan Steen, *Girl with Oysters*, c.1660, Mauritshuis, The Hague.

■ Judith Leyster, *Serenade*, 1629, Rijksmuseum, Amsterdam.

■ Rembrandt, *Portrait of a Man at his Desk*, 1631, The State Hermitage Museum, St Petersburg.

■ Anthony Van Dyck, *Portrait of Marcello Durazzo*, 1621, Galleria Franchetti alla Ca'd'Oro, Venice.

A DK PUBLISHING BOOK
www.dk.com

TRANSLATOR
Anna Bennett

DESIGN ASSISTANCE
Joanne Mitchell

EDITOR
Louise Candlish

MANAGING EDITOR
Anna Kruger

Series of monographs
edited by Stefano Peccatori and Stefano Zuffi

Text by Stefano Zuffi

PICTURE SOURCES
Archivio Electa, Milan; Alinari, Florence
Elemond Editori Associati wishes to thank all those museums and
photographic libraries who have kindly supplied pictures, and would be pleased
to hear from copyright holders in the event of uncredited picture sources.

Project created in conjunction with
La Biblioteca editrice s.r.l., Milan

First published in the United States in 1999 by DK Publishing Inc.
95 Madison Avenue, New York, New York 10016

ISBN 978-0-7513-0730-6

Library of Congress Catalog Card Number: 98-86757

First published in Great Britain in 1999
by Dorling Kindersley Limited,
9 Henrietta Street, London WC2E 8PS

A CIP catalogue record of this book is available from the British Library.

ISBN 0751307300

2 4 6 8 10 9 7 5 3